USING EUROPE, ABUSING THE EUROPEANS

CONTEMPORARY HISTORY IN CONTEXT SERIES
Published in association with the Institute of Contemporary British History

General Editor: Peter Catterall

Other titles include:

Peter Catterall and Sean McDougall (*editors*)
THE NORTHERN IRELAND QUESTION IN BRITISH POLITICS

Harriet Jones and Michael Kandiah (*editors*)
THE MYTH OF CONSENSUS: New Views on British History, 1945–64

Using Europe, Abusing the Europeans

Britain and European Integration, 1945–63

Wolfram Kaiser
Deutsche Forschungsgemeinschaft Research Fellow and Lecturer
University of Vienna
Austria

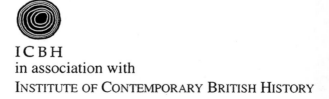

ICBH
in association with
INSTITUTE OF CONTEMPORARY BRITISH HISTORY

First published in Great Britain 1996 by
MACMILLAN PRESS LTD
Houndmills, Basingstoke, Hampshire RG21 6XS
and London
Companies and representatives
throughout the world

A catalogue record for this book is available
from the British Library.

ISBN 0–333–64942–7

 First published in the United States of America 1996 by
ST. MARTIN'S PRESS, INC.,
Scholarly and Reference Division,
175 Fifth Avenue,
New York, N.Y. 10010

ISBN 0–312–16350–9

Library of Congress Cataloging-in-Publication Data
Kaiser, Wolfram, 1966–
Using Europe, abusing the Europeans : Britain and European
integration, 1945–63 / Wolfram Kaiser.
p.   cm. — (Contemporary history in context series)
"In association with the Institute of Contemporary British
History."
Includes bibliographical references and index.
ISBN 0–312–16350–9 (cloth)
1. Europe—Relations—Great Britain.   2. Great Britain—Relations-
–Europe.   3. European Economic Community.   I. Title.   II. Series.
D1065.G7K35   1996
303.4'824041—dc20
96–23297
CIP

10   9   8   7   6   5   4   3   2   1
05   04   03   02   01   00   99   98   97   96

Printed and bound in Great Britain by
Antony Rowe Ltd, Chippenham, Wiltshire

To Susanne

Contents

General Editor's Foreword

International relations, as with politics, involves the making of sometimes unpalatable choices. The balance of the literature on Britain's European policy in the period covered by this book has tended to suggest that Britain made the wrong ones, blinkered by great power illusions reinforced by its role in the Second World War. While by no means entirely dropping this approach, Wolfram Kaiser here offers, however, a much more sophisticated analysis of the motive forces behind and the course of Britain's European policy 1945–63.

For the six countries which negotiated the establishment of the European Economic Community in 1955–7, integration was a positive choice offering clear advantages. These advantages were both economic and political. The creation of a customs union gave the Six enhanced access to their principal markets in other member states and helped to increase trade. In what the former President of the European Commission, Jacques Delors, has described as the marriage contract on which the EEC was founded between its two principal members, France and the Federal Republic of Germany, the French received support and better access to markets for their agriculture in return for opening up the French market in industrial products to the Germans. This reciprocity of economic interests also chimed with the other founder members. At the same time the founding of the EEC also served the political purposes of its members, for instance in providing a means for the rehabilitation of Germany and Italy after the Second World War or for the French to guard against an over-mighty Germany.

The choice was not so apparent at the time for British policy-makers. The burden of national interest did not point unambiguously in a European direction. The British interest was felt to be to maximize their influence not just in Europe, but through the Commonwealth and with the United States. Instead British participation in a process of European integration seemed likely to impact detrimentally on the Commonwealth, reducing the British room for manoeuvre on the international stage. It might also have reduced their influence on the United States, which was no less of a risk if political integration among the Six without Britain and with strong United States encouragement went ahead, creating a new power centre which would at the same time close off Britain's options in Europe. None of these eventualities seemed as appealing as the status quo. Instead the talks which began at the Messina conference in 1955 seemed to threaten Britain's influence and interests in Europe in the short term and its transatlantic influence in the medium term. Accordingly Britain initially hoped that its problems would be solved by the failure of the negotiations. Far from exercising positive choices, as was the case with the Six, British policy remained in this period characterized by such negative responses to events. The Plan G proposal of 1956, for instance, was a reaction once the strength of American support for the customs union negotiations and growing chances of those negotiations succeeding became clear, a sign of the British government attempting to secure the least worst option rather than a real policy departure.

The same, as Wolfram Kaiser shows, is true of the eventual decision to negotiate on entry terms to the EEC in July 1961. This has sometimes been characterized in the existing literature as marking a substantial shift in British policy, reflecting both the diminishing economic importance of the Commonwealth and mounting concern about the risk of being frozen out of a prosperous EEC. Such shifts were certainly occurring. Simply by being there the EEC had transformed and narrowed Britain's policy options. By 1961 the best option could no longer be that the EEC be stillborn; instead the best (or the least worst) option seemed increasingly for Britain to join. This, however, was not just because of its effects on Britain's economic interests but its political interests as well, in particular its relationship with the United States. In order to secure that relationship the British were now prepared to pay the price of at least showing willing in the face of continuing American support for European integration. But what this demonstrates as well is that the twists and turns of Britain's European policy took place against a background of continuity in calculations of national interest, calculations to which that European policy was always subordinate.

Britain's problem in European negotiations was making those interests accord sufficiently with the national interests of other European states. This proved impossible with the scheme for a European free trade area encapsulated in Plan G, although from Britain's point of view it seemed to fit much better with its existing foreign economic policy. The problem for Britain, as Plan G as well as the first EEC application of 1961 demonstrates, was that the choices it would have preferred were increasingly not realistic options, particularly after the EEC became a reality.

This book, the third in the *Contemporary History in Context* series, is the first detailed analysis of the dilemmas of British policymaking at the time. Using newly released documents at the Public Record Office and other archives, it scrutinizes the interdepartmental conflicts and debates, and the party political and business inputs which went into the policy-making process. It also shows the growing sophistication of British policy-making, not least the appreciation by 1961 of the need to offer something in return when pursuing your own national interests on the European stage, in this case Macmillan's attempts to win de Gaulle's support through some sort of nuclear deal. At the same time it clarifies the bases on which European policy options were evaluated. The result is a book which adds significantly to our understanding of the relationship between Britain's perceived interests and the course of its European policy.

Peter Catterall
London, 5 January 1996

Acknowledgements

In the course of this project I have received generous assistance from many sources. I am particularly grateful to Vernon Bogdanor, Anthony Nicholls and John Prest of the University of Oxford from whom I have learnt much about British history and politics. I have been fortunate enough to work with Wilfried Loth in the Study Group on Europe of the Kulturwissenschaftliches Institut in Essen, with William E. Paterson at the Europa Institute of the University of Edinburgh and with Bernd-Jürgen Wendt of the University of Hamburg, who have provided much encouragement. Numerous colleagues have talked to me over the years about Britain and European integration. I am indebted, among others, to Werner Abelshauser, Anne Deighton, Alan S. Milward, Andrew Moravcsik, Gustav Schmidt, Clemens Wurm and John W. Young for stimulating discussions. A special thank you to Peter Catterall, James Ellison and Jonathan Zatlin for their detailed and valuable comments on the manuscript. I would also like to thank the staff of the Public Record Office in London, the Bodleian Library in Oxford, the Birmingham University Library and, in Cambridge, the Trinity College Library and the Churchill Archives Centre for their valuable assistance. Finally my warmest thanks go to my wife and to my parents.

List of Abbreviations

ABCC	Association of British Chambers of Commerce
AED	Anthony Eden Diaries
BAOR	British Army of the Rhine
BLO	Bodleian Library, Oxford
BOT	Board of Trade
CAB	Cabinet Office
CAC	Churchill Archives Centre, Cambridge
CAP	Common Agricultural Policy
CCI	Consultative Committee on Industry
CEEC	Committee of European Economic Cooperation
CND	Campaign for Nuclear Disarmament
CPA	Conservative Party Archives
ECSC	European Coal and Steel Community
EDC	European Defence Community
EEC	European Economic Community
EFTA	European Free Trade Association
EPB	Economic Planning Board
EPC	European Political Community
EU	European Union
FBI	Federation of British Industry
FRUS	Foreign Relations of the United States
FTA	Free Trade Area
FO	Foreign Office
GATT	General Agreement on Tariffs and Trade
HMD	Harold Macmillan Diaries
IGC	Intergovernmental Conference
MAC	Mutual Aid Committee
MAFF	Ministry of Agriculture, Fisheries and Food
MLF	Multilateral Force
NATO	North Atlantic Treaty Organization
NFU	National Farmers Union
NUM	National Union of Manufacturers
OECD	Organisation for Economic Cooperation and Development
OEEC	Organisation for European Economic Cooperation
OFD	Overseas Finance Division (Treasury)

PREM	Prime Minister's Office
PRO	Public Record Office
SACEUR	Supreme Allied Commander Europe
T	Treasury
TCL	Trinity College Library, Cambridge
TUC	Trades Union Congress
ULB	University Library, Birmingham
WEU	Western European Union

Introduction

Upon taking over from Margaret Thatcher as Conservative Party leader and Prime Minister in November 1990, John Major insisted that he wanted Britain to be 'at the heart of Europe'. Rather than reluctantly following the leadership of others, particularly France and Germany, Major intended to shape the future development of what in 1993 came to be the European Union (EU). But it soon became apparent that the Major government lacked the necessary political strength to play a more constructive role within the EU. This was demonstrated in both the crisis in the European Exchange Rate Mechanism in 1992, which resulted in the withdrawal and devaluation of the pound sterling, and the internal controversies within the Conservative Party in 1992–3 over the ratification of the Maastricht Treaty.[1] With a majority of 21 after the 1992 general election that was falling rapidly, Major became increasingly preoccupied with containing the adverse domestic political consequences of the Conservative Party's deep split over Europe. Facing the 1996–7 Intergovernmental Conference (IGC) on EU reform, his government became increasingly paralysed.

The controversial debate over Britain and Europe within the Conservative Party, between the parties, in the media and the public since the signing of the Maastricht Treaty is a reminder of the steadily growing, immense importance of the European issue in British postwar history – not only for British foreign policy, but also in domestic politics. This book argues that in order to appreciate the continuing problems in Britain's relations with its EU partners, it is necessary to understand the unexplored ambiguities in British policy towards European integration in the first two decades after 1945, which has had significant long-term effects, and above all in Britain's first application for membership in the European Economic Community in 1961.

Much of what has been written on Britain and European integration after 1945 is preoccupied with identifying the reasons for Britain's seemingly negative and unique reaction to the virtuous initiatives of the six founding members of the European Coal and Steel Community, created in 1951–2, and of the European Economic Community, established in 1955–7.[2] The task of the historian of British European policy resembles that of a pathologist concerned with identifying the syndromes responsible for Britain's dysfunctional behaviour. The simple approach to this task is what one critic has dubbed the 'Casablanca method of "rounding up the usual suspects"'.[3] These suspects include Britain's role as belligerent and victor in the Second World War, the so-called special relationship with the United States and, finally, the Commonwealth. More ambitious studies have attempted to identify the key determinant, usually the alleged atavistic attachment of the British political elite to the concept of national sovereignty, which prevented participation in more closely integrated organizations in Western Europe.

This 'awkward partner' school is reminiscent of the strong tendency among German historians of the 1960s and 1970s to interpret modern German history in terms of a *Sonderweg* – a historically unique departure from the apparently normal path of democratic virtue – leading from Frederick the Great to Bismarck to Hitler. The contemporary British equivalent to this approach is the alleged continuity in the abnormal detachment from developments on the European continent and – after 1945 – from European integration, from Palmerston to Neville Chamberlain to Thatcher. Like its German academic counterpart, the British *Sonderweg* thesis suffers from two major methodological deficiencies. The first is that it is based on the normative assumption that the path taken by the Six in the 1950s was not only successful but natural, and also morally superior to the British preference for trade liberalization within intergovernmental institutional structures. Implied is that on several occasions the British governments simply 'missed the bus'. Evidence which suggests a more differentiated analysis and judgement has often been ignored and this tendency has in the past diverted attention from the actual interests and intentions of British policy-makers – including, for example, the importance of party political influences. In the ritual search for proof of Britain's abnormal attitudes to European integration, public utterances of British politicians about the importance of maintaining national sovereignty, for example, have too often been taken at face value. Yet in reality they have seldom reflected the real motives behind British European policy.

The second main methodological deficiency of the *Sonderweg* thesis is that in order to make it sound convincing, it must lack a comparative perspective. To give an obvious example, one reason that is sometimes cited for the alleged 'awkwardness' of Britain in European matters is its putative 'unique' role as the only island in the EU – as if the Republic of Ireland, which for its own specific reasons has tended to be much more enthusiastic about EU membership, did not exist. Much of what has been written on Britain and Europe after the Second World War takes no note of the European policies of the six founding member states of the European Economic Community, or of what has been written about them. Otherwise, to give just one example, it would be so much more difficult to interpret Britain's general preference for intergovernmental cooperation as a sign of its alleged awkwardness. As would become clear, the British government had in fact come to terms with the implications of majority voting by 1961, whereas Charles de Gaulle provoked a serious constitutional crisis in 1965–6 specifically in order to prevent the transition to majority voting at the beginning of stage three of the integration programme. Of course, the *Sonderweg* thesis also completely ignores the European policies of other democratic West European states, who became Britain's partners in the European Free Trade Association in 1959–60 and who also did not want to join an integrated economic community with the long-term aim of political union.

For some time now access to archival sources has greatly facilitated a more differentiated analysis. Although most of the recent writings on Britain and Europe still lack a comparative perspective, they have contributed to a more appropriate historical treatment of British European policy during 1945–55. After overviewing British policy towards the reconstruction of Western Europe during this first decade after the war, this book will carry the historical debate forward by analysing and reinterpreting the evolution of British policy towards European integration from the Messina conference in 1955 to the failure in 1963 of the first British application for full membership in the European Economic Community. Among other aspects, it will draw attention to the importance both of the prevailing transatlantic motivation behind British policy and of domestic political considerations. The application is shown to have been the result of a dual 'appeasement' strategy by Macmillan: externally, it was designed primarily to seduce the new Kennedy government into continuing the so-called special relationship and to provide Britain with a modern, credible nuclear deterrent, while at home a conditional application was regarded as the best medium-term strategy to hold the Conservative Party together and to split Labour over Europe. In both respects, even a failed application was seen to be advantageous in some regard.

This is the first historical study of the European Union in its formative years which considers Britain's role in the integration process through a detailed analysis of British government records. These include records from the Prime Minister's Office, the Cabinet, the Foreign Office, the Treasury, the Board of Trade and the Ministry of Agriculture, Fisheries and Food. The records of the Conservative Party, which was in government throughout the period 1955–63, are also utilized, as are private papers, official papers, autobiographical accounts and personal interviews, among others with Edward Heath, who led the British negotiating team in Brussels from 1961 to 1963.

1 Building and Defending a British Europe, 1945–55

Having won the war, Britain could certainly not accept being treated by the United States as 'just another European country', Foreign Secretary Ernest Bevin protested in June 1947 to William L. Clayton, the chief American negotiator in the Geneva trade talks.[1] Perhaps Britain was the weakest power of the 'Big Three' of Yalta and Potsdam, but it was surely still a world power with world-wide interests and responsibilities.

Without doubt the Second World War had drained Britain's economic and financial resources dramatically. By 1945 Britain had run up a huge external debt. The cumulative deficit in the balance of payments on current account from 1939 to 1945 was some £10 billion. Half of this had been met by the United States under lend-lease, but the other half had to be found by borrowing and by selling British foreign investments.[2] At the same time, due to the war effort, British exports had collapsed to only 30 per cent of the prewar level. It was therefore unclear how Britain could find the means to settle accounts with its principal supplier, the United States. When the Americans terminated lend-lease in August 1945, Britain was on the verge of bankruptcy. The full extent of the new dependence on the United States was obvious. After protracted negotiations in Washington, agreement on a new American loan was eventually reached in December 1945. In return for the loan, the British government had to support the American project for a multilateral trading system with convertible currencies. It had to accept the Bretton Woods Agreement and agree to the introduction of sterling convertibility by mid-1947. While the conditions of the loan itself were generous in commercial terms, they were resented in Britain where it was generally felt that, due to its war effort, Britain deserved much better treatment.

In addition to the new economic limitations on Britain's international role, the intensifying East–West conflict produced a bipolar world system which led to a further marginalization

1

of Britain in the confrontation between the two new superpowers, the United States and the Soviet Union. But while
Britain's material resources were limited and its international
influence obviously diminished, it was nonetheless the general
view, shared by the governing Labour Party and the
Conservatives, that Britain would naturally continue to be a
world power. After victory over Germany and Japan, it remained the unquestioned central assumption of British
foreign policy that, in the words of a senior official in the
Foreign Office:

> It must be our objective to maintain our position as a great
> Power, and this has, indeed, been our main purpose
> since 1900, when British power was at its zenith. It can be
> argued ... that our resources are no longer equal to this
> task, ... but if we accepted a lesser role, it would be so
> modest as to be intolerable.[3]

The British foreign policy elite hoped that the evident
decline in material resources could be compensated, at least
to some extent, by what they saw as intangible and imponder-
able resources of international influence; these Britain allegedly possessed in abundance, such as prestige, diplomatic
experience and skill as well as national will. To support the
claim of continued world power status, the British also developed a new foreign policy doctrine for the postwar period, the
'three circles' concept. This doctrine, which was not controversial between Labour and the Tories, soon became the
guiding principle of British foreign policy in the first decade
after the war, with repercussions for the period after 1955 and
particularly for Britain's policy towards Western Europe.
According to this new foreign policy doctrine, as it was
explained by Anthony Nutting, the Conservative Under-
Secretary of State in the Foreign Office, in a speech delivered
in the House of Commons in November 1951:

> The position of Britain is ... quite unique, for we are part,
> and an essential part, of ... the three great unities of the
> world. The unity across the Atlantic, the unity within the
> British Commonwealth and Empire, and the unity with
> Western Europe.[4]

Britain, or so it seemed, was the indispensable economic
and political hinge between these three centres of power, or
'circles', within the Western world, the transatlantic relationship with the United States, the Commonwealth and Empire
and Western Europe. This mediating position of Britain within
the West was now the primary legitimizing source of a British
seat at the negotiating table of the two superpowers and, more
generally, of continued world power status. Continued British
world power status after the war seemed so natural as well as
morally justified that subsequent British governments never
really analyzed whether and how British economic and political interests in the three circles could ultimately be reconciled.
As Harold Macmillan has conceded in his memoirs, not
much thought was given to the crucial question as to how the
apparently unchallengeable British leadership roles in the
Commonwealth and Western Europe and Britain's wartime
role as junior partner of the United States could be sustained
and best combined.[5] In the immediate postwar period the
British claim to a leadership role in Western Europe initially
did not seem out of place. The rest of Western Europe was
economically weak and politically unstable. Moreover, at that
time the continental Europeans still looked to British leadership in the postwar reconstruction of Western Europe. But as
time went by, the initial working hypothesis of a natural and
durable British leadership role in Western Europe degenerated into a rigid ideology which was to prevent an earlier and
anticipatory adaptation of British European policy to the new
economic and political circumstances which were rapidly
changing at Britain's expense. Within the three circles, the
Commonwealth and Empire initially continued to play a
central role.[6] The economic importance of this circle for
Britain was particularly great in the immediate postwar period.
The Commonwealth temporarily took approximately 50 per
cent of British exports, with a peak around 1950. The volume
of exports to the Commonwealth was initially lower in absolute terms, but higher as a percentage of overall British
exports when compared with the interwar years after the
introduction of Commonwealth preferences at the 1932
Commonwealth conference in Ottawa. British economic recovery initially rested heavily on the expansion of trade with

who have commonwealth?

the Sterling Area, which was largely identical to the Commonwealth, and only to a lesser extent on the recovery of trade with Western Europe. It was by increasing imports from the Sterling Area, which could substitute for imports from America, that Britain hoped to reduce its shortage of dollars. Moreover, its Commonwealth exports could earn Britain some gold and dollars directly from certain Commonwealth states such as South Africa. At the same time, Britain was still the most important export market for several Commonwealth states, particularly Australia and New Zealand. Commonwealth free entry ensured exporting their agricultural produce to Britain without tariffs and without quantitative restrictions. The relatively greater economic importance of the Commonwealth for Britain during the immediate postwar period, however, was largely the result of the distorting effects of the war on trade patterns. British trade with the Commonwealth was stimulated by the remaining preferences and the provisions of the Sterling Area, which favoured trade transacted in sterling. Moreover, intra-European trade was still impaired by quantitative and other restrictions and by the general dollar shortage which affected not only Britain, but also most other West European countries.

In the wake of the economic recovery of Western Europe and the dynamic expansion of world trade in the 1950s, the importance of the Commonwealth and Empire for British trade began to decline. The preferences were no longer so significant to influence trade flows. After the war the United States initially intended to force Britain to abandon the preferences altogether as part of their wider scheme for a liberal world trading order. The Commonwealth preferences were eventually allowed to continue; any extension, however, was prohibited by the no-new-preference rule of the General Agreement on Tariffs and Trade (GATT). The preferences were subsequently undermined by tariff reductions in the GATT as well as by the renegotiation of some of the bilateral trade agreements between Britain and individual Commonwealth states, whose trade patterns began to change in favour of greater trade with the North American and Pacific regions before the Europeanization of British trade patterns became evident from the mid-1950s onwards. As a result, the average preference margin in intra-Commonwealth trade

declined from roughly 12 per cent in 1945 to only 6 per cent
in 1955. The importance of the Commonwealth and Empire
for Britain was not, however, restricted to the economic
sphere. The wartime alliance of the Dominions with Britain
appeared to have cemented the political bonds which kept the
Commonwealth together. British politicians still generally saw
Britain as the natural centre of a group of states bound together by history, common traditions and culture rather than
elaborate institutions, which could play a useful political role
in the world. Leadership of the Commonwealth initially still
seemed the most suitable basis for Britain's claim to a continued world power role. In the first decade after 1945,
however, the hope, entertained most of all by the Empire wing
of the Conservative Party, that Britain might be able to achieve
a much greater degree of economic and political unity within
the Commonwealth, proved increasingly illusory. The internal
character of the Commonwealth already began to change
significantly with the independence of the Indian subconti-
nent in 1947–8. Moreover, the other Commonwealth states
had learned the lesson of the Second World War that their external security could no longer be guaranteed by Britain, but
only by the new superpower, the United States. The formation
of the ANZUS Pact in 1951 made clear the extent to which
Britain's political importance for the foreign and security
policies of the other Commonwealth states had already diminished. Due to American insistance, Britain was excluded from
this Pacific defence treaty between Australia, New Zealand and
the United States.

Because of the growing heterogeneity of the economic and
political interests of the Dominions, by the mid-1950s the
greatest political importance of the Commonwealth for
Britain was its function as an international status symbol independent of its actual relevance in international affairs. It still
appeared that to lead the Commonwealth could compensate
at least partially for Britain's latent economic and political
weakness and thus help to legitimize a special international
role. When Whitehall subsequently judged its economic and
political usefulness more pragmatically during the latter half
of the 1950s and the early 1960s, the Commonwealth remained influential in party political terms. For the Empire
wing of the Conservative Party it was still the most important

circle of Britain's external relations. At the same time, the political Left within the Labour Party hoped that the increasingly multicultural Commonwealth could be transformed into an economic and political bridge between the first and the third worlds. At a more general level, the historical and cultural ties remained significant for the British sense of identity beyond the ever-declining economic and political importance of the Commonwealth for Britain.

By contrast to the Commonwealth circle, the transatlantic relationship, if anything, grew in importance until the mid-1950s, as the new economic and security hegemony of the United States in the Western hemisphere became more apparent. The less significant the Commonwealth became as a legitimizing basis for Britain's claim to continued world power status, the greater the importance the Conservative governments of the 1950s attached to what Winston Churchill had first coined the 'special relationship' with the United States. In the British view, they were perfectly placed to give valuable assistance to the Americans due to their great diplomatic experience and world-wide contacts. The governments in Washington were encouraged as much as possible to draw upon these special qualifications which, the British believed well into the 1960s, set them apart from other West European allies and made them the ideal junior partner of the United States in the leadership of the West. During the immediate postwar period, the bilateral relationship was of course extremely important to both governments with regard to the reconstruction of Western Europe and, more generally, the organization of the postwar order.[7] Cooperation was particularly close in security policy and, more particularly, within the North Atlantic Treaty Organization (NATO) after its creation in 1949. In view of the desolate economic and political situation in the other West European states and of its remaining military strength and continuing world-wide responsibilities, Britain naturally remained by far the most important partner of the United States after 1945. When the British exploded their first nuclear bomb in 1952 and decided to develop the hydrogen bomb in 1955, their special transatlantic role was strengthened and seemed secure for the foreseeable future. The 'special relationship', which was always more special to the British than to the Americans, was increasingly seen as the real key to a con-

tinued British world power status. Of the British Prime
Ministers after 1945, Churchill and Macmillan, who both had
family ties to the United States, were particularly keen to cultivate the British role of junior partner in the wartime alliance.
Whenever serious conflicts in the bilateral relationship
erupted, such as over the Suez war in 1956, they were particularly anxious to adjust British policy to American interests in
order to secure continued special treatment.

From the very beginning, however, Britain and the United
States were not cooperating on equal terms. It became immediately clear after the end of the war that the Americans felt
under no moral obligation to make special concessions to the
British with respect to the organization of the Western world
or, more particularly, of Western Europe due simply to the
wartime alliance. In economic matters this became abundantly
clear with the termination of lend-lease and the subsequent,
hard negotiations over a new American loan. What was widely
regarded in Britain as unfair and condescending treatment by
the new superpower was continued when the United States
unilaterally terminated the bilateral wartime nuclear cooperation in the Manhattan project and thus forced Britain to
develop its own nuclear deterrent independently and of
course at a much greater price. The McMahon legislation,
passed by Congress in 1946, forbade the American government to pass on any nuclear know-how to other countries,
including Britain. It was only amended in 1958 to allow the resumption of Anglo-American cooperation in nuclear matters.

More importantly, the transatlantic relationship was also
complicated as a result of fundamental differences over important issues. Anglo-American conflicts were particularly pronounced in questions of economic and trade policy. These
included, for example, constant American pressure on the
British to abandon or at least to reduce the remaining preferences as well as conflicting conceptions of the reconstruction
and political integration of Western Europe and the British
role in this process. The refusal by the Attlee government and
subsequent British governments to lead Western Europe into
economic and, ultimately, political integration was arguably
the most important source of division between Britain and the
United States until the British EEC application of 1961.
Another source of friction was the pressure which the United

States applied on the British to accelerate the process of decolonization. The latent conflict between British colonial policy and the economic and political hegemony of the United States, which saw the development in the European colonies almost exclusively from the perspective of the East–West conflict, finally culminated in 1956 when the Eisenhower government forced Britain to break off the Suez war.

Of the three circles, Western Europe was initially considered much less important than either the Commonwealth and Empire or the transatlantic relationship. Directly after the war, it was not seen as an asset of British foreign policy, but as an enormous additional economic burden. The occupation zone in Germany drained British financial resources so much that the British were content to merge it with the American zone in July 1946. In addition, while British exports to Western Europe at 25 per cent of total British exports occupied a larger share than they had in the 1930s, they grew more slowly until 1950 than British exports to the Commonwealth. Moreover, trade with Western Europe did not greatly help the British to close the dollar gap, a problem that was shared by most other West European countries. The initial necessity to reduce imports from the United States and to increase exports to countries where Britain could earn dollars led the British to underestimate the much greater long-term potential for increased trade in Western Europe in the wake of its economic recovery by comparison with the Commonwealth.

When explaining the lack of British enthusiasm for closer association with Western Europe directly after the war, it is not sufficient, however, to point to the different economic needs of Britain which were as much the result of external pressures as of conscious foreign economic priorities of the government in London. Whatever its economic merits, the mental barriers against closer British association with Western Europe, which were prevalent in the political class and the public at large, should not be underestimated in their importance for European policy-making. The Second World War had reinforced the psychological de-Europeanization of the interwar period. Since the early 1930s external forces had had an integrative effect on British national identity. The rise of fascism and communism followed by the Second World War and, perhaps to a lesser extent, the threat posed by the Soviet

Union after 1945 created a sense of common purpose which greatly strengthened the unifying feeling of Britishness. This had repercussions, for example, for the perception of the British constitutional framework with its centralized government and a strong executive which apparently provided the ideal institutional setting for surviving the Nazi threat; after the war, it provided for the introduction of far-reaching welfare state reforms by the Attlee government. The fact that the British had overcome the external challenges and were now realizing progressive and apparently exemplary domestic reforms helped to create a degree of societal complacency and intellectual arrogance *vis-à-vis* the continental Europeans. This was to burden British European policy for a long time. The domestic debate on the future of Britain after 1945 was in a striking way self-referential and largely lacked a comparative European perspective. In every sense, Britain seemed so obviously superior when compared with the other larger West European democracies after the war. The strength of communist parties, in particular in France and Italy, did not inspire confidence in the continental Europeans. The crisis of the Fourth Republic in France, in particular the threat of a military coup in connection with the explosive situation in Algeria during the late 1950s, seemed to confirm that Britain was the only reliable stronghold of democracy. At the same time, the dominant view among the British political class concerning the Federal Republic remained in the 1950s that a return to some form of authoritarian government could certainly not be ruled out for the post-Adenauer period. For Britain it seemed unattractive to share its destiny with that of the unstable continental European countries which had all lost the last war, in the British view, either in 1940 or in 1945.

Britain's prevalent intellectual ambivalence regarding the efforts on the continent at closer economic and political unity during the first decade after the war is also evident in the European policy of the self-proclaimed pro-European Churchill. The opposition leader, who was often accused of neglecting domestic affairs after 1945, initially gave important impulses for closer economic and political cooperation among West Europeans. Only one year after the war, he suggested in his famous Zurich speech held in September 1946 that Franco-German reconciliation should form the basis of a kind of 'United States of Europe'. He was subsequently among the first to support German rearmament within the framework of a European army in 1950. Churchill's views as to how the new Western Europe should be organized, however, remained extremely vague. He was even more imprecise and ambivalent when defining the role of Britain in this new Europe, which he hoped to create. The Conservative leader seems to have believed that Britain should cooperate as closely as possible with the continental Europeans in economic, political and military matters, as long as the institutional structures of any new organizations were strictly intergovernmental. Because it was expected to strengthen the West in the global confrontation with the Soviet Union, it was generally in Britain's best political interest to support the integration process in Western Europe, even when it went beyond cooperation between sovereign states; in any case support should be provided as long as the process did not infringe upon British economic interests or undermine the British leadership role.

Due to its world-wide interests and responsibilities, however, Britain could not itself participate in such further integration. It was, after all, only partially European. In February 1930 Churchill had argued in a newspaper article on the Briand Plan for closer unity in Europe: 'We are with Europe, but not of it. We are linked, but not compromised. We are interested and associated, but not absorbed … We belong to no single continent, but to all.'[8] If anything, the Second World War had strengthened this sense of separateness. Churchill's conception of a semi-distanced British position in Europe was not really controversial among decision-makers in London or between the parties during the 1940s and the early 1950s. Both Labour and the Tories saw the urgent need to strengthen the West European states economically and politically in view of the economic crisis and the developing Cold War in order to make them immune against the domestic influence of communist parties and resistant against Soviet expansionism. After a while, the anti-communist and anti-Soviet thrust was at least as characteristic of the Attlee government's European policy as that of the Conservative governments of the 1950s. Unlike Labour, leading Conservatives, while in opposition, at least contributed to the mobilization of public support for the European idea. In 1946 Churchill charged his

son-in-law Duncan Sandys with the organization of an inter-
party group of well-known individuals which would promote
the idea of European integration in Britain and in Western
Europe. On 16 January 1947, Sandys presented the British
United Europe Committee. The committee included
Conservative members, such as Robert Boothby, but also
several Labour politicians as well as representatives of trade
unions and churches and academics. The Labour Party
National Executive Committee, however, urged Labour
members not to participate. With some justification, it feared
that Churchill was keen to use the committee as a platform for
attacking the Attlee government. As a result, when the United
Europe Movement constituted itself on 14 May 1947, it was
dominated by Conservative and Liberal members. But while
the Conservatives initially played a leading role in getting the
European movement off the ground in Britain and Western
Europe, which led to the Hague Congress in May 1948, they
too were ultimately not prepared to support British participation in more closely integrated West European organizations like the European Coal and Steel Community (ECSC)
which France, the Federal Republic, Italy, the Netherlands,
Belgium and Luxembourg set up in 1951–2. As leader of the
opposition, Churchill sometimes attacked Bevin publicly for
his allegedly insufficiently 'European' foreign policy. But when
the Conservatives took office once again in 1951, they did not
change the established policy in any significant way and
implicitly confirmed the degree of consensus which existed in
British European policy. The refusal of the Churchill government even to contemplate a more positive policy towards the
ECSC or plans for a European Defence Community (EDC)
underlined that, while Churchill's general support for
European integration was an important part of his foreign
policy belief system, the previously displayed rhetorical
support for a *greater British role* in Western Europe had been
primarily motivated by domestic tactical considerations.

After taking over from Churchill during the Potsdam conference in July 1945, the Attlee government was first confronted with the task of defining Britain's future bilateral
relationship with France. One crucial question was whether
Britain ought to conclude a military alliance with France,
which in the immediate postwar period was initially designed

mutual security against a revived Germany. -British relationship was, however, burdened with sions over crucial issues, particularly over the rmany. French plans to separate the Ruhr and the Rhineland from Germany, the British believed, would strengthen nationalist feeling in Germany, ruin its economy and ultimately drive the Germans into the arms of the Soviet Union. To the French, the merging of the British and American zones, seen foremost as an economic necessity in London, seemed geared towards undermining their demands on Germany. Franco-British cooperation was therefore initially restricted to economic consultation. The political deadlock was only overcome when Foreign Secretary Ernest Bevin and Leon Blum, Minister President in a short-lived Socialist-led government in France, met in London in January 1947. Despite Blum's subsequent loss of office, a Franco-British treaty was eventually signed at Dunkirk in March 1947. It was a fifty-year alliance against German aggression and, as such, marked the first long-term British security commitment on the European continent. It was, however, not followed up by concrete cooperation in military and strategic matters and was soon overshadowed by the growing East–West tensions.[9]

Scholars have debated whether British foreign policy before the creation of NATO aimed exclusively at securing American military involvement in Europe in a wider Atlantic security framework, or whether the Attlee government seriously considered the concept of Western Europe as a 'third force' with a greater degree of independence from the United States. Some have argued that since at least early 1946 British policy aimed primarily at the formation of a transatlantic alliance with the United States against the Soviet threat.[10] Others have suggested that at least Bevin was definitely interested in closer cooperation among the West Europeans in order to establish Western Europe as an equal partner of the Americans.[11] This debate, however, tends to deflect from three fundamental characteristics of the British approach to European integration. First, even the clear majority of the Labour Party never supported those 'third force' concepts which advocated Western Europe's equal ideological distance from the United States and the Soviet Union with respect to the political organization of the state or the economic and social structure of

society. Secondly, unlike some advocates of the 'third force'
concept on the continent, particularly in France, the Attlee
government certainly assumed throughout that any greater
West European cooperation would take place within a wider
Atlantic framework. In foreign policy terms, too, equal distance from the United States and the Soviet Union was generally rejected apart from a minority on the Left of the Labour
Party. Finally, although Bevin or others in the Attlee government may have toyed with the idea of greater British involvement in Western Europe, they always regarded this primarily
as an additional foreign policy tool for Britain to match the
power of the United States and the Soviet Union. They never
wished to achieve greater interdependence by integration
within Western Europe.

The various 'third force' ideas were soon obsolete in 1948–9
due to the intensifying East–West conflict. On 17 March 1948,
the Netherlands, Belgium and Luxembourg, who had already
formed the Benelux customs union, joined Britain and France
in signing the Brussels Pact, an extension of the Dunkirk
Treaty. The Brussels Pact was primarily a military alliance,
which at that time was already effectively directed more
against the Soviet Union than a revived Germany, but it also
included provisions for greater cooperation in economic and
cultural matters. By mid-1948 talks began between the Brussels
Pact powers and the United States about an Atlantic defence
organization which would lead to the creation of NATO in the
following year. Within the Brussels Pact, the Attlee government was soon confronted with demands for a greater degree
of political cooperation. Following up on the Hague Congress,
leading European politicians, such as the French Foreign
Minister Robert Schuman, urged the British to agree, among
other demands, to a European parliamentary assembly which
would initially be consultative, but might later assume decision-making powers. French interest in the project at that
stage was motivated primarily by the prospect of the creation
of a West German state which raised the issue of the best institutional structure for the future containment of Germany with
much greater urgency than hitherto.[12] The Attlee government
strongly believed that the proposal was unrealistic. It also disapproved of the potential supranational implications and
feared that the assembly would provide an ideal platform for

the Conservatives to attack the government. The Brussels Pact
powers eventually decided on 26 October 1948 to charge a
Committee of Inquiry to study the question. The compromise
solution reached on 5 May 1949 provided for the creation of a
ministerial council combined with a consultative assembly.
When compared with the initial proposal, the result was highly
disappointing to most continental Europeans. Moreover, when
the new Consultative Assembly of the Council of Europe first
met in Strasbourg on 10 August 1949, it soon turned out that
the value of its work was much reduced as the British members
did indeed primarily extend their domestic political shadow-
boxing to the new European forum. It also became immediately obvious that the British government would try to
undermine progress towards any meaningful degree of political integration among the member states.

  The central British aim of securing American commitment
for the defence of Western Europe had hardly been achieved
in 1949, when the West Europeans were already confronted
with the question of German rearmament which became
much more urgent with the North Korean attack on South
Korea on 25 June 1950. The possibility of German rearmament within a European structure had already been vented by
the German Chancellor Konrad Adenauer in late 1949 and by
Churchill in a speech to the House of Commons on 16 March
1950. The American government, however, now suggested the
formation of an integrated NATO military force with German
troops. Without any meaningful degree of political integration
having been achieved in Western Europe, the French were
now confronted with the question of how to make the domestically unpopular German rearmament politically more
acceptable, an issue that from then on was to overshadow the
integration process during the first half of the 1950s. After
highly controversial internal discussion and despite continuing disagreements, the French government finally decided on
19 October 1950 to counter the American demand with the
proposal of German rearmament within the framework of a
European army. According to the Pleven Plan, the Federal
Republic would be doubly discriminated against in such an
army. It would not be a member of NATO. It would also have
no troops outside the common command structure and no
access to the higher echelons. The discriminatory elements of

the Pleven Plan secured a majority in the French Assemblée Nationale in a vote on 25 November 1950, but they were not acceptable to the Germans, who preferred the full integration of the Federal Republic into NATO; neither were they acceptable to the Americans nor the British who believed that such a European army would be militarily ineffective and politically unstable in the long term. A breakthrough was only achieved when the Americans finally decided to support the creation of a European army in order to make German rearmament politically more acceptable in France and elsewhere in Western Europe. They now linked German support for the EDC with the end of the occupation in the Federal Republic. At the same time, they induced the French government to accept German equality, including a German defence ministry and general staff and the inclusion of all troops of all member states in the common command structure.

From the beginning, one central question was how a European army would be controlled politically. The idea of a European Political Community (EPC), which was pushed primarily by the Italians, was eventually linked to the EDC project in Article 38 of the EDC Treaty. Detailed discussions on a suitable institutional structure did take place, but decisions were deferred until after the ratification of the EDC.[13] In the 1951–2 EDC negotiations, the supranational elements of the Pleven Plan were watered down. The idea of a European defence minister, for example, was dropped. Doubts over the military efficiency of the European army were dispelled with the decision that its command centres would be assigned to the European headquarters of NATO and that in the case of a crisis, the NATO Supreme Commander Europe (SACEUR) would command the EDC troops. The EDC Treaty, which emerged from the meeting of EDC foreign ministers on 26–7 January 1952 and from the conference of the American, British and French foreign ministers on 13–19 February 1952, was eventually signed in Paris on 27 May 1952.[14]

When the question of German rearmament was first raised by the Americans in the summer of 1950, it was supported by the Attlee government. When the Pleven Plan began to be discussed, however, it was obvious that the British had severe doubts about the military efficiency of a European army, and that they were not themselves prepared to participate. It soon

turned out that this policy remained fundamentally unchanged when the Conservatives once more took office in late
1951.[15] On 28 November 1951, Foreign Secretary Anthony
Eden stressed publicly that Britain could never join a
European army. It has rightly been pointed out that there was
never any chance that a Conservative government would
reverse the basic decision of the Attlee government against
British participation.[16] The Churchill government was divided
only about how best to safeguard British leadership of Western
Europe. Foreign Secretary Anthony Eden supported the EDC
because he believed that it was the only politically feasible
road to German rearmament, and because the United States
advocated it. In May 1952, when the Six signed the EDC
Treaty, Eden agreed to sign a fifty-year mutual security treaty
with the EDC in the hope that this would ease the ratification
process in France. In contrast, those in the Conservative Party,
like Churchill and Macmillan, who appeared more pro-
European in their public statements, in fact privately hoped
that the EDC would fail, thus allowing Britain to regain the
diplomatic initiative in Western Europe with an alternative
plan. They were primarily concerned about the possible domination of European institutions by the Germans.[17] The British
government tried to avoid the impression in public that it
wanted to sabotage the EDC because, for military and political
reasons, it preferred the alternative option of German NATO
entry. In April 1954, the British eventually agreed to an association treaty with the EDC which provided for some institutional links and the inclusion of one British army division into
an EDC corps. But throughout the negotiations and the subsequent ratification process, the British sounded negative about
the EDC and their reserved attitude ultimately contributed to
its failure. This finally came after the French military defeat at
Dien Bien Phu in May 1954, when the United States refused to
support the encircled French troops, with a negative vote in
the French parliament on 30 August 1954. The failure of EDC
seemed to vindicate earlier British doubts. The main issue,
German rearmament, was still unresolved. The British government now proposed an intergovernmental solution, namely
that the Brussels Pact be extended to Italy and the Federal
Republic in order to create a suitable European framework for
German rearmament and the accession of the Federal

Republic to NATO, thus making it politically more easily digestable in France. The British proposals had already been discussed within Whitehall before the failure of EDC, which had been foreseeable for some time, and were accepted at the London conference in September 1954. The Brussels Pact was thus transformed into the Western European Union (WEU) in 1955. German accession to NATO now proved acceptable to the French. After the failure of their own plan, they feared that the Americans and the British might implement German rearmament without them. It was also made much more acceptable by the German renunciation of nuclear weapons as well as the willingness of the British to commit themselves for the first time to the stationing of a substantial number of British troops and aircraft on the continent. The failure of the Six alone had allowed the British government temporarily to regain the initiative in Western Europe.

Defence issues played such a prominent role in European integration during the early 1950s largely because of the external pressures of the Cold War and, more particularly, the Korean War of 1950–3. They burdened the integration process politically. They also overshadowed the more important field of European integration with a much greater direct impact on Britain: economic integration which provided a 'durable economic peace settlement' in Western Europe.[18] After the war the Marshall Plan was the first major initiative for the systematic and comprehensive economic reconstruction of Western Europe. On 5 June 1947 the American Foreign Secretary George Marshall announced the readiness of the United States to provide further aid to the European economies provided that this aid was used in a coordinated way rather than being allocated to the individual states for different and unrelated purposes.[19] The central aim of the American government was not purely the short-term economic recovery of Europe, but rather its long-term economic and political reconstruction. The Americans wanted to induce the Europeans to integrate into one economic area, preferably in the form of a customs union. It was hoped that such economic integration would increase output and productivity in Europe and eliminate the problem of dollar deficits, while also providing a suitable economic framework for the rebuilding of the German economy. The ultimate aim, however, was the political integration of Europe. As the Cold War developed, the Americans hoped that integration would make Western Europe independent of American aid and would strengthen it against the Soviet threat. Hence, the Marshall Plan increasingly developed into a tool of American containment policy.[20]

Marshall Plan aid was initially also offered to the Soviet Union. After a meeting of the Soviet, British and French foreign ministers in Paris on 27 June 1947, however, Joseph Stalin rejected the offer. When it turned out that the governments of most East European states were interested in the Marshall Plan, Stalin forbade them to participate. As a result, the governments of 16 West European states began negotiations over the American proposal in Paris on 12 July 1947. The American government hoped that this Committee of European Economic Cooperation (CEEC) would provide the stepping stone for full economic and, ultimately, political integration. It soon turned out, however, that the interests and aspirations of the West European countries were extremely diverse and incompatible with the original American design.

One crucial problem was the future of Germany. Here, the French held views very different from those of the Americans or the British. The French government, for example, intended to make France the leading steel producer in Europe with the aid of German coal. At the beginning of the negotiations in Paris it thus rejected out of hand the demand to increase West German steel production which the Americans and British envisaged as a central pillar of the economic reconstruction of Western Europe as a whole. At the subsequent meeting of the three Western occupation powers in London in August 1947 the French were forced to accept increased German steel production. In return, however, the Americans had to promise to support in principle the creation of a Ruhr authority which would supervise the production and distribution of German coal. The final conference report was passed on 22 September 1947. The Americans were disappointed over the distinct lack of enthusiasm among the West Europeans for the initial comprehensive concept for economic integration. The Truman government now devised the aid programme independently. It was limited to four years, and American aid had to be approved by Congress on a year-to-year basis.

Negotiations over the institutional structure for the administration of the Marshall Plan began in Paris at the end of
January 1948. With respect to institutional matters, French
and American policies were actually very similar. The governments of both countries wished to see a strong executive
which would administer the distribution of American aid, de-
ciding autonomously about the national economic recovery
programmes. The French, Italian and Benelux governments
hoped that a supranational construction would provide a suitable institutional framework for the recovery of West Germany
and that it would have a pacifying and integrative effect on
postwar Western Europe. But the British government was
totally opposed to such a structure for the new organization. It
had welcomed the American offer to provide further aid in
principle. But it staunchly defended its extra-European
economic interests, particularly the economic link with the
Commonwealth through the Sterling Area and the preferences; moreover, it had no intention of giving up its independent decision-making powers to a supranational European
authority.

Because of the highly diverse interests of the key West
European states, comprehensive economic integration was not
achieved and the institutional structures of the newly created
OEEC were entirely intergovernmental. The organization did
get an executive committee which, however, was made dependent on the OEEC Council of Ministers with no provisions for
majority voting. As all other member states, Britain thus retained a veto right. The OEEC Treaty generally provided for
the possibility of strengthening the powers of the organization, but this was thwarted by the British and other member
states. The OEEC's responsibilities were largely limited to the
administration of the Marshall Plan and trade liberalization
through the reduction of quantitative restrictions. Instead of
the new organization providing a stepping stone towards comprehensive economic and, ultimately, political integration, as
had been the original American intention, the integration
process soon focused on Franco-German cooperation in one
specific industrial sector, namely coal and steel.

After the Western occupation powers' decision in July 1948
to set up a West German state, France slowly moved towards
what was a less ambitious concept than that of the Americans,

namely Franco-German association, which would deal with the crucial question of French access to German resources of coke and coal. This would enable the regulation of steel markets and provide a suitable starting point for Franco-German reconciliation and cooperation. The government in Paris was initially still reluctant to proceed with any plans for economic integration without Britain. The French Socialists in particular were keen on the participation of a Labour-led Britain. However, when French attempts to instil a greater degree of political integration into the Council of Europe were continuously obstructed by the British, this stimulated the search for an alternative core Europe concept without Britain. Moreover, the election of Adenauer in the Federal Republic, who strongly supported the Western integration of the Federal Republic over unification, provided a window of opportunity. If missed, this might lead either to the full equality of the Federal Republic and its ultimate economic and political domination of Western Europe without adequate economic or institutional constraints, or to the neutralization of a unified Germany.

The French only decided to take the initiative at the end of April 1950, when it became clear that at the forthcoming conference of the foreign ministers of the three Western allies, the Americans and the British would demand lifting the existing limits on West German steel production. Schuman now took up the proposal of Jean Monnet, head of the French reconstruction plan, for a European coal and steel authority, a plan which had recourse to previous deliberations in Paris about possible cooperation in coal and steel in Western Europe. Schuman secured Adenauer's support on 8 May and that of the French Cabinet on 9 May. His initiative was more smoothly approved by the French government not least because the Socialist ministers had left the government in February 1950. Limited economic integration in coal and steel, the French hoped, would avert the expected steel crisis in Western Europe and assist the French plan for domestic economic modernization by securing access to German coal. It would also promote Franco-German reconciliation, where more ambitious plans, such as for a customs union, still seemed unrealistic for economic and political reasons.

The French government had devised a plan which did not require British participation. Indeed, while Adenauer and the American Foreign Secretary Dean Acheson were consulted before the plan was launched, the British government was not. The French, moreover, linked their initiative to a demand for a supranational accord in order to avoid a situation, such as over the creation of the OEEC and the Council of Europe, in which the British could join negotiations without any real desire to accept a meaningful degree of political integration and could water down any proposals made by others. The Attlee government was first told of the French plan when Schuman and Acheson flew to London on 11 May 1950. The British initially hoped that they could win time by suggesting that they might be associated in some way with future negotiations over the French proposal; however, talks over a possible formula for British participation were unproductive.[21] On 1 June Schuman imposed on the British a one-day deadline to accept his invitation to a conference on the creation of a common coal and steel authority, which the British finally rejected. The Attlee government did not wish to commit itself to the supranational principle or to an open-ended integration process. Moreover, cooperation with the West Europeans in coal and steel did not seem urgent in economic terms because British production of coal and steel was still very high by comparison with the six continental European countries. The Labour government was also unwilling to surrender newly nationalized industries to European control, particularly at a time when the potential partner states were all dominated politically not by Socialist, but by Christian Democrat parties. It also appears that Bevin and others in the London government believed that the Schuman Plan was likely to fail, and that this would eventually present Britain with an opportunity to rescue the continental Europeans with an initiative to their liking. Negotiations among the Six began in Paris on 20 June. A first draft treaty was ready by mid-December, and the treaty establishing the ECSC was signed on 18 April 1951. The influence of the High Authority of the ECSC, which Monnet had wanted to give key powers, was now in fact limited by the ECSC Council of Ministers with important powers as well as by a parliamentary assembly and a court.[22] In 1954 Britain concluded a consultative association treaty with the ECSC.[23] While the ECSC was the first West European organization formed among the Six without British participation, it was limited to one industrial sector where it did not harm British core economic interests. As the economic importance of coal and steel was to decline continuously, the ECSC in itself was no serious threat to British leadership in economic matters which still seemed secure within the wider OEEC structure. When the EDC collapsed in 1954 and was replaced with the dual WEU and NATO solution for German rearmament, this appeared to the Conservative government also to remove the more serious threat to British leadership of Western Europe in foreign policy and defence matters. During the first decade after the war the British had been highly successful in shaping Western Europe in accordance with their special economic needs and political interests and in containing more ambitious plans for more far-reaching economic and political integration. This was largely due to the initial French reluctance to proceed without Britain and to the failure of the EDC. At the end of 1954, a British Western Europe, led by the London government, seemed secure.

However, the British diplomatic success of 1954 soon proved a Pyrrhic victory. It strengthened the sense of nonchalant loftiness with which the British had long since been following the efforts of the Six. It led the Foreign Office in particular to underestimate the chances of further progress in European integration in other areas than defence where it would soon turn out to be potentially much more damaging to Britain's economic interests and, ultimately, its political influence in Western Europe and to its world power status. The Six's decision at the Messina conference in June 1955 to proceed with further economic integration has usually been explained as the attempt after the breakdown of the EDC project to 're-launch' the idea of European integration in the economic field.[24] More recently, it has been stressed that the proposals for horizontal integration in the form of a customs union among the Six as well as for further sectoral integration did not come out of the blue but had in fact been debated for some time parallel to the EDC and EPC talks between 1950 and 1954.[25] The first proposals for a West European customs union by the French and Italians in 1947 still aimed at organizing Western Europe as a political unit, led by France, to provide security against a revived Germany. On Bevin's initiative, Britain actually joined a Customs Union Study Group, which was established by most of the states participating in the Marshall Plan talks.[26] Within Whitehall, however, the Treasury and the Board of Trade argued that a customs union would lead to full economic union with Western Europe, thus destroying Britain's role as a world trading power. It seems that what Bevin had in mind at the time was an economic link between Western Europe and the Commonwealth and Empire, tying together manufacturing countries and raw material producers.[27] The idea of a union of West European states with their colonies reappeared later and seems to have played an important role in the formation of French policy towards economic integration in the mid-1950s. In 1947–8, however, Bevin's views continued to be opposed by the economic ministries and soon vanished over the creation of the OEEC.

Like the French and Italian initiatives, American proposals for a European customs union in the 1940s, although not directed against Germany, were also of a highly political nature. They were designed to complement in the economic field the military and political elements of a Western security system which would encompass the Federal Republic of Germany, once it was formed in 1949. Only in the 1950s did the potential economic advantages of a customs union in freeing and stimulating trade in Western Europe gain in importance. By fostering economic interdependence, by stimulating growth and by creating greater prosperity, a customs union was now also expected to increase the stability and security of Western Europe in a more general sense than only to contain German economic power. The customs union idea was taken up again by the Dutch in the so-called Beyen Plan of September 1952 which forms the intellectual 'bridge' leading from the ECSC to the European Economic Community (EEC).[28] After the breakdown of the EDC in 1954, the Benelux governments once again returned to the idea and produced a memorandum on 18 May 1955 in which they proposed the creation of a common market among the Six in the form of a customs union. The customs union project was also supported by one section of the German Economics Ministry, from where very similar proposals emanated which the Bonn government initially presented in a separate memorandum.[29] Proposals for further sectoral as opposed to horizontal integration included those for integration in transport and nuclear policy, ideas which by 1955 had also been debated for some time both within and outside the OEEC.

To discuss the various proposals for closer economic integration, the Six, represented by their foreign ministers, met in Messina on 1–3 June 1955. In the final conference communiqué they declared their intention to create a common market among themselves in the form of a customs union with common institutions and progressively closer cooperation in economic and social policy. In addition, and as a quid pro quo to the French, who were initially very sceptical about the customs union proposal, they also agreed in principle to create an atomic energy authority.[30] The foreign ministers charged a newly created expert committee under the direction of the Belgian Foreign Minister Paul-Henri Spaak to analyse the technical problems involved in setting up a common market and to present the results in a final report, before negotiations between the governments could start. The Spaak Committee finished its deliberations in November 1955.[31] The final report was subsequently drafted by a small group of senior officials and eventually published on 21 April 1956.[32] It had in fact been turned by Spaak into a 'political plan for action' rather than a purely technical report.[33] At their conference in Venice in May 1956 the Six discussed the report and principally supported its recommendations. They agreed to start negotiations which finally led to the signing of the Rome Treaties on 25 March 1957 and thus to the creation of the EEC and Euratom.

It is important to point to the degree of continuity in thinking about the various proposals for economic integration in Western Europe. To explain the Messina initiative and its ultimate success, it is not, however, sufficient to argue that economic integration, which got 'briefly and only by fortuity mixed up with the military problem, was able to resurface where it had been submerged'.[34]

Particular reasons can be identified as to why the various schemes for economic integration, which had been aired before, were revitalized so soon after the failure of the EDC

and as to why the customs union project was eventually acceptable to the French, who were initially very reserved about the
prospect of greater German competition in industrial products in their market. The Messina initiative was certainly
designed to contribute to West European security through fostering economic interdependence. This motive, however, had
gained in importance because, unlike the much more closely
integrated EDC and EPC, military integration of the Federal
Republic into NATO and WEU did not seem to go far enough
in the control of the Federal Republic through integration.
Other motives for supporting the Messina initiative varied by
country. They included the belief that economic integration
would be politically less sensitive in France than military
integration with the Federal Republic. Another important
motive was that economic integration and interdependence,
while economically valuable in itself, would increasingly foster
political cooperation and interdependence among the Six, the
ultimate aim of many involved in European integration.
Moreover, the Messina initiative was to demonstrate that the
Six were capable of successful independent action after the
humiliating experience of the EDC failure and the subsequent
rescue by the British and Americans with the creation of the
WEU and German accession to NATO. This was a significant
psychological factor which, despite the diverging economic
interests among the Six, helped to sustain the increasing determination, particularly on the part of the French, in 1955–7
to proceed, if necessary, without Britain; later the French government believed that it was even preferable to proceed
without Britain.

In a more general sense, the Messina initiative was also a
protest against the British Europe which had emerged with
the creation of the OEEC and the accession of the Federal
Republic to NATO, a Western Europe that was largely organized along intergovernmental lines and restricted to trade liberalization. The initiative reflected the determination of the
Six after the creation of the ECSC to emancipate themselves
further from intergovernmental economic cooperation
through the OEEC, which was so effectively controlled by the
British government with the help of those countries, such as
Sweden and Switzerland, who did not wish to participate in
more integrated organizations either because of their

neutrality or for economic reasons. The low tariff countries among the Six became increasingly annoyed over the lack of British willingness even to discuss tariffs within the OEEC, while many among the Six were also disappointed over the total depoliticization of the OEEC, orchestrated by the British, which made it so unsuitable for any politically meaningful economic integration in Western Europe. The Six did acknowledge the progress made in OEEC towards the progressive abolition of quantitative restrictions in West European trade. The low tariff Benelux countries, however, regarded this as insufficient and had demanded for some time that tariff cuts should also be discussed in the OEEC. The British, however, strictly rejected this on the grounds that tariffs should be dealt with exclusively by GATT. They wished to prevent a regionalization of tariff negotiations and wanted to protect their own relatively high tariff barriers as well as the remaining Commonwealth preferences. In 1955, however, the Benelux countries only agreed to the further extension of the volume of West European trade to 90 per cent, on which quantitative restrictions were to be abolished, under the condition that these would be followed by OEEC tariff cuts to be extended to third countries on a most-favoured-nation basis. They did so only to find the British as uncompromising as ever in the OEEC Ministerial Council meeting in February 1956. This British fundamentalism greatly annoyed the traditionally anglophile Benelux governments. Others who played a crucial role in the Messina process, such as Spaak, had given up hope that the organization might still prove useful in fostering closer political unity among its members. It was obvious that the British had systematically undermined any attempt to instil a political element into the OEEC and that, moreover, they had no intention to change their policy on this in the foreseeable future. The OEEC, Spaak made plain to the British government during a visit to London in November 1955, was 'like a boutique' in which each member could take what suited its particular interests. In contrast, the Six wanted a more closely-knit community.[35]

When the plans for further economic integration were first aired among the Six, the British failed to grasp the continuity with previous discussions or the main economic and political motives as to why the Six were now aiming at the quantum

leap from the more limited sectoral integration in coal and
steel to the much more ambitious scheme for a customs
union. It became clear early on that this would be supplemented by agreements on agriculture and nuclear policy.
Pronounced complacency after the failure of the EDC in 1954,
combined with the arrogant belief that the Six were bound to
fail without British support or even guidance, also led the
British to underestimate the extent to which the Messina initiative represented a substantial revolt against a British
Western Europe. Strictly limited to intergovernmental cooperation and trade liberalization, a British Western Europe
had to conform to both the extra-European interests and responsibilities of the British and the needs of the three circles
doctrine. It was not designed to serve the economic and political interests of the Six.

2 What Bus? The Messina Conference, 1955

At Messina, the Six decided to invite Britain to join the preparatory talks in Brussels and possible subsequent negotiations. As the failure of the EDC was partly attributed to Britain's refusal to participate, it initially appeared that at least the benevolent support of the British government was a necessary precondition for the success of any attempt at further integration. Unlike the Schuman Plan of 1950, British consent to a supranational authority was not made a precondition for participating in the talks. The failure of the EDC had led to a reorientation among the Six towards functional integration, which would progress in stages and leave important powers to the member states. Although the Benelux memorandum suggested that the common market be administered by a strong central authority, the exact division of power between such an institution and the national governments remained wide open.

The Cabinet discussed the invitation of the Six on 30 June 1955.[1] Ministers agreed to follow the proposal of the Chancellor of the Exchequer, Rab Butler, that the advantages and disadvantages of British membership in a West European customs union should be evaluated by a working group of the interdepartmental Mutual Aid Committee (MAC) which was responsible for questions of international economic cooperation. In the Spaak Committee Britain was to be represented by Russell Bretherton, Under-Secretary of the Board of Trade. Due to the preparatory character of the Brussels talks, the Foreign Office expected that it would not be necessary to make a decision on membership in a customs union before autumn. Between July and October 1955 the governmental debate on British European policy took place almost exclusively at the official level. The MAC Working Group included officials from the Foreign Office, the Commonwealth Relations Office, the Colonial Office and the Ministry of Agriculture, Fisheries and Food; however, the representatives of the economic ministries – the Treasury and the Board of Trade – dominated the internal discussion. Under the chairmanship of Burke Trend, Under-Secretary of the Treasury, the Working Group met ten times to discuss various memoranda submitted by the ministries involved, concentrating on the possible economic consequences of British membership in a customs union. Wider foreign policy considerations were given only scant attention and were left largely to the Foreign Office.

To assess the economic balance of membership, Trend argued, short-term dangers had to be weighed against potential long-term benefits.[2] The main problem appeared to be the necessary structural adjustments in those economic sectors insufficiently prepared for the much greater competitive pressures that would accompany the abolition of tariffs within a customs union. According to the Board of Trade, the problem sectors included horticulture and certain so-called strategic industries such as chemicals. These industries were regarded as essential for national defence and were still protected by the high tariffs of the 1932 Import Duties Act and, in some cases, of the Key Industries Duties of the First World War.[3] The resulting transitional unemployment could perhaps be limited with the help of an adjustment fund which at that time was already under discussion in Brussels. Nonetheless, the officials argued in their final report that participation in a West European customs union would probably result in regional economic disparities within Britain and could – even in the long term – disadvantage certain regions with a high concentration of uncompetitive industries.[4] At the same time, most leading officials in the economic ministries saw considerable long-term advantages in British participation in a customs union.[5] They believed – as did advocates of economic integration in continental European countries – that the general benefits of a customs union included a more efficient allocation of resources, the production in greater units, an improved competitiveness in relation to producers from third countries and an increased trade among the member states, all of which was expected to lead to greater economic growth.

The key feature of the envisaged customs union was the abolition of internal tariffs and the introduction of a common external tariff *vis-à-vis* third countries. Consequently, the MAC

Working Group concentrated on assessing the possible effects
of membership on British trade. In their first memorandum
the officials from the Commercial Relations and Exports
Department of the Board of Trade concluded that membership would result in considerable additional export opportunities for British industry in the rapidly growing West
European market. At first sight, however, participation in a
West European customs union seemed incompatible with
British trade patterns.[6] After all, only 14 per cent of British
exports went to the Six and only 25 per cent to Western
Europe as a whole. By comparison, almost 50 per cent still
went to Commonwealth countries. In theory, at least, participation in a West European customs union with a common
external tariff would lead to so-called negative preferences for
Commonwealth products in the British market, that is tariff
discrimination by comparison with products from within the
customs union.

While ministers still regarded the preferences as essential
for the political cohesion of the Commonwealth in 1955,
senior officials of the Board of Trade concluded that the economic benefits of the various preferential trade agreements
with the Commonwealth countries were hardly significant any
more. The main advantage the other Commonwealth countries derived from the preference system was free entry for
their agricultural products, which amounted to 50 per cent of
Commonwealth exports to Britain. Although the preparatory
talks in Brussels showed that compensatory concessions would
be necessary to induce European agricultural exporters, such
as France, to agree to the proposed industrial customs union,
the Six did not aim at free trade in agriculture. The economic
ministries thus speculated that in case of British participation
special arrangements could be negotiated that would safeguard the main export interest of the Commonwealth countries. An additional 40 per cent of Commonwealth exports to
Britain were raw materials, which were mostly tariff-free in the
Six. As a result, Britain's Commonwealth partners would only
lose the preferences on their industrial exports, losses that
would mainly affect Canada.

British firms, on the other hand, almost exclusively exported industrial products to the Commonwealth. The Board
of Trade reckoned that if Commonwealth trade interests

could indeed be safeguarded in negotiations in Europe, most British preferences in the Commonwealth markets could also be retained. In any case, the preferences were now rightly seen as having only a marginal effect on trade flows. According to the Board of Trade, the main competitive advantages of British exporters in the Commonwealth markets were not slightly lower tariffs; rather, they were cultural connections, long-standing trade contacts and the advantageous regulations of the Sterling Area, which limited trade in currencies other than sterling.[7] Senior Board of Trade officials regarded the remaining preferences primarily as pawns in future GATT negotiations. Equal access to the West European market was widely judged as much more important in the long term.[8]

A further erosion of the preferences was seen as inevitable, not least because of pressure from other Commonwealth countries. Since 1938 the British share of exports by other Commonwealth countries had declined from 39 to 27 per cent. In 1956 64 per cent of New Zealand's exports still went to Britain, but it only received 31 per cent of Australian and 17 per cent of Canadian exports.[9] The Australian and the Canadian economies became increasingly integrated in the Pacific and the North American economic spheres respectively. Britain's policy of expanding its domestic agricultural industry left little room for an increase in agricultural exports to Britain which remained of paramount importance for Australia and New Zealand. Equally, with respect to their growing industrial exports, it was inadvisable for Commonwealth countries to concentrate unduly on the relatively small and slowly growing British market. For most Commonwealth countries the existing trade links increasingly lost significance when compared to the benefits gained from British investment and capital exports.

For a prognosis of the economic balance of membership in a West European customs union, the Industries and Manufactures Department of the Board of Trade was asked to assess the likely trade gains and losses of individual sectors.[10] The department's divisions had close contacts with the various sectors, mainly with export-oriented firms, and tended to represent their views within Whitehall. Overall, the divisions expected British industry to be extremely apprehensive about its ability to sell successfully in a West European common market, a market that was regarded as much more competitive than the weaker Commonwealth markets in which British firms enjoyed natural trade advantages. The Industries and Manufactures Department expected major new export opportunities in only coal and steel, automobiles and mechanical engineering. But even for these sectors the Board of Trade officials were wary of German competition in the home market once British producers were no longer protected by tariffs of up to 50 per cent. Massive German inroads into the British market were expected, for example, in automobiles and optical products. Officials also reckoned with increased American exports to Britain, for example in construction and office machinery, as the common external tariff would have to be considerably lower in certain sectors than current British tariffs, thus strengthening the competitiveness of third-country producers in the British market. Among the main losers in a common market, the chemical industry, which in 1955 was already running a trade deficit with Western Europe, was predicted to fare disastrously. In fact, it later exported quite successfully to the Six even when confronted with a tariff disadvantage in the 1960s. The pronounced defeatism of the Industries and Manufactures Department, at a time when Britain was still comfortably the world's leading export nation, was not shared at all by senior Board of Trade officials like Bretherton. It nonetheless contributed to the highly ambivalent overall judgement in the final MAC report, which made clear that any prognosis of likely trade gains and losses was speculative and depended primarily on the assessment of the general competitiveness of British industry. Moreover, the economic balance also depended on the details of a possible treaty, including for example the levels of the common external tariff, which officials could not possibly foresee before the start of negotiations. The economic ministries thus concluded that the economic consequences were so unpredictable that there was no clear economic case for participating in the establishment of a West European customs union. In their economic report the Treasury and Board of Trade also considered the wider implications of participation in a common market for economic policy-making.[11] Officials reckoned with a progressive loss of sovereignty which, however, was not in principle seen as problematic. They expected that the government could negotiate terms which would be economically acceptable and politically marketable. In particular, the Board of Trade was less worried about the inevitable loss of Britain's independent power to conclude trade treaties than about the exact levels of the common external tariff. In some sectors Britain would have to lower existing tariffs considerably which, in combination with the necessary reduction of Commonwealth preferences, would temporarily diminish Britain's bargaining power *vis-à-vis* third countries such as the United States. At the same time the Board of Trade appreciated that the unified negotiating power of a West European customs union in GATT and elsewhere would far surpass that of individual West European states.

Should the government have decided in favour of membership in a customs union, the Treasury wanted to see very strict rules limiting the use of quantitative restrictions by member states, particularly France, to reduce balance of payments problems. For Britain this would have meant even greater reliance on tax and interest rate policy to protect sterling. Equally, the Treasury was very keen on a competition policy to control the use of national subsidies and to prevent the formation of cartels. Anticipating the internal market programme of the 1980s, the Treasury even expected that in order to make the common market work, some degree of standardization would be necessary regarding non-tariff barriers such as industrial norms. By comparison the Treasury expected no significant changes in finance and monetary policy. The harmonization of taxes, for example, was regarded as equally unnecessary and undesirable. Finally, officials pointed out that if the Sterling Area were to be kept intact, the government could not agree to open the London capital market to member states of a customs union without a major improvement in Britain's balance of payments situation. They insisted that capital export controls would have to remain in place for the foreseeable future, a measure which they regarded as invariably preferable to the use of quantitative restrictions in trade.

The economic ministries also discussed whether a free trade area might not be preferable to a customs union, if Britain participated in a common market. The main difference between the two was that in a free trade area internal tariffs were to be abolished while national external tariffs remained in place. The Economic Section of the Treasury, comprised of independent economic experts on leave from British universities, argued strongly in favour of a customs union which they expected to offer greater long-term benefits.[12] But the Board of Trade view prevailed; a free trade area was preferable as the more conservative and politically acceptable approach in so far as it allowed Britain to retain its national autonomy in foreign trade policy and helped to safeguard the remaining Commonwealth preferences.[13] When the MAC Working Group submitted its internal report in October 1955, it was already clear, however, that the Six wanted a customs union and that the free trade area was therefore not a realistic alternative. The Board of Trade position is nonetheless significant as it foreshadowed the so-called Plan G which was later propagated by the ministry in the spring of 1956 during deliberations within Whitehall about a counter-initiative to the Messina proposals. In their analysis the economic ministries compared participation in a West European common market with the status quo. Their decision not to recommend membership because it offered no clear economic advantages was made on the basis that the Messina initiative, as predicted by the Foreign Office, was doomed once the British withdrew from the preparatory talks in Brussels. The economic ministries were concerned, however, lest the Six manage to set up a customs union without Britain. In his June memorandum Butler had already warned that such an economic bloc would damage Britain's trade interests and its strong political position within the OEEC, the main forum for economic cooperation in Western Europe.[14]

The economic ministries saw numerous dangers. For one, German industry would gain a decisive competitive advantage in a common market of the Six. As a result, British producers would lose important export opportunities in one of the most rapidly growing markets in the world, while their tariff preferences in the stagnating Commonwealth markets were continuously being eroded. Moreover, continental European producers could make use of all the advantages of a much larger home market to improve their competitive position in third markets. Perhaps the British government would retain more freedom in economic policy; without influence on the policies of the Six, however, formal independence might soon prove worthless. The government could be tempted to defer necessary but politically inconvenient structural adjustments in the British economy without the disciplinary effect of membership in a common market. In the long term it would thus be even more questionable whether British industry could continue to compete on equal terms in world markets.

Just how dangerous exclusion from a common market of the Six would be remained controversial. The final MAC report was a compromise document, influenced by the Foreign Office as well as the protectionist ministries, particularly the Commonwealth Relations Office. Even this memorandum concluded, however, that 'it can be argued, with some reason, that the disadvantages of abstaining would, in the long run, outweigh the advantages.'[15] Earlier in the internal Whitehall discussions Treasury and Board of Trade officials had prophetically warned that 'if the six countries went forward with a common market on their own, it might have unfavourable effects on United Kingdom industry after a few years, and we might then be forced to join on their terms.'[16]

In 1955 the economic ministries already operated against the backdrop of Britain's relative economic decline in comparison to the Six. Even taking into account their different starting positions after the war, average British growth rates were relatively low between 1950 and 1955 at 2.9 per cent when compared with 4.4 per cent in France, 6.3 per cent in Italy, 9.1 per cent in the Federal Republic and an average of 6.2 per cent in the Six.[17] During the same period most West European countries also fared much better in terms of investment rates and productivity increases. The public did not begin to perceive Britain's relative decline until the early 1960s. On the other hand, the officials in the economic ministries were well aware of some of the structural weaknesses of the British economy and were concerned about British industry's competitiveness in Western Europe, particularly in comparison with German industry. If British producers continued to concentrate on the weaker Commonwealth markets, officials thought, their capacity to adjust might well diminish further. In this respect the Messina initiative was indeed recognized at the official level as a serious challenge, unintended by the Six, to British economic and trade policy.

The economic ministries, however, had not yet advanced beyond the stage of selective therapy, such as drastic cuts in military spending in the wake of the 1957 Defence White Paper. Some issues were still taboo, including the anchor role of sterling in the Sterling Area which forced the British government to defend its overvalued currency with a deflationary tax and interest rate policy which affected economic development adversely. In 1955 the Treasury and the Board of Trade could only agree on warning against the possible exclusion of Britain from a common market of the Six. They never challenged the Foreign Office's self-proclaimed supremacy in European policy-making which judged the question of membership in a West European customs union exclusively on foreign policy rather than economic grounds. In the end, even most officials in the Treasury and the Board of Trade agreed that the issue was primarily political. While assessing the economic benefits of the remaining preferences very pragmatically, senior Board of Trade officials indicated in the same memorandum that the preferences were probably still politically and psychologically important enough to exclude the possibility of British participation in a common market in Western Europe.[18]

The economic advantages and disadvantages of participation in a common market were analysed quite extensively in the MAC Working Group and in the MAC itself. In contrast, the political part of the final MAC report was prepared by the Foreign Office without prior interministerial discussion and after only very selective consultation with some senior officials in the Treasury, including the Head of the Overseas Finance Division, Otto Clarke. Clarke rejected common market membership outright and, along with other Treasury officials, he remained unconcerned about the possible adverse economic effects of exclusion from a customs union of the Six. The Foreign Office completely ignored the discussion within Whitehall about the economic aspects of the issue. The wider political arguments were presented in such a way as to lead to the seemingly inevitable conclusion that participation in a common market in Western Europe was incompatible with Britain's world power role.[19] The Foreign Office memorandum simply confirmed the traditional policy of Britain since Churchill's 1946 Zurich speech of encouraging integration from outside whenever it went beyond intergovernmental co-operation, excluding the possibility of British participation. In principle, the Foreign Office argued, the Messina initiative was worth welcoming because it was supported by Britain's most important ally, the United States, and could potentially contribute to binding the Federal Republic further to the West. Generally, European integration was seen as valuable psychologically for the political cohesion and stability of Western Europe.

The Foreign Office then proceeded to explain that Britain itself could under no circumstances participate in a common market, because membership would result in a one-sided emphasis on the European role, destroying the equilibrium in the three circles of Britain's foreign relations. Membership in a West European customs union, the Foreign Office maintained, would endanger the political cohesion of the Commonwealth; it would undermine Commonwealth confidence in British leadership, and it might even call into question the very existence of the Commonwealth. In any case, the political consequences would be so damaging as to exclude absolutely the possiblity of British participation in setting up a common market in Western Europe. In retrospect Nutting, Minister of State at the Foreign Office in 1955–6, argued that the government did not want to participate in a common market and that the Commonwealth was merely a welcome excuse.[20] Nutting was right in so far as the Foreign Office played up the potential adverse effects on the Commonwealth in order to prevent a major debate about the future priorities of British foreign and trade policy. But in the view of most officials and politicians, the Commonwealth still fulfilled the important function of contributing significantly to the legitimation of Britain's continued claim to a world power role. The Commonwealth was an important foreign policy status symbol which helped to compensate for Britain's relative economic and political decline and to justify a special role alongside the United States and the Soviet Union.

In its memorandum the Foreign Office also claimed that participation in a common market in Western Europe would endanger Britain's special relationship with the United States,[21] a peculiar argument since the Foreign Office actually admitted that the Eisenhower government would certainly welcome a British decision to take the lead in setting up a common market in Western Europe, just as it had initially hoped for British participation in the EDC. In fact, the Foreign Office was well aware of the American position on the Messina initiative. Even before the Messina conference the Foreign Office had been advised by the American Embassy in London that the Eisenhower government supported the new initiatives without reservation. In anticipation of possible British objections the State Department had even told the Foreign Office that they saw absolutely no danger of any overlap with the work of the OEEC.[22] Subsequently, the State Department actively supported the Six in insisting on the continued exclusion of the OEEC Secretary General from the Brussels talks.[23]

In the political part of the final MAC report, the Foreign Office did not even attempt to explain its transatlantic argument. The warning, however unfounded, that the special transatlantic relationship was at stake, did allow the Foreign Office to manoeuvre around a politically sensitive issue: citing transatlantic interests, it could more easily forestall serious discussion about British participation in a common market with France and the Federal Republic, which saved Britain the appearance of having declined to a medium-sized power, overstretched economically and militarily. Other arguments were relatively less important. The Foreign Office maintained, for example, that the creation of a common market, with or without Britain, would endanger Britain's privileged political position within the OEEC. The British government controlled the OEEC so well that in alternating alliances with other member states, it had succeeded for some time in preventing a political strengthening of the organization or OEEC tariff negotiations. The Foreign Office was determined that this bastion of intergovernmental cooperation, comprising all of Western Europe, should not be undermined. Finally, the Foreign Office warned against the possibility that a West European common market, even if largely intergovernmental at the outset, could always develop into a more integrated organization later. Even before the Messina conference, Assistant Under-Secretary John Coulson had noted that 'there can of course be no question of our entering any organisation of a supra-national character.'[24] Despite the failure of the

EDC, Foreign Office officials remained haunted by the ghost of a European federation in which Britain would lose its sovereignty, and this ghost proved useful in deterring certain ministries and cabinet members from calling into question the main political premises of the established British European policy. Constitutional theory, however, was no longer in step with the political reality of an increasingly interdependent world, in which Britain depended on the protection or cooperation of other states, notably the United States, for its external security and its economic affluence. The economic ministries no longer supported the Foreign Office's dogmatic division into strictly intergovernmental and other, partly or fully federal organizations. They were not, in principle, unduly disturbed by the prospect of a substantial loss of sovereignty within a common market. In foreign economic policy, particularly in GATT, they had operated for some time with institutionalized transfer of sovereignty. Despite the existence of NATO, the Foreign Office, in contrast, was still only very slowly getting used to the loss of Britain's independence to project power, which was to become obvious in the Suez war of 1956.

Among the ministries involved, only the Board of Trade was prepared in 1955 to consider an innovation in Britain's relationship with the Six. Its senior officials were highly critical of the political arguments used by the Foreign Office. These were more relevant to the present than to the future, Bretherton argued in an internal circular in November.[25] Moreover, because of Bretherton's reports from Brussels, the Board of Trade feared that the self-confident prediction of the Foreign Office might be proved incorrect, and that the Messina initiative would not sooner or later simply collapse as a result of French intransigence. The President of the Board of Trade, Peter Thorneycroft, was the leading champion within the government of a liberal foreign economic policy. He wanted Britain to get away from the preference system. At the Conservative Party conference in 1954 Thorneycroft had helped to defeat a motion for the expansion of existing preferences, illegal under GATT, which was the beginning of the end of the ideological defence by the Conservative Party of imperial preference. For Western Europe Thorneycroft strongly preferred a free trade area, as did the German

Economics Minister Ludwig Erhard. Thorneycroft believed that a customs union would encourage what he regarded as the undesirable regionalization of the world economy. The Board of Trade also feared that under French protectionist influence, a customs union might degenerate into a preference system.

Under the influence of his senior officials, Thorneycroft became primarily concerned with avoiding Britain's exclusion from a customs union of the Six. He wanted the government to keep its options open until it was clear whether the Brussels talks would indeed falter.[26] The Board of Trade had indicated previously in the interministerial discussions that, if necessary, it would support participation in a customs union as a founding member, once the success of the Messina initiative could be foreseen. This would avoid the economic dangers of exclusion and enable Britain to influence the development of the new organization effectively from the outset. By autumn, the Board of Trade was forced to decide between participation and a final negative reply to the Six. At this stage the Board of Trade saw such grave dangers in possible exclusion from a common market of the Six that in the final meeting of the Economic Steering Committee of senior officials, Permanent Secretary Frank Lee opted for membership.[27] Lee's vote was a symbolic gesture because it had been clear all along that the Board of Trade was in a minority of one. Thorneycroft thus refrained from intervening again at the ministerial level when the Economic Policy Committee decided at its meeting of 11 November 1955 to withdraw from the Spaak Committee.[28] In order to safeguard Britain's trade interests Thorneycroft now had to prevent the emergence of a customs union of the Six.

In the Treasury the views of senior officials varied much more than in the Board of Trade. Some believed strongly that in the long term, the economic arguments were all for membership – or that at least the economic dangers of exclusion had to be avoided. The most innovative were the experts in the Economic Section and the chairman of the MAC Working Group, Burke Trend.[29] Their opponents usually insisted that the political arguments put forward by the Foreign Office excluded the possibility of membership anyway. Otherwise, they tended to emphasize the benefits of the Commonwealth preferences and the implicit link between the preferences, the

Sterling Area and the wider political stability of the Commonwealth. The warning that a reorientation of trade policy might fatally undermine the cohesion of the Sterling Area was highly speculative, and was thus only referred to in passing in the MAC report. The school of economic thought which asserted the supremacy of currency over trade policy was, however, still influential and included such senior figures as Clarke. Their arguments lined up nicely with those of the Foreign Office and contributed significantly to the overall negative position of the Treasury, strongly supported by Butler himself, who was opposed in principle to membership which to him appeared incompatible with Britain's role at the centre of the Sterling Area and of the Commonwealth.

By comparison, the Foreign Office was very cohesive, taking for granted both the primacy of the political argument about Britain's world power role and its departmental prerogative in European policy over the economic ministries. The degree of departmental arrogance which the Foreign Office habitually displayed is best exemplified by an ironic comment made by the Permanent Under-Secretary of State for Foreign Affairs, Ivone Kirkpatrick. He remarked laconically in a draft letter to the British Ambassador to Bonn, Frederick Hoyer Millar, 'there are in Whitehall economists who will undertake to prove that the United Kingdom ought to join in setting up a European Common Market! It was left ... to the Foreign Office to supply the spectacles of political reality.'[30] Kirkpatrick's remark and the political part of the final MAC report reflect a very strong belief in the primacy of foreign policy. The Foreign Office simply ignored the economic aspects of the issue. It is doubtful whether it actually had the necessary expertise to appreciate the dangers of exclusion from a customs union of the Six. It generally lacked economic aptitude, particularly after it had been stripped of its Economic Intelligence Department during Churchill's peacetime government.[31] The ministry was still run by a special elite with a pronounced *esprit de corps*, whose members had mostly studied philosophy or classics at Oxford or Cambridge. They were educated to rule the Empire and not to manage its disintegration or to search for a new role for Britain in the world. They were particularly ill-prepared for the new challenges of an increasingly interdependent world economy.

Instead of presenting fairly the political pros and cons of each course, the Foreign Office attempted in its report to manipulate government policy by giving a one-sided picture. Trend, the chairman of the MAC Working Group, complained bitterly in a letter to Clarke that the Foreign Office deliberately suppressed important political arguments which did not fit its overall assessment, in order to sustain its wider argument against British membership in a West European customs union. In particular, Trend mentioned the fear shared by Foreign Office officials in the previous interdepartmental discussions that a common market without Britain would be dominated economically and eventually also politically by the Germans.[32] The Head of the Mutual Aid Department, Alan Edden, had in fact admitted as early as June 1955 that British participation would help 'to hinder the possible emergence of an integrated continental Europe dominated by German economic power'.[33]

At the level of senior officials and ministers, the Foreign Office precluded a thorough debate over Britain's future policy priorities with what seemed a conclusive argument, namely that the Messina initiative, just like the EDC, would eventually collapse as a result of French obstruction. The Foreign Office initially argued only that success was unlikely.[34] In a meeting of the Economic Steering Committee on 1 November 1955, however, the Deputy Under-Secretary of State, Harold Caccia, went one step further. He declared categorically that according to the most recent reports from the British Embassy in Paris, the French government was sure to torpedo the customs union plan eventually.[35] The challenge was, or so it seemed, how to allow the Brussels talks to transpire without damaging the transatlantic security and defence system.

During his eight months as Foreign Secretary, Harold Macmillan never intervened once to challenge the substance of the Foreign Office approach. This is particularly interesting given that the current situation provided a much greater chance than the Schuman Plan to attain institutional structures for possible new organizations in Western Europe which would be acceptable to Britain. When he assumed the position of Foreign Secretary, Macmillan was still regarded by some colleagues as a Europhile, a reputation gained during what

Butler called 'his Strasbourg goose days':[36] from 1949 to 1952 Macmillan was one of the British delegates in the Parliamentary Assembly of the Council of Europe, where he supported British participation in a West European organization for coal and steel, albeit one for which he suggested a more intergovernmental institutional structure than that of the ECSC. Later Macmillan carefully cultivated his European image. In his memoirs he emphasized, for example, that while Minister of Housing under Churchill, he had supported a more constructive European policy, and that Foreign Secretary Eden had been responsible for Britain's negative policy towards the plan for a European army.[37]

In 1955, however, Macmillan's approach differed very little from that of the new Prime Minister Eden. Ministers came and went, but Foreign Office policy remained unchanged. Macmillan shared the view that membership in a West European common market was incompatible with Britain's world power role. Once he moved to the Foreign Office, from which half the world had once been ruled, much of the Europeanness Macmillan had previously displayed was suddenly gone. Macmillan, too, wanted the government to keep its options open, but only, in his own words, as an 'insurance policy'.[38] On 19 September 1955, on the margins of an internal Foreign Office memorandum, he remarked about the Messina initiative: 'This is our second string – we may need it. The "one-world approach" isn't going with a swing at the moment. It may even bankrupt us.'[39] Most of the time, however, Macmillan hoped that the spectre of a common market of the Six would simply disappear before long. As late as mid-December 1955 he confidently predicted in his diaries that the French would 'never' join a common market.[40] Without British participation the plan seemed doomed.

The British government was so certain of the eventual failure of the Six that the Messina initiative was never once discussed by the Cabinet. For the officials it was sufficient to know that within the Cabinet there was little or no support for any fundamental reorientation in government policy towards Europe. The implicit consensus, shared by Macmillan, was that, for the time being at least, participation in a common market in Western Europe was neither in Britain's wider political interest nor politically feasible. Thus it was no realistic

possibility. The political part of the final MAC report, by reit-
erating most of the arguments used in previous internal evalu-
ations of Britain's priorities in Western Europe, rather
conveniently seemed to confirm the traditional assumptions
underlying the established policy. The Prime Minister never
even bothered to enquire about Messina. All Eden did was to
advise the Cabinet Office to downgrade Trend's interdepartmental group of officials from subcommittee to working
group.[41] Only one year after the failure of the EDC, most
British ministers were, if anything, bored by the apparently
futile efforts of the Six. In any case, the government was preoccupied with seemingly more urgent matters, such as the
crises in Cyprus and Egypt and summit diplomacy.

Lacking a supranational nexus, as they had in 1950, the Six
had placed the British government in a serious dilemma.
Edden, of the Mutual Aid Department, concluded even before
Messina that the only honest solution was for the government
to accept the invitation but to make absolutely clear that
Britain could not actually participate. Edden was convinced
that the government should not negotiate if it was not even
prepared to consider membership.[42] Britain should merely
send an observer to the Spaak Committee who would follow
the talks among the Six.[43] If, contrary to expectation, the Six
succeeded in setting up a common market, then Britain could
always consider some form of association later. Edden's recommendation reflected the consensus view of the Foreign
Office. Butler also agreed and suggested to the Cabinet that
they appoint an observer.[44] The Six should be assured of the
British government's broad political support, he argued.
Otherwise, one had to be extremely cautious when trying to
influence the talks, in order to safeguard British economic
interests. In particular, the government would have to insist in
its written reply to the Six that 'there are, as you are no doubt
aware, special reasons which would *preclude* this country from
joining a European common market.'[45]

If the Six were to succeed in setting up a common market,
the line taken by the Foreign Office and Butler was unlikely to
protect Britain's economic interests in Western Europe.
Substantial economic association with a customs union was
clearly not as easy to negotiate as a purely consultative form of
association with a sector organization such as the ECSC on

which Britain and the Six had agreed in 1954. The Foreign Office approach would, however, have made British government policy comprehensible for the Six. At least, it would have safeguarded Britain's strong diplomatic position in Western Europe after its major contribution in 1954 to the creation of the WEU and to the NATO entry of the Federal Republic. Instead, on 22 June 1955 the Foreign Secretary intervened by telegram from Washington, where he was meeting with the American President Dwight D. Eisenhower and Secretary of State John Foster Dulles. Without actually committing Britain to the principle of a customs union, he demanded that the government send a delegate and keep all its options open *vis-à-vis* the Six as long as possible.[46] Macmillan reckoned that, once more, the plans of the Six would collapse. The British government would then conjure up another emergency plan, this time for intensifying economic cooperation, and thus prevent the disintegration of Western Europe.

Macmillan succeeded only in so far as the Cabinet decided on the compromise solution of sending not an observer or a delegate but a 'representative', and only mentioning in passing in the written reply that Britain had 'special problems' with the proposal for a West European common market. Bretherton was sent to Brussels, and was later supported by a Treasury official and a Foreign Office diplomat from the British Embassy in Belgium. By accident a new European policy had emerged which Bretherton described in retrospect as 'cooperation without commitment',[47] a purely tactical innovation which soon proved a Pyrrhic victory for Macmillan and which led to a diplomatic fiasco for the British government.

The initial obstacles were of a domestic nature. Macmillan was able to convince his colleagues to agree to sending a representative only by implying that this was a tactical move on his part to influence the Brussels talks. As long as Bretherton was under tight control of the interdepartmental official and ministerial committees in London, he could put in a word or two to the Spaak Committee, without any commitment. But once the Brussels talks reached a more advanced stage by late summer, the Commonwealth Secretary Harry Crookshank and Butler demanded that the government should now withdraw Bretherton and make absolutely clear to the Six that it would not join a customs union. Bretherton continued to sit on the

Spaak Committee for a few more weeks, but the interdepartmental decision to withdraw him was inevitable.[48] Not only did
strong internal opposition from the Empire wing of the
Conservative Party prevent Macmillan from keeping all
options open until at least the French elections in early 1956,
his vague idea somehow to manipulate the Brussels talks was
immediately boycotted from within Whitehall. In addition to
Bretherton's small team, several ministries were asked to send
representatives to the various subcommittees of the Spaak
Committee, but some were withdrawn after only a few weeks.
Some senior officials either believed that the Brussels talks
were irrelevant to the respective British sectors, such as transport, or they hoped – as the Foreign Office thought – to gain a
free hand to criticize the plans of the Six in the OEEC.[49] By
the beginning of August the British were no longer represented in the Sub-Committees for Civil Aviation, Energy and
Post and Telecommunications, and the Treasury sent an internal circular demanding that ministries should at least ensure
that they were being kept informed of the Brussels talks.[50]

Macmillan not only faced internal obstruction. The Six also
declined to play by his rules. They wanted political support,
but did not really expect British participation. Their assessment was confirmed during the preparations for a ministerial
meeting in Nordwijk on 6 September 1955 to discuss the
progress made in the Brussels talks. Macmillan was invited,
too, but he allowed his officials to concoct an excuse for him,
citing the urgency of the Cyprus conflict, and the Foreign
Office proposed to send just Bretherton instead.[51] When the
Dutch subsequently insisted on the participation of a minister
rather than an official, the Foreign Office gladly turned down
the invitation, arguing that the government did not want to
commit itself.[52]

On 3 October 1955 the Belgian Foreign Minister declared
that the final report of the Spaak Committee would be prepared only by representatives of the Six. Whether or not he
meant to exclude Britain, as is sometimes argued,[53] is an irrelevant issue because the British, including Macmillan, had no
interest whatsoever in contributing to the Spaak report. All
they were looking for at this stage was that the British views, as
represented by Bretherton and his colleagues in Brussels,
would not be recognizable as such in the report and that, if

possible, the British government be given advance copies before the next ministerial meeting of the Six.[54] Finally, in the last session of the Spaak Committee on 7 November 1955 Bretherton simply read out word by word a Foreign Office statement which claimed that the British government would not participate in a customs union and, moreover, that they saw the danger of considerable overlap with the work of the OEEC. The Six were not surprised. Spaak commented ironically that some governments apparently could not understand the new context for European integration that had been created by the Messina conference,[55] but separation was peaceful – as long as the British refrained from torpedoing the Messina initiative.

The Six also ensured that the British would not be allowed to manipulate the Brussels talks without commiting themselves to participation. Bretherton had initially believed that the British government could steer the Brussels talks in any direction, provided it was prepared to participate fully.[56] However, he continued to get entirely negative instructions from London. With the Foreign Office continually ignoring Bretherton's warnings that the Six might well succeed without Britain, the Macmillan strategy of cooperation without commitment degenerated into a farce of Shakespearean proportion. Bretherton's position in Brussels became first uncomfortable and then untenable. Within the Board of Trade, Lee was extremely annoyed that his official had apparently been placed in Brussels as a diplomatic alibi, and by late September was already hoping for the end of the 'elaborate and embarrassing comedy of manners' which Macmillan had staged.[57]

Towards the end of the preparatory talks, the Six ceased to listen to Bretherton, whose interventions were basically restricted to two points: first, Bretherton had been told to propagate the concept of a free trade area instead of a customs union. When the Dutch Foreign Minister Johan Willem Beyen conveyed the invitation of the Six in London on 21 June 1955, he had already made clear, however, that the Six wanted a customs union.[58] At the end of July Bretherton confirmed from Brussels that a free trade area was absolutely out of the question,[59] but he was nonetheless forced to bring up the idea over and over again. Secondly, after frequent interventions in London by the British representative in the OEEC, Hugh Ellis-

Rees,[60] Bretherton was asked to warn at every possible junc-
ture against overlap with the work of the OEEC and to get the
consent of the Six, particularly the French, to the participation of the OEEC Secretary General René Sergent in the
Spaak Committee.[61] Sergent was eventually admitted to a few
sessions and allowed to read a statement at the final session,
but Bretherton's only diplomatic success in Brussels was hardly
more than a British face-saving exercise *vis-à-vis* third countries within the OEEC. As regards substance, Macmillan, with
his elaborate strategy of cooperation without commitment,
had not only failed in every respect, but he had even succeeded in making the Six rightly suspicious of British motives.
Everything now depended on the prediction of the Foreign
Office coming true, that the Messina initiative would collapse
as inevitably as capitalism would, according to Marx. But
would it? Only the British Ambassador to Paris, Gladwyn Jebb,
was certain that the French would veto the plan for a customs
union. Others were sceptical. Bretherton actually suggested in
his very first message from Brussels that there had been clear
signs that the Six were determined to make the Messina initiative a success.[62] In late 1955, when Spaak and a small group of
officials began to draw up their report, victory of the more
Europe-friendly centre-left seemed more likely in the forthcoming French elections. The economic ministries thus got increasingly agitated about the economic dangers of exclusion,
while the Foreign Office was primarily concerned about its
hegemonic institutional position within the OEEC, a position
which stood to be undermined by a customs union of the Six.
In a meeting of the Mutual Aid Committee at the end of
October 1955 all ministries agreed, therefore, that the
common market 'if possible, should be frustrated ... We
cannot count on the project collapsing of its own accord.'[63]
While the Board of Trade already wanted a constructive coun-
terproposal, the Foreign Office successfully pressed the line
that the Brussels initiative should be redirected into the orbit
of the OEEC where the British government would let it bog
down. 'Embrace destructively',[64] Gladwyn Jebb termed the
new OEEC strategy which, according to the decision by
the EPC on 11 November 1955, was to include *démarches* to the
governments in Washington and Bonn. These were delivered

one week later.[65] In both letters the Foreign Secretary stressed British displeasure with the Messina initiative and particularly with the plan for a customs union, as the union was allegedly incompatible with global trade liberalization and portended a politically dangerous split in Western Europe. Writing to Dulles, Macmillan also emphasized the potentially adverse economic effects of a customs union of the Six on third countries like the United States. As for the Germans, Macmillan relied on the scepticism of Erhard and of industry circles over a customs union which, they believed, might develop protectionist tendencies under French influence. Macmillan hoped that by expressing to Foreign Minister Heinrich von Brentano his strong reservations about a customs union of the Six, he would achieve a change of mind in Bonn. 'If we were to give them a lead', the Foreign Office argued, 'the Germans might ... adopt a more realistic policy ... and decide not to join a common market and concentrate on co-operation through OEEC.'[66]

Macmillan's European soap bubbles would soon burst. In his reply Dulles spelled out the motives of United States policy towards European integration since the Marshall Plan, emphasizing in particular the significance of the Messina initiative for further binding the Federal Republic to the West. Dulles confirmed that his government saw no danger of overlap with the OEEC at all, declaring that for broad political reasons the United States would continue to support the Six and their Messina initiative, even if a customs union initially developed some protectionist tendencies.[67] Dulles' answer could hardly have come as a surprise to the Foreign Office officials who were concerned with questions of European integration. State Department policy towards Western Europe had been well established and the American approach to Messina was well known to both the Foreign Office and the Foreign Secretary. Macmillan nonetheless believed that his personal intervention alone could lead to a sudden volte-face in American policy. He had an almost mystical belief in the intensity of the 'special relationship', which would not even be undermined by the experience of Suez.

While Dulles' straightforward negative reply did not lead Macmillan to reconsider British leverage over the American government, when British and American interests were so obviously mutually exclusive, he did immediately call off the OEEC policy designed to sabotage the Messina initiative. Under no circumstances could the British government allow itself to get involved in a fundamental conflict with Washington. At the end of 1955 all British embassies in Western Europe were instructed to stop plotting against the Six, and to indicate reserved diplomatic support instead.[68] During their visit to Washington in February 1956, Eden and the new Foreign Secretary Selwyn Lloyd tried one last time to convince the Americans that a customs union of the Six would split rather than unify Western Europe. Eisenhower and Dulles were unimpressed. Having returned to London, Eden mentioned in passing at a Cabinet meeting that the Americans were unfortunately just as enthusiastic for the Messina initiative as for the EDC.[69]

The Germans, on the other hand, had repeatedly been assured of strong American support for the Messina initiative when Macmillan's *démarche* reached Bonn. During the NATO Ministerial Council meeting on 17 December 1955 Dulles told Brentano, as well as Spaak and Monnet, that Macmillan's diplomatic attack was best ignored.[70] With the full support of Adenauer, the German Foreign Minister subsequently acknowledged only the receipt of the British *démarche* and proceeded to tell Macmillan, without further comment, that the German government was determined to continue the talks.[71] Macmillan's assessment of the likely German reaction to the OEEC strategy was accurate only in that the Messina proposals were indeed highly controversial in the Federal Republic. German industry recommended first the strengthening of economic cooperation through the OEEC. Leading industrialists were doubtful about the efficiency of possible supranational institutions, feared French protectionist influence within a customs union and wanted to avoid restrictions on the civil use of nuclear energy, as envisaged by the French.[72] Moreover, a cross-party consensus on integration had yet to emerge. The Social Democrats had opposed the EDC because it allegedly prevented German unification. They were only just beginning to revise their European policy.[73] Within the government the national-liberal wing of the smaller coalition partner, the Free Democrats, was opposed to further integration for similar reasons. The Messina proposals posed a divisive intra-party issue which even contributed to the split of the party leadership in 1956. The sceptics included leading members of the ruling Christian Democrats as well. The young Minister of Atomic Energy, Franz Josef Strauß, for example, strongly disapproved of the project for a European atomic energy authority. This, he felt, would hamper the future economic and, potentially, the military use of nuclear power by the Federal Republic.

Moreover, Economics Minister Erhard was opposed to the customs union idea for the same reasons as Thorneycroft. In February 1956 during a meeting in London he openly conveyed his scepticism to Macmillan.[74] When the British subsequently devised Plan G, Erhard even told Nutting that, personally, he would be happy to drop the customs union completely for a free trade area.[75] After the failure of the free trade area negotiations in December 1958 Erhard actually encouraged the British to set up the European Free Trade Association (EFTA) in order to create political pressure on the Germans, and supported a wider economic arrangement between the EEC and the EFTA. In Erhard the British certainly had an important ally, but the British government erred in relying too much on his support, at least until the breakdown of the OEEC negotiations. This error came despite frequent warnings – not the least from the British Embassy in Bonn – that Erhard's influence over German European policy was limited and that political motives would ultimately decide the issue. From Messina Coulson had reported to the Foreign Office that despite Erhard's critical remarks in public, the official German position was unchanged.[76] The final MAC report stated explicitly that the Economics Minister had apparently been overruled by Chancellor Adenauer for whom economic arguments counted little.[77] Reginald Maudling, the British representative in the free trade area negotiations, would conclude later that Adenauer even seemed to take pride in not understanding the economic problems of European integration which were then determining the British approach to the free trade area proposal.[78] Adenauer was keen to show that before NATO entry, his support for European integration had been more than simply a machiavellian pretext for achieving the reacceptance of the Federal

Republic into international organizations as an equal partner. Adenauer started to focus on the Messina initiative at the end of 1955. He grew increasingly frustrated with the obstructionist policy of Erhard and others. As a result, in January 1956, he sent an internal circular to all ministers in which he claimed the chancellor's constitutional power to determine policy guidelines, and demanded unconditional support for 'a clear and positive German policy towards European integration'.[79] Adenauer hoped that in proceeding with the plans for a customs union and, if necessary, an atomic energy authority, he might facilitate Franco-German reconciliation – already a central part of the Federal Republic's *raison d'état*, but always underestimated in London. Contrary to the British with their free trade area plan, Adenauer was prepared to pay a high economic price in the EEC Treaty for partnership with France through contributing, for example, to the financing of French overseas territories. Moreover, on a visit to Paris in November 1956 during the height of the Suez crisis, he was also pleased to declare his solidarity with the interventionist policy of the Mollet government. This policy was in fact highly contested within the Federal Republic. Adenauer's declaration came just as the British government, without consulting the French, decided to withdraw its forces.

On receiving the British *démarche*, the Germans and the Americans had immediately notified the other ECSC states. Their governments were therefore fully prepared for Ellis-Rees' announcement on 6 December 1955, in which he informed the representatives of the other OEEC states of Britain's reservations to the Messina initiative. That December, Macmillan arrived in Paris ill-prepared for, first, the WEU Ministerial Council meeting and, then, for the NATO Council meeting in Paris. He was promptly attacked at the WEU meeting by the representatives of the Six, with Spaak leading the charge. Nobody had expected British participation, he said, but neither had they foreseen such a frontal assault by the British government on the Messina initiative.[80] Beyen was equally bitter, particularly since he had visited London two weeks previously and had been told at that time by Butler that, while membership in a West European customs union was no 'short-term possibility', it might well be feasible at some later stage.[81] This misunderstanding was later explained by Butler, who indicated that it was all due to his contempt for Beyen; because he thought the other arrogant, Butler had tried to keep their conversation as superficial as possible.[82]

The sharp reaction from the Six, including such anglophile politicians as Spaak and Beyen, was not surprising. The change from benevolent neutrality towards the EDC to the active attempt to sabotage the Messina initiative marked a dramatic innovation in British European diplomacy. Of all ministers the supposedly europhile Macmillan was responsible. He had not only signed the letters to Dulles and Brentano, but the letters had been his idea, and represented an *ad hoc* volte-face of established Foreign Office policy which could only have been initiated at the very top of the ministry.[83] Macmillan instinctively feared the long-term dangers of British exclusion from a common market of the Six, and therefore his decision to sabotage the Messina initiative, once it no longer seemed so obviously doomed, was even logical. His *démarches* in Washington and Bonn had been, however, utterly unprepared and for that reason alone were destined to fail. Moreover, Bretherton had participated in the preparatory talks in Brussels without once intimating opposition in principle, so that Macmillan should hardly have been surprised to see the Six, as well as the Americans, perplexed and even enraged. It seems that Macmillan had not even consulted the British Ambassadors in Washington and Bonn who very probably would have advised against the *démarches*.[84] Hoyer Millar in Bonn actually sent an angry letter to Kirkpatrick afterwards asking whether it had truly been in the best British interest for the Foreign Office suddenly to press Adenauer to do the exact opposite of what the Americans had been asking him to do for years. All Macmillan had achieved at the end of 1955 was the creation of justified suspicion among the Six as to the British motives in Western Europe, which was later to burden the free trade area plan and other British initiatives, and to raise among the Six the traditional unpleasant spectre of perfidious Albion.

There had been ample warning that Macmillan's attempt to redirect the Messina initiative into the OEEC would result in a fiasco. At the end of October 1955, Trend explained to the MAC that the continuation of talks within the OEEC was not a viable option, since the Six wanted to go beyond sector integration and aimed at a full customs union that, moreover, would be entirely compatible with GATT. An offer to discuss tariffs in the OEEC would also easily be recognized as a red herring, since for years the British government had vehemently refused any tariff-related discussions in the OEEC.[85] Bretherton, in speaking to Thorneycroft, even declared the OEEC idea as nonsense.[86] At that stage the economic ministries were already beginning to think about substantial initiatives. Trend thought that Britain might make an offer in atomic energy where British technology was far advanced.[87] The Board of Trade, on the other hand, was already thinking about some wider form of association with a customs union of the Six, but they had not yet developed a substantial concept.[88]

Following the disaster of his interventions in Washington and Bonn, Macmillan refrained from intervening in Britain's European policy until after his move to the Treasury in late December. Macmillan initially only thought of a new tactical manoeuvre. On 19 January 1956, Leslie Rowan, Second Secretary of the Treasury, noted that the new chancellor 'thinks that it is important. In his view it is not so much that it need contain any very startling ideas but rather that it would provide an alternative for discussion in Europe.'[89] A few days later, just before Eden's and Lloyd's final attempt to influence Eisenhower in Washington, Clarke explained once more Macmillan's view: 'The interim report on the counter initiative is not and ought not to be a very hopeful document ..., rather ... a tactical objective than ... a piece of major strategy.'[90]

The British government has often been accused of having acted recklessly in 1955, of having 'missed the bus' which apparently took the Six directly from Messina to the Italian capital for the signing of the Rome Treaties in March 1957.[91] However, the historical analysis of this political judgement proves it to be misleading in two major respects: first, it was not at all clear in 1955 that the bus, which the Six boarded at Messina, was actually roadworthy, nor that driver and passengers would be able to avoid a major diplomatic accident on the way. In 1955 not all roads led to Rome. The success of the Messina initiative was not at all guaranteed. Spaak, for example, begged Macmillan as late as February 1956 during a visit to London to save his project, threatened with failure, in order to prevent a major political crisis in Western Europe.[92] It had in fact appeared initially that the French government might make no move at all without close British cooperation, leaving the British government in a strong position as West European mediator. The British could hardly foresee in 1955 that the Suez débâcle would accelerate the reorientation of French European policy towards closer cooperation with the Federal Republic at the expense of Britain.

Secondly, the bus analogy is misleading because, although the British government did examine the bus, however superficially, no minister seriously considered buying a ticket. The accusation that Britain 'missed the bus' is usually linked with the allegation that the government was comprised of convinced 'Europeans' who were looking for a greater role for Britain in European integration, but did not get their way. It has been suggested, for example, that British ministers at the time can be divided into 'Europeans' and 'Atlanticists'[93] or into European 'optimists' and 'pessimists',[94] an assessment that is wide of the mark. Much more accurate is the judgement of Spaak's adviser Robert Rothschild that Eden and Butler were very much and Macmillan perhaps somewhat less opposed to British membership in a West European customs union. Macmillan merely sensed the political dangers of exclusion. Eden had publicly declared a few years previously that he could 'feel in his bones' that the British people were not Europeans.[95] Macmillan felt in his bones that such an attitude might turn out to be disadvantageous in the long term. Even in the early 1950s Macmillan's concept of European 'unity' had been extremely vague. Once he became Foreign Secretary, he could not make up his mind to support a more constructive approach towards the Messina initiative, which he disliked and only very reluctantly began to take seriously at all. Within the government it was only the best diplomatic tactics that were controversial. British participation in a customs union as a founding member was therefore never an open option in 1955.

Membership in a more strongly integrated West European organization still seemed incompatible with the vague aim of British foreign policy to retain the traditional world power role. Most leading politicians – and not only of the governing

Conservative Party – continued to believe strongly that Britain had always been a world power and would have to remain so in future.[96] The great power syndrome, which prevented a more substantial re-evaluation of British economic and political interests and *long-term* aims in Western Europe, was rooted in strong traditions of political mentality. In terms of foreign policy, Conservative leaders after the Second World War still saw themselves in the tradition of Palmerston and Disraeli. They felt an almost moral obligation to uphold the legacy of Britain's period of greatness before 1914, a legacy which was deeply ingrained in the minds of the older generation of British politicians and which had been successfully conjured up by Churchill during the Second World War, glossing over the long-term decline in Britain's economic, political and military power base. From this perspective, to surrender established claims, particularly the claim to a world power role, appeared almost as a betrayal of a national history of imperial greatness. Certainly no Conservative leader wanted or could politically afford to be guilty of such betrayal. Whenever the retreat from established economic or political positions was inevitable, the retreat had to be presented to the public as at least complying with traditional policy objectives.

The British claim to a special position in international politics, defined increasingly in comparison to France and the Federal Republic, seemed to most Conservatives to be not only historically founded, but historically just. Indeed, why should Britain, having successfully fought Nazi Germany, continue to lose economic and political power only ten years after the war, while the West Germans attained economic success and were beginning to gain political influence, particularly with the Americans. Only the psychological underpinning of British policy can account for the British attitude towards the Messina initiative in 1955. The mental roots of British foreign policy explain why the British Cabinet refused outright to consider making a more substantial economic and political commitment in Western Europe as an *equal* partner, and instead became obsessed with defending the threatened status quo as long as possible. The Foreign Office even admitted that in ten or 15 years the economic and political conditions of a decision about membership in a West European customs union might be completely altered. It nonetheless made no serious attempt to base policy towards the Messina initiative on Britain's medium- and long-term interests. Most Whitehall officials, particularly in the Foreign Office, moved within an intellectual context which was at least as narrow as that of the politicians above them. As in other administrations, British officials worked on the basis of an implicit consensus about the limits within which recommendations would have to be made.[97] This inherently conservative consensus – which for British foreign policy involved the application of the three circles doctrine – was particularly pronounced in Whitehall for historical reasons and had been greatly reinforced by the psychologically affirmative experience of the Second World War. Those officials who moved outside the traditional intellectual context were marginalized in the policy-making process. They included, for example, the professional advisers in the Economic Section.[98] Bretherton was another victim. In Brussels the Board of Trade official was kept in a diplomatic quarantine by the Foreign Office after he began to dispute its assertion that the Messina initiative was doomed.[99] Many senior officials and ministers were inclined to ignore reports from within Whitehall and other evidence conveyed to them from outside, for instance from the State Department, which contradicted their prejudices and implied the necessity of fundamental change. The resulting streamlining of recommendations in the final MAC report, particularly in its political section, appeared to add legitimacy to the policy favoured by most ministers to 'wait and see', as it was explicitly termed in the MAC report. This policy was arguably typical of the phenomenon that:

> the fear of making positive decisions is perhaps the main characteristic of a power in decline ... The policy of *attentisme*, that is, waiting for events to happen instead of shaping them, is perhaps to be expected of a nation which refuses to look into the future because of the fear of what it might discover.[100]

Even if, however, the institutional and mental structures of European policy-making had been more flexible in 1955, domestic political reasons would have made it highly unlikely for the Eden government to make a decision in favour of participation. Public opinion, interest groups and the

Conservative Party were totally unprepared for such a major policy innovation. The Messina conference had hardly been noticed by the media. Despite Bretherton's participation in the Brussels talks, even the serious press reported very little about the work of the Spaak Committee.[101] Most journalists apparently shared the Foreign Office view that less than one year after the failure of the EDC, the new initiative of the Six was also doomed. Only after the publication of Plan G for a West European free trade area (FTA) were developments in European integration covered more widely in the press, but media reports tended to focus on the economic dangers of exclusion from a customs union of the Six.

The major economic interest groups were also unprepared for the idea of British membership in a customs union in Western Europe. The problem of Britain's relationship with the ECSC and later with the European Economic Community mainly affected industry, so that it was the Federation of British Industries (FBI), comprising almost 300 associations and 7000 individual companies, which was primarily concerned with monitoring British trade policy. The FBI also included the National Farmers Union (NFU), which had close connections to the Conservative Party. In addition to the FBI, there were also the less influential National Union of Manufacturers (NUM) and the Association of British Chambers of Commerce (ABCC). The NUM represented the interests of small and medium-sized companies and generally supported more protectionist policies. The ABCC, on the other hand, stood for the interests of export-oriented businesses and had particularly close ties with the Board of Trade.

Within these organizations interest in European economic integration only increased markedly from 1957 onwards. Later on, after the failure of the FTA negotiations, leading FBI functionaries and industrialists increasingly advocated a redefinition of British policy towards the Six. By contrast, in 1955 when the Spaak Committee met in Brussels the question of possible British membership in a West European customs union was hardly discussed within industry. According to the then FBI President Harry Pilkington, the matter was deliberately avoided because it was likely to prove politically divisive. Since it seemed clear that among the FBI membership there would be no majority in favour of participation anyway, the

FBI leadership wanted to avoid an unpleasant internal polarization.[102] The FBI did, however, at least set up a working group of its trade policy committee, which later included representatives from the NUM and the ABCC. The members of this working group were asked to follow the Brussels talks and to evaluate the potential impact of a customs union of the Six on British industry.[103] Despite the fact that Britain was actually represented in the Spaak Committee by Bretherton until November 1955, no consultations took place between government and industry. Neither the government nor the FBI sought such consultations because British participation in a West European customs union seemed out of the question for political reasons alone. In their regular meetings with officials of the economic ministries in 1955, the FBI representatives never even raised the topic of the Brussels talks. Only in early 1956, worried by Macmillan's counter-productive attempt to torpedo the Messina initiative, did leading FBI functionaries personally intervene. They approached the Board of Trade at the highest official level in order to express their anxiety about the economic dangers of exclusion from a customs union of the Six.[104] Neither did the trade unions speak to the government representatives about British European policy. In 1955 they still considered participation in a West European customs union out of the question, as it appeared incompatible with Britain's Commonwealth trade relations. In addition, the trade unions assumed that Britain's welfare state and social security provisions were generally superior to those on the continent. They feared that these provisions would be eroded as a result of economic integration with the Six. According to the trade unions, British employers would argue that these provisions represented an unfair competitive disadvantage in comparison to companies from the Six.

Finally, in 1955 no substantial party political support existed yet for British membership in a West European customs union which, the Six suggested, would later become more integrated politically as well. In fact, the Messina initiative was not mentioned in the House of Commons until June 1956 when Boothby submitted a written parliamentary question about British European policy, which led to a short adjournment debate in early July.[105] Within the ruling Conservative Party the ideology of imperial preference may have been on the retreat, but the Commonwealth link was still widely regarded as politically and culturally important. For this reason alone it is likely that in 1955 a decision by the Eden government to participate in a West European customs union would have caused a major upheaval within the Conservative Party.

Although, from a historical perspective, British membership was not an open policy option in 1955, the government was surely reckless in following the Foreign Office line and in basing policy on the assumption that the Six would never succeed without full British cooperation. The alternative view, put forward by Bretherton and others within Whitehall, that the Six were at least determined and perhaps even likely to succeed, was actually made explicit in the economic section of the final MAC report. Accordingly the Eden government alone was responsible for any adverse economic effects of Britain's self-exclusion from the EEC and for the loss of political control over the European circle of British foreign policy which had looked so secure in 1954. Had the government taken the Messina initiative seriously from the very beginning, it might have anticipated the conclusion reached in spring 1956 that Britain could not afford exclusion from a customs union of the Six. A free trade area, albeit with a certain degree of institutional cohesion and with compensatory concessions to the French, might have been a realistic concept in 1955 – either instead of a customs union, or – as seems more likely – as a wider trade roof above it. The British government did not 'miss the bus' in 1955; rather, it failed to steer the bus towards a destination other than that of the customs union of the EEC Treaty. If, however, the government was not prepared to pursue such a more active and innovative course, everything pointed to the established approach, supported by Eden, Butler and others, of benevolent neutrality towards the efforts of the Six. Instead, with its amateurish diplomatic manoeuvres, the government completely destroyed its European credibility among the Six and considerably burdened any future policy initiatives. It is perhaps ironic that of all leading politicians, the allegedly pro-European Macmillan was primarily responsible for this failure in British policy.

3 Best of All Worlds: The Free Trade Area Plan, 1956–7

Shortly after the OEEC fiasco officials in the Treasury and the Board of Trade began to examine possible alternatives to the customs union of the Six. Having supported this course in the first place, the two ministries took up the initiative within Whitehall. Consultation between individual officials started as early as November 1955. Now at the Treasury, Macmillan began to encourage the evaluation of substantial counter-proposals. Impressed by the aggressive reactions of the Six, as well as the Americans, the new Chancellor hoped to lead the government out of its self-inflicted isolation in Western Europe and to regain the diplomatic initiative. In early 1956 the government was still looking for a counter-initiative to prevent a customs union of the Six. The new British policy was initially only a new tactical variant of the OEEC strategy. From the point of view of several officials and ministers, the so-called Plan G for a West European industrial FTA, developed in spring 1956, retained a destructive function for some time, in some cases perhaps even until Suez. Plan G did, however, undergo an astonishing functional metamorphosis during 1956. For different reasons Macmillan and Thorneycroft, in particular, became determined to pursue the FTA proposal, even if the Six failed to set up a customs union. What started out as an alternative for discussion, turned into a possible re-placement project and eventually ended up as a concept for a trade roof over the EEC.[1]

Macmillan initially wanted to buy time for a more fundamental re-evaluation of British European policy. On 1 February 1956, he sent a short note to Sir Edward Bridges, Permanent Secretary of the Treasury, revealing the anti-German component of his future, more active policy:

> Are we just to sit back and hope for the best? ... For perhaps Messina will come off after all and that will mean Western Europe dominated in fact by Germany and used as an

61

instrument for the revival of German power through economic means. It is really giving them on a plate what we fought two wars to prevent ... I don't want this matter to slide. I believe it may be one of the most difficult that we have to deal with in the next few years.[2]

Five days later, in a note on the margins of a Treasury document, the Chancellor demanded an innovative step forward for the first time: 'The real difference is whether [the counter-initiative] is a rearguard action or an advance. I am anxious for an advance which would be recognized as such.'[3] In mid-February Macmillan called upon senior Treasury officials to discuss British European policy.[4] Still under the impression of strong American support for the Six, he told them that economically speaking the failure of the Messina initiative might still be the best outcome, but that for political reasons it had become undesirable for it would endanger the political cohesion of Western Europe. To prevent exclusion Britain now had to move closer to Europe. Since Macmillan had no idea how this could be achieved, he charged several senior officials to develop a number of policy options in an informal interministerial working group. In 1955 the officials engaged in pro forma debate over the advantages and disadvantages of a given alternative. They were now expected to develop a new policy without detailed formal instructions other than that it would have to be viable in the long-term and politically acceptable within the government. The acceptability would depend not least, according to Clarke, on the right Whitehall strategy. If the new Chancellor wanted a constructive policy, Clarke noted, the Treasury should consult only the Board of Trade and the Foreign Office. To exclude in the initial stages the more protectionist ministries of Commonwealth Relations, Colonies and Agriculture, Fisheries and Food would prevent the new initiative from being watered down through interministerial compromises before it even reached the ministers.[5]

When the informal Clarke Working Group finally met for the first time at the beginning of March, the Foreign Office was represented, but largely indifferent to the intensive discussion among officials from the two economic ministries. Relieved of Macmillan, the Foreign Office had immediately fallen back on its traditional policy of benevolent neutrality.

Emphasizing the positive contribution of European integration in binding the Federal Republic to the West and in strengthening Western solidarity in the global conflict with the Soviet Union, the Foreign Office was once more in step with the State Department. The renewed policy reversal also suited the new Foreign Secretary Lloyd whose appointment was widely interpreted as an attempt by Eden to replace the independent-minded and unsuccessful Macmillan with an obedient mandarin.[6] Under Lloyd the contribution of the Foreign Office to the deliberations of the Clarke Working Group was restricted to a suggestion of the institutional rationalization of Western organizations, following up on the Eden Plan of 1952. The Foreign Office initially advocated a merger of the OEEC and the Council of Europe.[7] Later on, in its 'Grand Design', it suggested that the reorganization include the parliamentary assemblies of the WEU and perhaps even NATO.

These Foreign Office ideas were ignored by the economic ministries because they certainly seemed a totally inadequate response to the economic challenge of the Messina initiative. As the Foreign Office was not really interested in economic projects, the interministerial debate devolved largely to the economic ministries who treated the new European policy exclusively under foreign economic premises. By now both ministries were agreed about the grave economic dangers of exclusion from a customs union of the Six. Bretherton spoke of a 'deadly danger',[8] and even Clarke, so relaxed in 1955, argued that if the counter-proposal was unsuccessful, Britain would surely have to 'kill the Messina project stone-dead'.[9] In an internal meeting at the end of April, senior Treasury officials could already foresee Britain's fate in Western Europe under the premises which determined the future European debate: 'On a longer view the question might become, not whether we should go into Europe to save Europe, but whether we should not have to move closer to Europe in order to save ourselves.'[10]

By comparison with the final MAC report, the detailed economic analysis had changed very little by spring 1956. Officials judged the economic benefits of the remaining Commonwealth preferences even more realistically than they had in 1955. The emerging consensus on this issue now even included the Overseas Finance Division (OFD) of the Treasury which had traditionally advocated a policy designed primarily to prop up the Sterling Area rather than to safeguard British trade interests. OFD Under-Secretary Frank Figgures, who later became the first Secretary General of EFTA, noted self-critically in a letter to Clarke in February 1956 that in the past the Treasury, and particularly the Overseas Finance Division, had enormously exaggerated the importance of the Commonwealth circle for Britain's foreign economic relations.[11] Later on, the economic ministries also increasingly saw the danger that third countries, such as Denmark or Austria, might become more and more economically dependent on a customs union of the Six, reducing British influence in Western Europe further.[12]

In trade policy, the British government found itself increasingly forced to fight on two fronts: while the Six were about to create a customs union, the Australian government demanded major changes in their bilateral preferential trade agreement with Britain, which was renegotiated in the summer of 1956.[13] According to Thorneycroft, the Australian move indicated a further strengthening of the centrifugal forces within the Commonwealth, which in the long-term were likely to affect its economic and political usefulness for Britain.[14] The parallel developments in the European and the Commonwealth circles threatened to further reduce British freedom in trade policy, already much diminished by comparison with the interwar period. Not surprisingly, the search for an escape route from Britain's European dilemma proved much more difficult than Foreign Office association rhetoric had suggested. A consultative treaty along the lines of British association with the ECSC was clearly useless. The economic danger of exclusion from horizontal integration by the Six were, of course, much greater than they were in the case of sectoral integration in coal and steel. What the economic ministries were looking for in 1956 was a coherent project which would avert the dangers of exclusion from a customs union of the Six and which was equally suitable as a replacement for the customs union if the Six failed, or as a trade roof should they succeed. The new initiative also had to be fully compatible with the three circles doctrine, affecting Britain's relationships with the Commonwealth and the United States as little as possible. Very early on in their deliberations the officials came to the conclusion that only a major initiative in the tariff sector could possibly fulfil all these conditions.[15]

One possible option, which the Board of Trade mentioned as early as November 1955, was substantial tariff reductions for products that were mainly traded within Western Europe.[16] According to this European Commodities Plan, OEEC states would define specific groups of products which were traded among themselves up to a certain percentage, for example 80 per cent, implying that only a limited trade interest of third countries was involved.[17] For these groups of products, tariffs between OEEC states would be reduced by, for example, 25 per cent.[18] This plan was, however, highly problematic in several respects. To begin with, it involved the politically divisive technical problem of defining the individual product groups, which would determine the balance of trade gains and losses for each state involved and virtually guarantee long, drawn-out negotiations. Furthermore, without automatic extension of the tariff reductions on a most favoured nation basis – not intended, in fact, by British officials – the plan was incompatible with GATT provisions. As such, it would have required special permission, for which the support of the United States would have been essential. Such support was, however, unlikely because the Americans were only prepared to accept substantial derogations from the principle of multilateralism in return for the political benefit of a more stable and politically cohesive Western Europe. In addition, the European Commodities Plan would have accommodated the trade interests of the low tariff countries such as Benelux, but it lacked the political substance which was important to many in the Six. Finally, the British government had prevented similar tariff negotiations within OEEC for more than two years, constantly referring to GATT. The Clarke Working Group concluded that such an abrupt about-face would therefore be perceived by the Six either as the British government's political surrender in the face of the Messina initiative or as a renewed attempt to sabotage it.[19]

Of the two other, more far-reaching suggestions for a counter-proposal which were seriously considered by the Clarke Working Group, some senior Treasury officials leaned towards a common preference zone of Western Europe and the Commonwealth. The influential Clarke, for example, admitted the need to upgrade Western Europe in Britain's foreign economic policy, but did not want to do so at the expense of the Commonwealth.[20] Perhaps, Clarke and others believed, the two circles could be merged economically by renegotiating the entire preference system with the Commonwealth and the OEEC states, a concept which was nicely compatible with the Treasury's foreign economic world power perspective. It was not a new concept, however. The possibility of some form of economic connection between Western Europe and the Commonwealth had been discussed on and off after the war. The Treasury proposal resembled a similar concept, propagated by Boothby in the Parliamentary Assembly of the Council of Europe. The concept evolved into the so-called Strasbourg Plan, which was now pulled out of the drawer again.[21]

By 1956 the preference scheme was totally unrealistic. To begin with, it would hardly have satisfied the hopes among the Six of creating greater political unity among themselves. It was also extremely difficult to negotiate and totally incompatible with the no-new-preference rule of GATT. What would effectively have amounted to the extension of the existing preferences in some form was a red rag to the Americans, who had only reluctantly agreed to the continuation of Commonwealth preferences after the war. Without American cooperation, even Clarke admitted, any project was doomed.[22] Furthermore, the economic interests of some Commonwealth countries were already diverging so much that their support for such a preference scheme was highly doubtful. It was equally questionable whether British industry would not actually suffer from such a foreign economic split by the government. British companies would gain tariff advantages in the West European markets *vis-à-vis* third countries, such as the United States, but would actually lose their tariff advantages in the Commonwealth *vis-à-vis* their continental European competitors. By contrast, the additional export opportunities both for the West Europeans and for some Commonwealth countries were regarded as much greater. It was unlikely that Britain could afford to pay the economic price for retaining the politically motivated role as hinge of both circles: Western Europe and the Commonwealth.[23] Finally, apart from all other technical and political problems, the Board of Trade officials intensely disliked the entire concept for dogmatic reasons; they wanted to escape the preference trap. In their view British dependence on the declining Commonwealth and Empire markets should have been sharply reduced. The counter-initiative in Western Europe had to further the envisaged reorientation in British trade policy.[24]

Even though the entire preference scheme was so obviously unsuitable, some officials, including Clarke, continued to support it in principle because, politically, it seemed the ideal escape route.[25] However, at the end of May 1956 when various plans for a counter-initiative were first discussed at the ministerial level, Macmillan declared the preference scheme antiquated and unrealistic.[26] Thus, even before wider consultations with other ministries, one of the two more far-reaching proposals was excluded. What remained was Plan G for an industrial FTA in Western Europe which emanated from the Board of Trade.[27] In 1955 it had appeared that non-participation in a customs union of the Six was the only option open to the British government. In 1956 the FTA proposal seemed the only option, if Britain wanted to avoid the economic dangers of exclusion from a customs union of the Six. In a meeting with senior Board of Trade officials in mid-May 1956, Thorneycroft concluded that Plan G was the 'inevitable' solution.[28]

The FTA concept had already been pushed by Bretherton in 1955, but then it was instead of a customs union and without British commitment to participate. The Six had dismissed the idea because the creation of a free trade area raised additional technical problems. They also assumed that the obtainable degree of institutionalization would not suffice to strengthen significantly the political cohesion of its members. The possibility of an association of Britain or other OEEC states with a customs union of the Six within a wider FTA was not seriously discussed in Brussels. Bretherton did recollect later, however, that he had been first confronted with this idea while talking privately to a Belgian delegate.[29] Bretherton mentioned the FTA idea within Whitehall for the first time in an internal Board of Trade memorandum. The memo insisted that officials think beyond the misconceived OEEC strategy of the Foreign Office to create more substantial alternative proposals.[30] Over the next three months, Bretherton developed the concept in greater detail, and then circulated a new memorandum throughout the Board of Trade, with a copy going to Figgures in the Treasury.[31] On 10 March 1956 Bretherton finally submitted the FTA proposal to the Clarke Working Group.

While Bretherton pushed the FTA proposal among officials, his personal role in the policy-making process should not be overestimated. Even though the deliberations of the Clarke Working Group were secret and until summer no systematic consultations took place outside Whitehall – with economic interest groups, for example – the officials were not working in a political vacuum. Bretherton was successful within Whitehall because his suggested innovation in British trade policy, which did not call into question the traditional foreign policy priorities, fell on fertile ground. The Board of Trade's search for a viable long-term concept which would avoid the dangers of exclusion from a customs union of the Six was facilitated in 1956 by the Conservative Party beginning to turn away from the imperial preference ideology. Modifications in the preference system, even if not forced upon Britain by other Commonwealth countries, were no longer regarded as heresy. Thus encouraged, the Board of Trade could more easily break old taboos. Moreover, even though no broader public debate was yet developing over Britain's European policy, experts outside Whitehall, particularly economists and foreign policy advisers, were very interested in the matter and, in some cases, they advocated almost identical concepts. For example, in late January 1956, James Meade – formerly Economic Adviser to the government, now Professor of Economics at the London School of Economics and Political Science – sent a letter to Figgures in which he advocated the creation of a wider FTA. Figgures passed the letter on to Bretherton.[32] Two weeks later, Meade published his concept in the *Manchester Guardian*.[33] In March 1956, the Oxford economist Roy Harrod also supported the FTA proposal in a personal letter to Macmillan, whom he knew very well.[34] Harrod even anticipated the necessity for partial tariff harmonization, later demanded by Italy and France. If anything, his and similar interventions from outside Whitehall can only have encouraged officials to develop Bretherton's proposal further in spring 1956.

According to Bretherton, the British trade initiative had to fulfil three main criteria in order to be politically acceptable: first, Britain had to retain its autonomy in foreign trade policy. Secondly, the Commonwealth preferences had to remain largely intact. Thirdly, the British initiative had to exclude the possibility of future supranational development of any new organizations. From this perspective a partial FTA seemed the ideal solution. According to the Adviser on Commercial Policy in the Board of Trade, Cyril Sanders, it was the 'natural development'.[35] To begin with, whereas a customs union involved the establishment of a common trade policy, members of a free trade area retained the right to negotiate their national external tariffs independently. The Board of Trade was primarily concerned that in a customs union the loss of Commonwealth preferences and the necessary reduction of British tariffs in certain sectors might not be reciprocated by third countries such as the United States. Plan G avoided this danger. Moreover, unlike a customs union, a free trade area would not lead to the introduction of negative preferences for Commonwealth producers in Britain in relation to West European competitors.

Officials considered a global FTA, comprising all sectors, to be out of the question. The complete abolition of all internal tariffs within such a free trade area would not have permitted preferential treatment of Commonwealth products in the British market. Yet, such treatment was considered essential both for political reasons and because Britain wished to retain its reciprocal preferences in the Commonwealth. Consequently, in his first memorandum Bretherton was already recommending only a partial FTA.[36] He initially thought of a solution along the lines of the European Commodities Plan.[37] According to this concept, certain product groups, where the Commonwealth share of the British market was higher than, for example, 20 per cent, would be exempt from the West European FTA. In contrast to the European Commodities Plan, however, tariffs in other sectors would not simply be reduced, but abolished altogether. The main problem here was once more the definition of product groups. For example, 80 per cent of imported cheese came from Commonwealth countries, but only 4 per cent of soft cheese. Moreover, such a free trade area seemed too restrictive in that it would cover

less than 50 per cent of British trade with West European
countries, or only slightly over 10 per cent of overall British
trade.[38]

Instead, the economic ministries came to the conclusion
that agricultural products, including industrially processed
products such as frozen fish, should be exempt in order to
avoid problems of definition. This solution allowed the continued tariff-free import of agricultural products from the
Commonwealth, 50 per cent of Commonwealth exports. As an
additional 40 per cent of Commonwealth exports to Britain
were in raw materials and would be largely unaffected anyway,
the Commonwealth would only suffer the loss of the existing
preferences on industrial exports to Britain. As a result,
officials reckoned, Britain could largely retain its preferences
in the Commonwealth. The industrial FTA thus seemed to be
the perfect trade cramp between Western Europe and the
Commonwealth; first, it would guarantee association with a
customs union of the Six, promoting British export interests
in Western Europe. Further, the retention of national tariffs
and the exclusion of agriculture would enable Britain to
protect its trade advantages in the Commonwealth. In addition, the partial FTA, which might comprise Denmark,
Sweden, Norway, Switzerland and Austria in addition to the
Six and Britain, also circumvented the danger that economic
cooperation might eventually lead to political integration.
During the summer of 1956, as officials in a subcommittee of
the Economic Steering Committee developed Plan G further,
they envisaged the lowest possible degree of institutionalization. Any future treaty was to reduce cooperation in matters
which extended beyond the administration of the FTA to an
absolute minimum. The FTA was to be integrated into the existing OEEC structures and each member retained a veto.[39]
Finally, when regulations of the FTA clashed with those of the
customs union of the Six, officials hoped to secure the legal
precedent for the FTA treaty.[40] The principle of unanimity was
in fact dropped before negotiations even began. Officials
feared that the veto right could not only be exercised by
Britain to avoid an undesirable political development of the
FTA, but by other members to prevent the enforcement of
the economic rules. The British believed in particular that the
French government would try to circumvent any agreement

that limited the use of quantitative restrictions to protect certain industrial sectors. Majority voting in certain clearly specified areas and restricted largely to the implementation of policies was thus seen as promoting the British interest.[41] Even with this pragmatic modification, the FTA concept was still compatible with the traditional Foreign Office doctrine that Britain could only participate in strictly intergovernmental organizations within Western Europe. It seemed that market integration in the form of a partial FTA, institutionalized as little as possible, was exactly tailored to Britain's economic and political interests.

The officials in the Clarke Working Group did not take into account the economic interests and political expectations of Britain's prospective partners in a West European FTA, who still had to be won over to the concept. The Clarke Working Group never discussed any fundamental modifications of the initial concept, which might have proved necessary in negotiations, but only minor concessions, primarily in agriculture. Industrial exporters such as Britain and the Federal Republic would benefit disproportionately from an industrial FTA, so other countries with major agricultural interests needed to be compensated. To the officials in Whitehall, strictly limited bilateral concessions appeared sufficient at first, with regard, for example, to the import of fish from Norway or bacon from Denmark.[42] Only when preparing the negotiations did officials devise a plan for a statute for agricultural trade. However, the statute promised West European agricultural exporters only that their exports to Britain would be stabilized at current levels, and would be reduced neither as a result of increased imports from the Commonwealth, nor because of higher subsidies to domestic agriculture.[43] This proposal proved hopelessly inadequate in the negotiations.

When the ministries of Commonwealth Relations, Colonies and Agriculture, Fisheries and Food became involved in the interministerial discussions in late spring 1956, officials could not even agree on such a limited offer. To these ministries the political scope for compensatory concessions seemed extremely narrow, because they had to be at the expense of either Commonwealth producers or British agriculture. Agriculture Minister Derek Heathcoat-Amory commented ironically that apparently the British, in order to successfully

negotiate a partial FTA, would either have to eat more or grow
less.[44] Even at the time of the preparatory interministerial
talks the Board of Trade made clear that a much more flexible
negotiating mandate was needed, one which allowed more
substantial concessions. Moreover, the success of the negotiations depended not only on the economic substance of the
British offer, but also on its diplomatic presentation. Officials
from the economic ministries argued therefore that the first
public proposal should already contain an offer on agriculture. If the British government wanted to regain the political
initiative in Western Europe, it would be foolish to insist on
the complete exclusion of agriculture.[45] In 1957–8 agriculture
was only one of several sensitive spots in the FTA negotiations.
The Spaak Report on the Messina initiative, published on
21 April 1956, argued that unlike the customs union plan, negotiations over a free trade area would be burdened by only
superficially technical problems, creating 'almost insurmount-
able practical problems'. The report already called attention
to the divisive origin problem, and warned that varying national tariffs within a free trade area could lead to massive
trade deflection. To avoid such trade deflection the Italians
and French later demanded not only a system of origin controls, but also a partial tariff harmonization in the OEEC
negotiations. This helped the Paris government to divert attention from its lack of political will to even proceed with the
FTA proposal at all. To retain hope for a successful outcome of
the negotiations, the British were eventually prepared to consider the establishment of a *de facto* customs union in certain
sectors.[46]

When they drafted the FTA concept in 1956, this and other
possible developments were not debated by officials. To make
sure that the initiative would be acceptable to the
Conservative Party, they carefully read the Beaverbrook press
and not the Spaak Report, even after its translation into
English. What counted was the agreement of the Cabinet and
subsequently that of the Conservative Party which would be
followed automatically, or so it seemed, by a rapturous reception among the Six. Officials and ministers neither considered
the different economic interests of the prospective FTA partners, particularly France, nor the political aspirations among
the Six for a greater degree of political cooperation or integra-

tion, which the British still hardly comprehended. The Treasury and the Board of Trade did not feel responsible, and the contribution of the Foreign Office to the Clarke Working Group was limited to the physical presence of its representatives. After all, the FTA proposal did not mark a major foreign policy reorientation towards a new political role for Britain in Western Europe. Whatever the Foreign Office was considering could only be a garnish to an essentially foreign economic construction. Macmillan shared this view. More than a year after the concept was devised by the economic ministries, the new Prime Minister realized that the FTA might never be negotiated purely on the basis of its economic merits. Yet, all he did to redress the balance was to tell the Foreign Office to find a suitable 'political gesture' to promote the closer association of Britain with Western Europe.[47]

The FTA proposal was a trade concept, and it was presented as such to the Cabinet. Nonetheless, its two main advocates within the government, Macmillan and Thorneycroft, had different motives for supporting the initiative. Thorneycroft was keen to get a coherent, long-term concept for British foreign economic policy.[48] The Board of Trade wanted to secure British economic leadership in Western Europe, which had seemed so secure in the OEEC, and at the same time to bring the centrifugal forces within the Commonwealth under its control as far as possible. But what was initially a pragmatic proposal to avert the economic dangers of exclusion from a customs union of the Six soon assumed an ideological thrust. Although a pronounced passion for political concepts might not generally have been part of the 'genetic code' of British officials,[49] the FTA initiative was clearly an exception in the case of the Board of Trade: there senior officials, particularly Lee, were trying to rid Britain of the protectionist legacy. They seized upon the necessity to devise a counter-proposal to the Messina initiative which, in connection with the Australian demands for a renegotiation of the bilateral preferential trade agreement, exerted the necessary external pressure allowing the Board of Trade to push through what was still a highly controversial reorientation of British trade policy. The innovative character of the FTA project became more and more important to Thorneycroft and senior Board of Trade officials. The FTA initiative thus developed into a concept for the modernization of Britain's foreign economic relations which, as a result of the larger internal market and the greater competitive pressures, might also promote the revitalization of British industry. The FTA proposal thus had nothing at all to do with European integration for the Board of Trade.

In contrast, this economic perspective was completely alien to Macmillan, even after his move from the Foreign Office to the Treasury. In his view the counter-initiative had to harmonize Britain's political interests and responsibilities in Western Europe and in the Commonwealth.[50] He perceived the customs union project as a frontal attack on Britain's pivotal role at the centre of Churchill's three circles. The FTA initiative had to help safeguard Britain's role as mediator between the United States, the Commonwealth and Western Europe. What mattered to the Chancellor was how Britain could retain the political leadership of the Commonwealth and Western Europe at the same time. As long as the counter-initiative promised to guarantee just that, Macmillan could not care less about its exact detailed economic content. In August 1956 he wrote to the Education Minister David Eccles, a friend from their days together in the Council of Europe, and asked him to summarize the political reasons for the FTA initiative.[51] The resulting memorandum, pathetically entitled 'Plan G and the Moment in British history', accurately reflects Macmillan's point of view. Eccles wrote:

> ... Looking at England from the inside we see that we have lost our sense of direction. ... We accept second-class status or we share first-class status by pooling our men and money with others ... who are willing to follow our lead ... We cannot abandon Western Europe either to the Germans or to the Russians, and ... the English want to join a show which they can run ... For all living things the rhythm of their being is the same: birth, flowering, seed-time and then the challenge 'death or resurrection?' ... We must do Plan G as the act of recreation of British influence overseas.[52]

Macmillan certainly wanted Britain to lead Europe, but as to where, he had no clue. He also did not know whether the Six, in particular France and the Federal Republic, would be happy with the role of assistant sheriff. Macmillan never thought much about what arrangements might be acceptable to the Six partly because it proved so difficult to get Plan G through the Cabinet in the first place. When Board of Trade and Treasury officials neared agreement on Plan G as the only politically feasible solution, they pressed Thorneycroft and Macmillan personally to take the initiative with their colleagues in order to prevent the FTA proposal from getting bogged down in endless interministerial discussion. Board of Trade officials hoped initially that they would be able to launch Plan G in the OEEC right after the first ministerial meeting.[53] However, when Thorneycroft and Macmillan informally met their colleagues at the end of May 1956, all they achieved was to convince them that none of the other options evaluated by officials was realistic.[54] Some ministers demanded that before going to the Cabinet Plan G should first be evaluated in more detail within a new interministerial framework including officials from other ministries. It was agreed that the new Sub-Committee on United Kingdom Initiative in Europe of the Economic Steering Committee[55] should produce a report which was ready two months later.[56] In the end, the counter-initiative was caught up in Whitehall despite all endeavours on the part of the economic ministries to utilize the most efficient tactics, while the government was losing precious time in Western Europe.

The Cabinet eventually first discussed Plan G after the summer break in mid-September 1956.[57] Thorneycroft and Macmillan presented a mixed menu of economic and political reasons as to why in their view no alternative existed to the FTA proposal, nearly causing it to appear as a new diplomatic all-purpose weapon. Thorneycroft deliberately de-emphasized its innovative character in terms of British trade policy in order not to antagonize colleagues on the Empire wing of the Conservative Party. According to him, Plan G was but a necessary adjustment to changing international circumstances to safeguard British trade interests in Europe, hardly affecting the Commonwealth.[58] By contrast Macmillan concentrated on the political reasons. In order to win over the Foreign Office, which was not interested in the economics of the new project, the Chancellor emphasized the contribution which a partial FTA could make to the political cohesion of Western Europe.[59] At other times he raised the historical spectre of German economic and political domination of Western

Europe which only an industrial FTA could prevent. Thorneycroft and Macmillan nonetheless encountered substantial opposition that was partly due to influential sectoral interests. For example, Butler, who was now Lord Privy Seal, was very concerned with domestic agriculture. He demanded that the legal and political guarantees to British farmers, still important electoral clients of the Conservative Party, must under no circumstances be undermined by bilateral concessions to West European countries in connection with possible trade negotiations. Butler thus insisted on the complete exclusion of agriculture from the FTA project as the absolute precondition for his approval of Plan G. On the other hand, the Secretaries of State for Commonwealth Relations and for Colonies, Lord Home and Alan Lennox-Boyd, opposed Plan G because they feared that it implied a major reorientation of British foreign policy at the expense of the Commonwealth. Pointing to the likely losses in Commonwealth industrial exports to Britain, Home even demanded agricultural compensations for the Commonwealth, including, for example, the introduction of guaranteed annual purchases of wheat from Australia.

The diverging agricultural interests could obviously not be harmonized. Concessions to West European producers to increase the chances of the FTA initiative and to the Commonwealth to compensate for the likely losses in industrial exports were impossible without reductions in domestic agricultural production. Faced with this dilemma, Thorneycroft and Macmillan gave absolute priority to the domestic and Commonwealth interests to pass Plan G through the Cabinet. Additional imports of fish and bacon were suddenly no longer issues. In their final memorandum Thorneycroft and Macmillan declared the agricultural interests of Britain and the Commonwealth 'so fundamental' that negotiations on a partial FTA could only begin on the condition that agriculture would be excluded categorically.[60] Thorneycroft and Macmillan had only delayed the inevitable political confrontation. It soon became clear that Britain would have to make substantial concessions on agriculture in order to get a package deal on the industrial FTA; having received the pledges in 1956, however, Butler and Home prevented necessary early changes in Maudling's mandate in the OEEC negotiations in 1957.[61]

Apart from sectoral interests, more fundamental political considerations were also important for the opponents of the FTA proposal. The Cabinet was unified in the strong belief that Britain had to continue to play a leading role in international politics, but the best policies to safeguard its status were highly controversial. The three circles doctrine was not contested; the relative weight of the Commonwealth and Western Europe, however, was an issue. Home, for example, feared that the FTA initiative would accelerate the disintegration of the Commonwealth ties, thus weakening Britain's world power role.[62] Macmillan, on the other hand, believed that in the absence of a credible alternative based on the Commonwealth, Plan G was the best and perhaps only policy to safeguard Britain's international status.

These differences of political judgement were so fundamental that Macmillan soon gave up hope for a fast decision in favour of Plan G and began to influence the Cabinet carefully in his direction through diplomatic initiatives. In July 1956 he was first granted permission to encourage a debate on European trade policy in the OEEC.[63] Soon after the FTA proposal was in fact being discussed in the newly created OEEC Working Group 17, officially recommended by Sergent but in fact initiated by Macmillan.[64] In September 1956 Macmillan elicited from the Cabinet permission to sound out Commonwealth finance ministers on Plan G during the annual ministerial meeting of the International Monetary Fund scheduled for early October.[65] On his return from Washington, Macmillan could report that the reception of the FTA proposal had been surprisingly positive. Commonwealth governments apparently hoped for increased West European investment in the Commonwealth and for greater export opportunities in a larger West European market. Even the Canadian government, informed in advance by Thorneycroft during a visit to Ottawa, did not react too negatively, although an industrial FTA in Western Europe was likely to hurt Canadian industrial exports to Britain.[66] Since Plan G was distortedly reported in the British press after the Washington meeting, Macmillan received Cabinet permission for a press conference at which he explained the proposal in greater detail, thus setting precedence for the final decision.

Not until November did the Cabinet agree formally to Plan G – two months after the first full discussion of the proposal and exactly one week after the British government had broken off the Suez war under pressure from the Americans. Meanwhile bilateral consultations with the Commonwealth countries had confirmed the positive impression Macmillan had perceived at the IMF meeting. Moreover consultations with representatives of the business associations, particularly the FBI, and of the trade unions had indicated broad support for a West European industrial FTA. The Eden and Macmillan governments maintained formal contacts with industry and trade unions in the form of joint committees. These primarily involved middle-ranking and senior officials, sometimes ministers, but did not have direct input into policy-making. In the Consultative Committee for Industry (CCI), chaired by the Board of Trade and meeting roughly every two months, representatives of both the business associations and the trade unions discussed economic and trade policy issues. In the Economic Planning Board (EPB), on the other hand, only the FBI and the TUC were represented aside from senior officials from both economic ministries. From 1957 onwards the EPB met regularly in order to discuss details of the FTA negotiations.[67] These negotiations were also the primary motive behind the creation of the Palmer Group, founded in February 1957, in which foreign economic policy issues, particularly the FTA negotiations, were discussed on an informal basis between leading industrialists in a personal capacity and senior officials from both the Board of Trade and the Treasury.

Neither in the CCI nor in the EPB was Plan G mentioned before Macmillan's press conference. With their mixed membership both committees were used by the government primarily for maintaining good relations with the business associations and the trade unions and for informing them about government initiatives. Concerning Plan G the more important meetings were held on an informal basis between senior officials and ministers on the one hand, and individual representatives of the business associations on the other. To sound out industry opinion Thorneycroft met with FBI representatives for the first time in July 1956.[68] In September he also met the ABCC Chairman Percy Mills.[69] As the economic ministries had expected, the main result of these informal consultations was that most functionaries also perceived the necessity of substantial association with a customs union of the Six. They differed primarily in their judgements of how competitive British industry would prove to be in a larger West European market compared with continental companies. As a result, they held very different views on which treaty provisions would be desirable and which political guarantees necessary for the protection of less competitive industries such as optics and precision mechanics.[70]

Only after Macmillan's press conference did the FBI and the ABCC send out questionnaires in order to ascertain more systematically the attitude of their membership to the FTA proposal. Of ten regional FBI associations, nine were in favour of the proposal; of the 664 companies responding to the questionnaire, 479 were in favour, 147 against and 38 undecided.[71] The degree of support for Plan G varied considerably between sectors and was naturally highest among export-oriented companies. Because of the threat of competition from Scandinavian producers only a majority of the paper industry opted against Plan G. By contrast the ratio of positive to negative replies was 3 to 1 in the metal-processing industry and chemicals, 4 to 1 in the machine-building sector and even 5 to 1 in the transport and construction industries. Support for the FTA proposal was often made dependent on conditions which were summarized in the FBI report. The FBI advocated, for example, strict anti-dumping laws and clear regulations for the origin problem. Certain sectors or companies demanded the harmonization of labour costs and transitional subsidies in order to increase their competitiveness in relation, for example, to German industry. These latter demands were, however, largely ignored in the economic ministries as rhetorical concessions of the FBI leadership to the less competitive and more protectionist-minded sectors and companies.[72] FBI representatives actually confirmed orally that the 'better elements' of British industry were almost all in favour of the proposal.[73] According to the FBI President Graham Hayman, their support was not due to a sudden conversion to free trade, but rather the reaction to the dangers of exclusion from a customs union of the Six.[74] In a separate internal opinion poll 90 per cent of ABCC associations declared themselves in favour of Plan G, as long as the government could ensure that the Commonwealth preferences remained largely intact.[75] The greater degree of support by comparison with the FBI can be explained by the fact that the ABCC represented the interests of export-oriented industry and was thus particularly interested in additional export opportunities in Western Europe.

The business associations had not been consulted by the government during the formative period of the policy-making process within Whitehall as the economic ministries did not want to see their project diluted either by the more protectionist ministries or sectoral industrial interests. The formal consultations with representatives of the business associations and the trade unions before the final Cabinet decision in November primarily fulfilled two political functions: first, Thorneycroft and Macmillan rightly hoped that they would help to persuade their colleagues that the FTA initiative would be politically acceptable to the country. The broadly encouraging response from the business associations was welcome, although the reaction of the Commonwealth governments was probably more important in convincing the sceptics in the government. Secondly, the business associations were also informed in advance because the economic ministries expected them to support the FTA proposal in the domestic political debate as well as *vis-à-vis* other associations and, if possible, individual politicians or parties in Western Europe.

The Conservatives took the political support of industry for granted.[76] Not least because of their financial contributions to the Conservative Party, industry deserved a certain amount of attention; however, business associations did not have the privilege of advance consultation in the initial policy-making process. By comparison with French industry's umbrella organization, the Patronat, which could directly influence French negotiating positions in Brussels and later in Paris, the government in London treated British industry like a stepchild. Simultaneously, the general approach of British business associations to their relationships with government was characterized by a largely passive, essentially unpolitical attitude. The world of politics remained alien to many in the FBI, the NUM or the ABCC. British industrialists did not aspire to political leadership, but instead felt much more comfortable in the more restricted technical world of tariffs and subsidies. Industry certainly expected to be consulted on a regular basis. To exert direct political pressure on officials or ministers was generally seen as unmannerly behaviour which was incompatible with the traditional gentlemanly relationship between industry and government. Intense concerns tended to be focused either upon sectoral issues, such as cotton, or on particular matters, such as the failings of the British Industries Fair. Moreover, unlike the German umbrella organization, the Bundesverband der Deutschen Industrie, the FBI leadership developed little independence from its membership, strictly limiting its potential capacity to act as an effective lobby. As a result, the FBI leadership was preoccupied with harmonizing the highly diverse views of its associations and individual companies on the FTA project.[77] The FBI found it difficult to agree internally and subsequently with the two other associations, the NUM and ABCC, on a compromise formula which could be published as an official statement of British industry on the FTA plan.[78]

Industry opinion nonetheless had an indirect supportive effect within Whitehall during the development of Plan G. In addition to the aforementioned committees, a network of personal contacts existed between representatives of industry on the one hand, and officials in the economic ministries and politicians on the other. Such contacts were certainly preferred by the Conservatives to the more formalized consultation mechanisms. Soon after the British attempt to sabotage the Messina initiative FBI representatives privately warned against the dangers of exclusion from a customs union of the Six. In February 1956 FBI Director General Norman Kipping sent to Lee a personal memorandum written by the FBI Overseas Director Peter Tennant.[79] In the context of Macmillan's failed OEEC strategy Tennant spoke freely of 'OEEC chauvinism' which he regarded as totally unjustified because the Six, aiming at far-reaching horizontal economic integration, had no intention to undermine the OEEC. Unnecessary interministerial rivalries and conflicts, Tennant argued, had made it impossible for the government to develop a viable long-term strategy in response to the Messina initiative. The government should now return to the established policy of benevolent support for European integration, keeping all options for participation open until the fate of the Messina initiative was known.

Lee accepted the criticism, but did not share the conclusion. In his view the time for non-committal participation in talks was long over. First, Lee replied to Kipping, the government had to come to a decision as to its long-term aims in Western Europe.[80] Senior officials were well aware of the unease among leading industrialists, exemplified by Kipping's initiative, at the prospect of exclusion from a customs union of the Six. If anything, it increased their determination to find a viable counter-initiative. In a retrospective analysis of the origins of the FTA proposal Clarke thus wrote about Plan G that Thorneycroft 'seized upon the idea of an industrial free trade area, with the support of an influential group in the Federation of British Industries'.[81]

By contrast, trade union opinion had no appreciable effect on the decision-making process. Consultations between government and representatives of the Trades Union Congress (TUC) were, at any rate, largely restricted to issues of economic and social policy. In foreign economic policy the Conservatives did not regard the TUC as a partner with equal rights to consultation. Macmillan and Thorneycroft only spoke to TUC representatives for the first time in October 1956 after the business associations had long been informed of Plan G. The official TUC response to the FTA project was positive.[82] As a result of their essentially pragmatic economic approach, the views of most individual unions were very similar to those of the respective business associations. Unlike industry, the TUC strongly opposed any curtailment of sovereignty in a West European FTA. The British variant of the idea of socialism in one country, which they still strongly supported, required that a future Labour government needed to retain complete freedom of action in economic policy. Otherwise, the TUC had two main demands: first, that in the envisaged FTA the living standards of British workers were to be kept at least at current levels. Any harmonization of income and social security provisions, which the TUC supported in principle, could only be upwards in the direction of what trade unionists believed to be the superior British standards. Secondly, the TUC demanded that the government insist in the negotiations that the maintenance of full employment be embodied in a future FTA treaty as a legally enforceable economic policy of the new organization. As early as March 1957 TUC representatives put forward a draft proposal for such a treaty provision.[83] During 1957–8 TUC representatives concentrated almost exclusively on this demand in their consultations with officials and ministers.[84] The government, however, had no intention to comply with these TUC demands. It was opposed in principle to the harmonization of social policy and, concerning full employment, the TUC was put off with the offer to include a non-binding general clause in the preamble of the FTA treaty. Later, in connection with the creation of EFTA in 1959–60, the TUC also concentrated on one specific demand. Trade union representation, the TUC argued, should be on a par with that of business associations in the EFTA Consultative Committee, which was to be the equivalent to the Economic and Social Committee of the EEC, only with more limited consultative rights. The government initially endorsed this view, but when business associations intervened at the highest level against the principle of parity, it later insisted on five representatives – two from the TUC, two from industry and one from the service sector[85] – so that here, too, the only TUC demand was eventually ignored by the Conservatives.

The generally positive response of the economic interest groups to Plan G in the autumn of 1956 considerably weakened opposition against the initiative within the Cabinet, but the last resistance only collapsed after the Suez débâcle. The joint military expedition of Britain, France and Israel had dramatically exposed both British dependence on American support and the political fragility of the Commonwealth. At the same time, the parallel ruthless suppression of the Hungarian Revolution by Soviet troops placed into the foreground once more the need to strengthen the unity of Western Europe, so that on political grounds Plan G now seemed a desirable concept even to former opponents. In September 1956 Macmillan noted in his diary on Plan G: 'What we are all agreed is that we cannot paddle in these dangerous waters. We must either stay on the bank or plunge boldly into the flood and strike for the opposite side.'[86] When British ministers did finally plunge into the flood in November

1956 – with the exception of Thorneycroft not boldly, but reluctantly – one year had passed since the economic ministries began to think about a counter-initiative and eight months since the Clarke Working Group first considered the various proposals. Meanwhile, at a ministerial meeting in Venice in May 1956 the Six had agreed on the Spaak Report as the initial basis for negotiations on a customs union and an atomic energy authority which started soon afterwards. After Suez the Six began to make substantial progress, so that when Plan G was eventually approved by the Cabinet in late November the British government was faced with the distinct danger that it would be presented by the Six with a fait accompli.

Several factors contributed to the extreme sluggishness of the policy- and decision-making process. To begin with, under Eden British European policy lacked the political leadership which would have eased the internal progress even of a politically more substantial counter-initiative than the FTA project. Without Eden's bored passivity Plan G would never have been bogged down to the same extent in interministerial rivalries. In addition, most ministers involved in British foreign policy were fighting battles of the past, but they were often moving on different battlegrounds. According to Macmillan, Britain was once more threatened – as after Austerlitz in 1805 – with a continental European 'bloc', a danger that could only be averted with the diplomatic riposte of the FTA initiative.[87] By contrast, Eden was less concerned with another Napoleonic menace, but instead preoccupied with avoiding another Munich in his relationship with Nasser, who in the dominant British view at the time was seen as the Hitler of the 1950s. Others in the Cabinet shared Eden's view of Nasser and Arab nationalism, but only the Prime Minister was so fixated in 1956 with the developments in the Near East that he hardly noticed the parallel developments in Western Europe. More than ever European policy seemed to Eden at best a secondary diplomatic theatre which, unlike the Egyptian challenge, could not seriously affect Britain's international status. In his diaries Eden mentions Plan G only once, describing it in passing as 'another very formidable issue'.[88] Otherwise, Western Europe remains *terra incognita* during 1955–6. In the Cabinet Eden intervened only once to express his regret that no counter-initiative based on the Commonwealth was feasible. He himself could only think of his old idea, thoroughly outdated by 1956, to offer Commonwealth membership to several West European states he liked, notably Belgium and the Netherlands.[89] Even after succeeding Churchill as Prime Minister, Eden remained the born diplomat who could move securely in diplomatic circles as long as the main purpose was to administer the status quo. He lacked the ability realistically to assess Britain's decline both in economic and military strength and political influence as well as the desirable open-mindedness to adapt quickly to rapidly changing circumstances. Policy innovation, based on a long-term strategic perspective, did not belong to Eden's strengths.[90]

The task of the supporters of Plan G was further complicated when European policy was increasingly overshadowed by the developments in the Near East, which initially slowed down the internal progress of the FTA project. The Suez crisis also began to preoccupy Macmillan when approximately six weeks before the war sterling first came under intense speculative pressure. Any innovation in British foreign economic policy, the Chancellor now feared, could lead to unpredictable reactions on the currency markets.[91] While in July 1956 Macmillan had aimed at getting Plan G approved by September, he was now happy to delay the final decision out of fear of endangering the stability of sterling and thus its world-wide role as a credible leading currency and potent symbol of Britain's world power status.[92] Moreover, Plan G was also overshadowed by the internal shadow-boxing over the succession of Eden whose replacement seemed increasingly likely during the Suez crisis and inevitable after the military retreat. In order to become Prime Minister, Macmillan needed to outmanoeuvre his main rival Butler. Whereas Butler's internal opposition to the Suez intervention was seen by many of his Cabinet colleagues as an unfortunate confirmation of his earlier support for Chamberlain's appeasement policy in the late 1930s, Macmillan proved a much more astute party tactician during the Suez crisis, first following Eden into the war with flying colours, but then demanding an immediate retreat when the United States intervened jointly with the Soviet Union against Britain and France in the United Nations Security Council.[93] His personal ambitions were also evident in his approach to the FTA proposal. According to Butler's apt retrospective analysis, Macmillan, by supporting Plan G, assumed the leadership of the disgruntled Young Turks who had set their eyes on a fundamental modernization of the Conservative Party in the post-Eden period.[94] At the same time, Macmillan was extremely careful not to antagonize the Empire wing of the party. He moderated his support for Plan G when opposition in the Cabinet hardened temporarily and acted like the future Prime Minister by distinguishing himself as internal mediator over Europe. Contrary to his convictions, in September 1956 he suddenly declared the arguments for and against Plan G as finely balanced and advocated a delay of the final decision. His apt moves on the chessboard of intra-party politics definitely eased his way into Number 10 Downing Street, but they may have prevented an earlier decision for the FTA proposal.[95]

Finally, the supporters of Plan G also had to battle against the pronounced inertia of Whitehall and the Conservative Party which rendered any change in government policy such as Plan G even more difficult. Thorneycroft, for example, was asked to prove conclusively that a West European FTA could be *absolutely guaranteed* to serve Britain's foreign economic interests better than the status quo. In August 1956 Butler demanded from Thorneycroft that the Board of Trade produce a detailed sector-by-sector calculation of the likely trade gains and losses without which he could not support Plan G. Thorneycroft, much lower than Butler in the internal pecking order, was so upset that he could not refrain from enlightening his more senior colleague about the appropriate attitude to political decisions in a rapidly changing world. He wrote:

Judgements of policy are inevitably concerned with matters of faith as well as with figures ... Like almost all major changes of policy Plan G would involve some uncertainties and risks. But there are also uncertainties and risks if we try to stay as we are. Our present relations with the Commonwealth, with Europe and with the U.S.A. do not make it necessarily any less risky to refuse to take risks. What is true is that a Government which seeks to shape events will have to accept responsibility for the results, though this may not be politically more damaging than watching events without any attempt to intervene.[96]

Thorneycroft's dynamic approach to politics was not easily reconciled with Whitehall's conservative decision-making culture. Innovation was difficult and in Europe it remained restricted to foreign economic policy in 1956. In the past the FTA plan has often been interpreted as a substantial shift of British policy towards Europe.[97] In historical perspective and in foreign policy terms it was an eminently conservative reaction to the dual economic and political challenge of the Messina initiative. Initially Plan G was a pragmatic concept to minimize the economic dangers of exclusion from horizontal economic integration of the Six. In Macmillan's perspective it soon became a concept for stabilizing the fragile geometry of Churchill's three circles and thus Britain's world power status. Thus considered the FTA initiative did not reflect a search among officials or politicians for a new British political role in Europe; rather, it was the search for the best means to safeguard the old world power role by securing for Britain the economic advantages of equal access to the rapidly growing West European market and political influence in Western Europe without a politically meaningful degree of institutionalization. The real modernizers in Whitehall were preoccupied with the economics of Plan G. Regionally confined and restricted to industrial products, Plan G adapted the pure liberal doctrine in a way which made it digestable for a changing Conservative Party. With the FTA initiative the Board of Trade hoped to sail safely between Scylla and Charybdis: on the one hand the outdated, one-sided Commonwealth orientation of British trade and, on the other, the possible long-term absorption into the customs union of the Six. Perhaps the modernization strategy provided the right answer, but it was to a question with which only Britain was faced. Usurped by the Board of Trade and the Treasury, British European policy had largely degenerated into a depoliticized matter of trade policy. As such, it was handled as a bipartisan issue by the government, with Macmillan taking great care to consult Shadow Chancellor Harold Wilson and others to secure full Labour support for the FTA initiative.[98]

4 Makeshift Solution: From FTA to EFTA, 1958–9

While the supporters of the FTA proposal strove hard to create the greatest possible party political consensus on the lowest common denominator, the government did not take the same care to launch Plan G skilfully in Western Europe. The main reasons for the failure of the FTA negotiations, which took place in Paris between October 1957 and December 1958, are not to be found in the course of the negotiations themselves. The various domestic constraints on the government were actually weakening in 1957–8, as it was increasingly accepted that Britain desperately needed a substantial form of association with the EEC, which came into existence on 1 January 1958. The business associations did not play a 'crucial restraining role'[1] in preventing necessary British concessions. Industry representatives were only informed *ex post facto* of government decisions to give way on certain crucial issues in the negotiations, such as partial tariff harmonization.[2] FBI representatives remained markedly cooperative throughout. They restricted their advice mostly to technical details of the FTA treaty. In its external relations in Western Europe the FBI also strongly supported official government policy, coordinating closely with officials its contacts with other business associations in France, the Federal Republic and elsewhere.[3] Only the homogeneous National Farmers Union exerted direct pressure on the government, managing to delay concessions on agriculture. Keen on a further expansion of agricultural production in Britain, which had grown by 60 per cent since 1945, the NFU even opposed the limited agriculture statute that Butler described in an internal note to Macmillan as 'dynamite' for rural constituencies.[4] The NFU had close contacts with officials in the Ministry of Agriculture as well as in the Conservative Party. During the negotiations in 1959, which led to the creation of EFTA, Macmillan argued in connection with necessary bilateral concessions to Denmark on the import of bacon that – particularly before a general election – 'the pig was an animal of electoral significance'.[5] Although the government did show considerable respect for NFU interests on domestic political grounds, it always managed to surmount NFU opposition when considered necessary for foreign policy reasons, such as over the agriculture statute or over bilateral agricultural concessions to Denmark and Norway.

The business associations only influenced the governmental decision-making process where the government itself was unclear as to the future course of European policy such as in the final phase of the FTA negotiations when failure looked increasingly likely. The FBI cooperated very closely with the other umbrella organizations from the so-called outer Seven: Britain, Sweden, Norway, Denmark, Switzerland, Austria and Portugal. In April and November 1958, two conferences of these umbrella organizations were held at which their representatives discussed the ongoing negotiations as well as possible alternatives to the original FTA plan.[6] In their consultations with the government leading industrialists first suggested to government representatives in the informal Palmer Group in May 1958 that there was a need to consider seriously such alternative projects, but officials insisted that it would be premature to do so at that stage.[7] After de Gaulle's veto FBI representatives did their utmost to convince the government to support the creation of an industrial FTA among the outer Seven. Should the government refuse to take the lead in setting up such an organization, industrialists feared that, in addition to the EEC, British industry might now be excluded from a second West European common market in the form of a Scandinavian customs union which was under discussion in 1957–9.[8] The FBI thus helped convince an initially rather reluctant government to favour EFTA as a makeshift solution. FBI representatives did, however, make clear throughout that they supported EFTA only as a bridge to the EEC and not as a desirable aim in itself.[9] British industry still wanted a wider common market in Western Europe in order to prevent exclusion from the EEC market. The fact that EFTA proved a diplomatic cul-de-sac soon after its creation contributed decisively to the change of opinion among British industry in favour of EEC membership.

During the FTA negotiations the British government also managed to contain Commonwealth interest in indirect participation in the negotiations at the expense of Britain, thereby removing another potential domestic obstacle to a successful conclusion. Because of the continous shift in their economic and wider geopolitical interests away from Britain, a parallel shift in British trade interests towards Western Europe seemed less problematic to the governments of some Commonwealth countries, such as Australia, than had initially been anticipated in London. The initial categorical exclusion of agriculture seemed to guarantee that the essential economic interests of most Commonwealth countries would be safeguarded. The original, undiluted Plan G would only seriously affect Canadian industrial exports to Britain. To safeguard its trade interests in Europe and to create a counterweight against an increasing, domestically sensitive economic dependence on the United States, the new Canadian government in June 1957 suggested that new efforts be made to increase the volume of intra-Commonwealth trade, including the diversion of 15 per cent of Canadian imports from the United States to Britain. The British did not, however, consider such trade diversion to be technically possible or in their best economic interest. As a purely tactical response to placate the Conservative imperialists, the British government proposed an Anglo-Canadian free trade area in autumn 1957, a proposal that – predictably – came to nothing.[10]

It soon became obvious during the FTA negotiations that the initial British concept could not be obtained and that the government in London needed to make substantial concessions to the Six as well as to other OEEC countries – a move which would also affect Commonwealth interests in agriculture. Nonetheless the governments of some Commonwealth countries perceived not only dangers, but also opportunities in the FTA negotiations. They hoped that, in return for further reductions of British preferences within their markets, they would be able to negotiate with the Six better access to the EEC market. The French demand in 1958 to include the existing Commonwealth preferences in the FTA negotiations temporarily appeared to offer a window of opportunity for such negotiations at the expense of the British.[11] Some Commonwealth governments clearly underestimated the extent to which in principle the Six were already committed to common agricultural protection as an indispensable element of the overall economic package of the EEC Treaty. The link between industrial and agricultural interests in Western Europe left little or no room for separate trade arrangements between individual Commonwealth countries and the Six. Through their demand the French had primarily intended to obstruct the FTA negotiations.

The Australian and New Zealand governments nonetheless came back to their idea of a separate deal with the EEC in connection with the talks between British and German, French and Italian officials in 1960–1 about a possible economic link between the EEC and EFTA. They rightly feared that the British government was quite happy to make bilateral concessions in agriculture at their expense. During a conference of senior economic officials of the Commonwealth in April 1960, for example, the Australian representative suggested that in any future European trade negotiations agriculture should be included in connection with a Commonwealth proposal for further reductions in the remaining preferences.[12] In February 1961 the British High Commissioner in Wellington reported that the New Zealand government was quite open-minded about the possibility of a British EEC application because it hoped that in the ensuing negotiations it could achieve better access to the EEC market for New Zealand agricultural produce in return for concessions on the remaining British preferences.[13] In the early 1960s the New Zealanders were still hoping for world-wide liberalization of trade in agriculture which they believed could be promoted with an agreement with the EEC.[14]

The main reasons for the failure of the FTA negotiations are in fact to be found in the initial British approach. As Maudling later observed, the chances for success were slim from the beginning.[15] If the British did manage to negotiate a trade roof above the EEC, officials and politicians in London increasingly recognized during 1957–8 that the Six would essentially determine its structure. Had de Gaulle not decided to break off the FTA negotiations at the end of 1958, any FTA treaty would certainly have had little in common with the initial Plan G. Even before it emerged from Whitehall, Plan G was diplomatically encumbered by Macmillan's disastrous attempt in November 1955 to destroy the Messina initiative. The fact had escaped neither Adenauer nor the new French Minister President Guy Mollet that the British decision shortly thereafter to call off the sabotage policy was not due to better understanding, but instead the result of the unequivocally pro-integrative policy of the United States. After this episode it was hardly suprising that every British diplomatic move in Europe was followed with suspicion by the Six. This included the anglophile Spaak and the Dutch government, who kept the British continuously informed on the negotiations of the Six. After the events of November 1955 it was easy for the British government to retreat; it was much more difficult, however, to find a place in the emerging West European structure. By the time Macmillan and Thorneycroft had recognized Plan G not as an alternative, but rather as a trade roof above a customs union of the Six, Spaak and others continued to regard the FTA project as a maliciously conceived diplomatic initiative intended to prevent the successful conclusion of the customs union negotiations.[16] Even after the Rome Treaties were signed in March 1957, such suspicions persisted. When the Foreign Office began to propagate once more the idea of a reorganization of the existing European institutions, perhaps even including NATO, the British policy seemed designed to drown Europe in the Atlantic.

Among the most suspicious of British motives was the first EEC Commission, which began its work in January 1958 under the Presidency of Walter Hallstein, the former State-Secretary in the Bonn Foreign Ministry. The Commission saw as its first priority to strengthen the EEC and to support its development towards a political community. If the FTA negotiations were successful, most Commissioners feared, then the EEC itself might degenerate into a *de facto* free trade area without the desired political cohesion.[17] According to the French Commissioner Robert Marjolin, the Commission was thus basically opposed to the creation of a wider FTA before the consolidation of the EEC.[18] As a result, it was all the more disadvantageous that the British government had failed to achieve parallelism between the customs union and the FTA negotiations. Because of the slow internal decision-making process Macmillan first begged Spaak in October 1956 to delay the customs union negotiations so that their outcome would not prejudice the FTA regulations, for example with regard to the timetable for tariff reductions.[19] The Belgian Foreign Minister made clear, however, that in view of the forthcoming Bundestag elections and because of the distinct possibility that the pro-European Mollet government in France might collapse any day, he was in fact keen on finishing the negotiations as early as possible. After all that had happened, he was not prepared to wait for the British government who could not even agree internally on a policy. The OEEC Council of Ministers eventually decided on 13 February 1957 that negotiations over the FTA proposal should take place. Ostensibly out of fear that the EEC and Euratom might be jeopardized, the French now refused to negotiate before the Assemblée Nationale ratified the Rome Treaties which it would eventually do on 10 July 1957 by a vote of 342 to 239. When the FTA negotiations subsequently began in Paris in October 1957, Maudling was under intense time pressure to make rapid progress, so that the first round of tariff reductions in the envisaged FTA could occur in parallel with the first EEC tariff reductions of 10 per cent scheduled for 1 January 1959.

In addition to these failures of British diplomacy in Western Europe, structural weaknesses of the initial Plan G were primarily responsible for the failure of the FTA negotiations: it was neither economically balanced nor politically attractive, particularly not to the French, the key government among the Six. The categorical exclusion of agriculture, which the British were actually prepared to abandon later in 1957–8, was welcome ammunition to those among the Six, who argued that the British wished to secure the best of all worlds without considering the economic interests of the Six. The problem that the initial Plan G was widely regarded as not economically balanced was accentuated by tactical errors of the British government. In its report, published on 10 January 1957, the OEEC Working Group 17 concluded that the creation of an industrial FTA was technically possible, but it also made abundantly clear that the British were alone in demanding the total exclusion of agriculture. All other governments called for special agreements on agriculture which would complement an industrial FTA.[20] Despite this, the British government published its White Paper on the FTA proposal only one month later and in it almost provocatively insisted once again on total exclusion as an absolute precondition for negotiations.[21] The French government in particular notified the British on several occasions, for example during the summit between Mollet and Macmillan in March 1957, that they could only ever agree to an industrial FTA if it were combined with major agricultural concessions by the British.[22] The British Cabinet nonetheless did not consider possible concessions until as late as August 1957.[23] At that time, however, it was already five minutes to twelve, as Maudling concluded after the first negotiating session in October. By insisting on its unrealistic maximalist position the British government had manoeuvred itself into a diplomatic cul-de-sac, from which escape was now only possible, if at all, by making greater concessions than might have been necessary twelve months earlier.

In January 1958 Maudling finally enlightened the Cabinet that in his view there was actually no support whatsoever in France for the FTA concept on economic grounds. Having agreed very reluctantly to the exposure to German competition in the customs union of the Six, potentially cushioned by extensive legal safeguards, the influential Patronat was violently opposed. The British government, however, was not much concerned with French opposition during the early stages of the negotiations. Macmillan believed that, if necessary, the French government could be 'forced' into the FTA.[24] As early as November 1956 he had argued that if the French proved difficult the other governments would simply threaten the creation of a free trade area without France.[25] As in the case of the OEEC strategy in 1955, internal criticism of the overconfident and britanno-centric view of the Foreign Office and of many in the Cabinet was conveniently ignored when, for example, in August 1956 Gladwyn Jebb in Paris sceptically asked whether 'the eleven, or so, other countries would be prepared to hold this collective pistol at France's head'.[26]

The EEC governments differed as to the desirability of an industrial FTA or of particular treaty provisions. Nonetheless, against the backdrop of the intensifying domestic political crisis in France, the organic development of the EEC created a high degree of internal solidarity among the Six towards the demands of the French during the FTA negotiations. After the ratification of the Rome Treaties the French held all the trumps, while the British were forced to make repeated concessions in order to avoid exclusion from the customs union of the Six. French obstruction policy concerning the FTA initiative had in fact been anticipated. In January 1957, for example, Spaak told Macmillan that the French government would only agree to the FTA, highly unpopular in France, if the treaty provisions were at least as advantageous as those of the customs union.[27] Subsequently Maurice Faure, French Minister for European Affairs, confirmed this on 6 February 1957 in the first official French statement on Plan G.[28] This warning was later underscored by the long lists of likely French demands for the FTA negotiations which Gladwyn Jebb sent to London the following spring and summer.[29]

There was also increasingly less support for an industrial FTA in France on political grounds as a result of the changing nature of Franco-German relations, a fact not much understood in London. A West European FTA without France, which Macmillan considered possible, was unthinkable for Adenauer. In view of his dominant position in the Bonn government, it was unrealistic to expect German support for such a solution or for a special legal status for France in an industrial FTA. This was an option that the British contemplated later, but which the German government regarded as dangerous for the political cohesion of the EEC.[30] By contrast, Adenauer could well do without British participation in West European institutions which he believed might actually complicate Franco-German *rapprochement*; and for him this was top priority. Although British and German trade interests were very similar, the political perspectives on European integration were not. Adenauer also neither liked nor understood the British whom he regarded, according to the apt observation of a British diplomat, as 'sea pirates', unreliable in European politics.[31] For the French, on the other hand, the new European organizations, the EEC and Euratom, had to contribute to the control of Germany through integration. The Fourth Republic governments initially thought that Britain would be an indispensable or at least useful counterweight to the Federal Republic; however, particularly after Suez, British participation in new European institutions was no longer regarded as necessary or even desirable to the same extent. Contrary to the FTA, the EEC presented many advantages to France. It offered, for example, the prospect of a socially tolerable route to economic modernization and of significantly increasing exports of agricultural products to the Federal Republic. In addition, Euratom would provide French influence over the development of the German nuclear industry. Finally the Rome Treaties also freed the French government from international isolation after the Suez war. Economically the British had nothing comparable to offer, and politically they were not nearly as prepared as the Germans were for close bilateral co-operation; instead they gave absolute priority to rebuilding transatlantic relations with the United States after Suez. While Macmillan nonetheless claimed political leadership of Western Europe for Britain, Adenauer was happy to leave it, at least symbolically, to France.

Preoccupied almost exclusively with the Suez crisis, the British government did not recognize the continuous change in Franco-German relations during and after 1956 and its fundamental significance for Britain's position in Western Europe. After the war British governments assumed that Franco-German conflicts would always enable them to assume the role, as in the case of the EDC, of an indispensable European mediator, thereby securing their political leadership in Western Europe. Franco-German *rapprochement* undermined this approach, which Adenauer described as a policy of 'divide et impera' when talking to de Gaulle in 1962.[32] Just how ingrained the belief in Britain's special mediating role was in the political mentality of the British foreign policy elite is best illustrated by Lloyd's remark to Spaak in May 1957 that without the FTA the EEC was destined to end in a disaster. Without Britain, he predicted, the Germans and the French would inevitably clash, thus leading to a political split among the Six and all of Western Europe.[33]

Lloyd's perception was historically rooted in British notions of a European balance of power, which had perhaps been successful in the eighteenth and nineteenth centuries, but was no longer very promising after the Second World War. In the bipolar world of the nuclear age the stability of the world-wide balance of power, to which the divisions of Germany and Europe were subordinate, did not depend on a few British nuclear weapons. At the very least the British government wanted to continue to tip the scales in Franco-German relations. The final failure of the EDC appeared to confirm Britain's mediating position, but after three wars in three generations the Germans and French decided to throw their weight onto the scale on the same side with the creation of the EEC and Euratom. The scale was suspended and, as a result, Britain lost much of its former influence in Western Europe.

Once the Community had come into existence and Franco-German cooperation intensified, the British government experienced even greater difficulties to safeguard its interests. In spring 1958, in connection with the so-called Carli Plan for tariff harmonization, the British eventually had to recognize that the Adenauer government was once more prepared to make substantial concessions to the French in the FTA negotiations and expected the British to do the same.[34] After de Gaulle came to power in May 1958 close Franco-German cooperation continued after a brief intermezzo of German irritation over de Gaulle's proposal for a political directorship of France, Britain and the United States in NATO. At their first meeting in Colombey-les-deux-Eglises in mid-September 1958 de Gaulle must already have told Adenauer of his intention to break off the FTA negotiations. At their meeting at Bad Kreuznach two months later the two leaders informally agreed that Adenauer would put aside German economic interests and effectively support a French veto, and that in turn de Gaulle would demonstrate strength over the Berlin ultimatum *vis-à-vis* the Soviet Union.[35]

It was not, however, only German economic ability and political readiness to make far-reaching concessions to the French that made life difficult for the British in Western Europe. French interests were also ideally safeguarded in institutional terms. As the EEC Treaty did not provide for the possibility of withdrawal of individual member states, the legal bounds uniting the Six could not have been tighter. In addition, foreign economic policy was an EEC competence, excluding national solo attempts. If the other Five wanted to keep open the option of a successful conclusion of the FTA negotiations, they would somehow have to try to induce the French to behave cooperatively. Not only Adenauer, but also the governments of the Benelux countries and Italy were fundamentally interested in strengthening internal solidarity within the EEC. Until and after the Ockrent Report of October 1958 they were thus prepared to make substantial concessions to French demands, particularly with respect to agriculture, in order to arrive at common negotiating positions. Because the British relied much more heavily on informal contacts and channels for consultations, they never quite grasped the institutional and legal dimensions of their emerging bilateral conflict with France even when the EEC began increasingly to act as a community.

If French consent to the FTA proposal was so essential and, if at all, only available on political grounds, it must be asked why the British government never made an additional political offer in order to improve the chances of the FTA initiative. Such an offer was in fact considered internally. Under the impression of alienation from the United States over the Suez war, the Foreign Office developed the proposal for a so-called Grand Design for Western Europe, which Lloyd placed before the Cabinet in January 1957.[36] Only the suggestion for an institutional revision of Western organizations became publicly known, but the Grand Design in fact proposed a radical reorientation of British foreign policy towards Western Europe. On 8 January 1957, explaining his ideas to the Cabinet, Lloyd declared that:

> the time is now ripe for a fresh initiative towards closer association between the United Kingdom and Europe. The F.T.A. might now be supplemented by proposals for closer political association and military association between the W.E.U. Powers within N.A.T.O. which should stop short of federation.[37]

After Suez Lloyd now reckoned with the development of a 'friendly rivalry' between Western Europe and the United States. As an integral part of it, Britain, Lloyd argued in his memorandum, should lead Western Europe which would develop into a third great power. It would be necessary to create a common WEU nuclear force around Anglo-French cooperation.[38] Lloyd did not support the idea, variously discussed within the Labour Party and in France, of Western Europe as a third force between the United States and the Soviet Union. The Grand Design concept lacked the anti-capitalist ideological or the anti-American foreign policy thrust of earlier third force proposals. Instead it was a Conservative British variant of the theme as to which role Western Europe could play in international relations in future. The Grand Design was not a mature plan, but rather an attempt at positioning after Suez; however, the tenor of a meaningful reorientation towards Western Europe 'with our immediate neighbours where we now most belong' was unmistakable. Throughout 1956 the Foreign Office had been largely uninterested in the counter-initiative. Under the shock of Suez it now advocated a substantial political supplement to the FTA.

The European option was, however, immediately rejected by the Cabinet. The Foreign Secretary received no support whatsoever for his concept. His colleagues agreed that absolute priority should be given to *rapprochement* with the United States, which was eventually achieved by Macmillan during his Bermuda meetings with Eisenhower in March 1957.[39] The decision was the result of the still dominant traditionalist perception of Britain's world power status, including a seat at the table of the two new superpowers, which in this form could only be secured with the benevolent support of the United States. The Macmillan government continued to look to Anglo-American relations for political assurance as well as psychological security. Domestic or external pressures were irrelevant to the decision against the Grand Design in general or British nuclear assistance to France in particular, an offer which would surely have lowered the economic price of the FTA and increased its chances of success. In the wake of Eisenhower's Suez policy the domestic political climate, marked by a considerable anti-American reaction, could not have been more favourable to a reorientation of British policy towards Western Europe. In relation to military matters there also was no Commonwealth alternative: even the Empire wing of the Conservative Party was not keen on creating a common nuclear force with South Africa and India. Finally the Grand Design, anticipating Kennedy's later concept, envisaged the creation of a European pillar within the Atlantic Alliance. As such it was fully compatible with United States security and European policy so that before the resumption of Anglo-American nuclear cooperation later in 1957, the Eisenhower government could well have been convinced to support the concept. The British Cabinet, however, never discussed the chances and limits of the Grand Design in any detail. The Suez war accelerated the decision in favour of the trade concept of Plan G. Unlike France, it did not, however, lead to a political reorientation towards Europe, as had been expected among the Six.[40] The crisis drastically demonstrated the narrow limits of independent military action of European nation-states and marked a parting of the ways in Anglo-French relations long before de Gaulle came to power in 1958.[41]

After the failure of the FTA negotiations the British government began to search for an alternative policy to avert or at least to reduce the potential adverse economic effects of self-exclusion from the EEC. In February 1959 Heathcoat-Amory, Chancellor since January 1958, once again explained in a Cabinet memorandum why in his view EEC membership was still no option for Britain.[42] The three main reasons were the necessary introduction of negative preferences in relation to the Commonwealth; participation in the future EEC agricultural policy, necessitating a fundamental change in the British subsidy system; and the inevitable loss of sovereignty in an organization which, in the long term, might develop into a supranational European federation.

With a view to the first internal EEC tariff reductions on 1 January 1959, perceived in London as trade discrimination against British exports, Macmillan had on several occasions threatened a trade war during the FTA negotiations. The British position, however, was politically and economically much too weak for a major confrontation with the EEC, particularly in view of the strong United States support for the Community. Through bilateral negotiations Britain and France eventually agreed on a transitional arrangement which included a further reduction in quantitative restrictions. Thereafter the British government began to support the creation of a small FTA of the outer Seven as previously advocated by leading industrialists. On 21 February 1959 the outer Seven held a first ministerial meeting in Oslo which was followed by another meeting in March and a visit to the seven capitals by Hubert de Besche, a representative of the Swedish government. On 7 May 1959 the Cabinet decided in favour of negotiations with the other Six which took place during the second half of 1959. Much ground had of course been covered already in the previous FTA negotiations. Moreover, the outer Seven were agreed on the institutional structure for a small FTA. The negotiations were concluded in November 1959 when the Stockholm Convention was initialled, leading to the creation of EFTA in May 1960. For the negotiations to succeed, the British government had to make bilateral concessions in agriculture, particularly concerning the import of bacon from Denmark and fish from Norway. Otherwise the EFTA Treaty resembled the initial British Plan G for strictly intergovernmental market integration in the form of an industrial FTA without strong institutions. The treaty included limited provisions for majority voting, an appeals procedure to deal with trade deflection and escape clauses intended mainly for balance of payments problems. In 1960 the EFTA Secretariat was set up in Geneva as a result of French opposition to Paris which the Seven had initially preferred mainly because it was the seat of the OEEC. In 1961 Finland became associated with the outer Seven in FIN-EFTA.

By agreeing to the creation of a small FTA among the outer Seven the British, in the words of Eccles, President of the Board of Trade, decided to marry 'the engineer's daughter when the general-manager's had said no'.[43] As in the case of Plan G almost three years earlier, negative reasons were decisive. The British did not support the creation of EFTA on the basis of its economic or political merits; they once again thought that there was no realistic alternative course of action.[44] To do nothing after de Gaulle's veto, ministers soon concluded, was out of the question, if only because it might be interpreted by other OEEC states as a sign of weakness and thus lead to a further decline in British influence and prestige in Western Europe.[45] Moreover, only if Britain led an institutionalized peripheral counter-alliance in Western Europe did it seem possible to preserve a more or less stable front *vis-à-vis* the EEC. Otherwise, the British believed, other OEEC states would eventually conclude bilateral association agreements with the Six or even join the EEC. Denmark, which depended to an equal extent on its agricultural exports to Britain and the Federal Republic, seemed particularly unreliable. If one stone in the row fell, others might follow suit. In his European domino theory Macmillan feared that 'if we cannot successfully organise the opposition group ... then we shall undoubtedly be eaten up, one by one, by the Six.'[46]

The creation of EFTA was designed to reduce the economic magnetism of the EEC. The government also hoped that it would create counter-pressure, particularly on the Germans who were still exporting more to EFTA countries than to those in the EEC. In 1959–60 27.5 per cent of German exports went to EFTA countries, two-thirds of which went to Scandinavia, Austria and Switzerland, and one-third to Britain. Whereas German industry gained tariff advantages within the EEC, the creation of EFTA led to tariff disadvantages compared to competitors from EFTA countries. The British hoped that the creation of EFTA would thus encourage Erhard and German industrialists, who were concerned about safeguarding German trade interests and had supported the original FTA proposal, to demand in stronger terms than before a reorientation of German European policy, including diplomatic pressure on the French to agree to a wider trade arrangement between the EEC and EFTA.[47] After all, the British never regarded EFTA as an aim in itself. The new organization was conceived as a bridge to the EEC in order to start renewed negotiations later which would be between two trade blocs rather than between the EEC on the one hand and individual OEEC states on the other, as had been the case in 1957–8.[48]

The outer Seven were initially united in their desire to secure equal access to the EEC market through some form of economic association with the Six short of membership. Otherwise their economic and political interests were very diverse and the new organization was much more heterogeneous than the EEC. As a result EFTA was not economically attractive or politically coherent and influential enough for the British government in the long term. Except for Scandinavia, the EFTA countries traded more heavily with the EEC than within EFTA. The EFTA market was also significantly smaller than the EEC. After the association of Finland EFTA was comprised of 41 million consumers outside Britain compared with 160 million EEC citizens. Moreover, the possibility of increasing British industrial exports was perceived to be limited in Denmark, Norway, Austria and Portugal. Significant opportunities for increased exports seemed limited essentially to Sweden and Switzerland. Both these EFTA members were, however, low-tariff countries so that the overall tariff advantages in EFTA were of limited use for Britain. Also, German industry disposed of certain advantages – geographical proximity, traditional trade contacts or, in the case of Austria and Switzerland, the common language – thus giving it an upper hand over British competitors.

Soon after the creation of EFTA officials in the economic ministries no longer believed that the new organization would be particularly useful for applying economic pressure on the Germans. Because of its close trade relations with the EFTA countries German industry was concerned with the division of Western Europe into the Six and the Seven, but it was always likely to suffer less in the EFTA market than British industry was in the larger and more rapidly growing EEC market. Moreover, German industry was generally more dynamic and better equipped to cope with the ensuing competitive problems. The Germans overtook the British in exports in 1958 and in industrial production in 1959.[49] The trade boom beginning in the EEC virtually guaranteed that any trade losses in EFTA could be regained by increased exports to the Benelux countries, France and Italy. In any case, as long as Adenauer was Chancellor, the extent to which economic pressure would translate into a dramatic change in German policy towards France was highly questionable.

British expectations that EFTA was not economically and politically cohesive enough to be a permanently viable unit rather than a temporary bridge to the EEC were first vindicated in 1960 by the hotly contested question of an acceleration of tariff reductions in the EEC and EFTA. Even before the Stockholm Convention was signed, the Wigny Report, named after the Belgian foreign minister, had initiated a debate within the EEC on an acceleration of the timetable for the reduction and eventual abolition of internal tariffs initially agreed upon in the EEC Treaty.[50] Acceleration, it was hoped, would strengthen the political cohesion among the Six in delimitation from the outer Seven's EFTA. The economic and political interests of the Six varied considerably over the issue of acceleration. In view of the stable economic development in France after successful internal reforms and the convertibility of the franc after a substantial devaluation in late 1958, de Gaulle was prepared to accept acceleration, but only if combined with an earlier introduction of the common external tariff. The Germans, who in this case would have had to increase their external tariffs considerably after having only just lowered them unilaterally by up to 25 per cent in 1957 because of their large balance of payments surpluses, were primarily interested in avoiding a deepening rift between the two blocs. The Dutch, finally, hoped to utilize acceleration as a first step to a wider West European FTA by proposing in the so-called Luns Plan a reduction of 20 per cent in the common external tariff; it would be extended on a most-favoured-nation basis, confirmed in the next GATT negotiations and combined with compensatory concessions by EFTA and third countries such as the United States.[51]

In March 1960 the EEC Council of Ministers decided in favour of acceleration in principle. The eventual compromise solution agreed upon on 1 July 1960 provided for the next internal tariff reduction of 10 per cent to be pulled forward by twelve months to 1 January 1961. In addition, subject to a multilateral solution being found in GATT later, the EEC lowered its common external tariff by 20 per cent and began with its introduction immediately. It was left to the member states to delay this step until 1 January 1961, and the Federal Republic was allowed not to reverse its previous 1957 tariff reductions by more than 50 per cent.

The EEC decision on acceleration put EFTA under pressure to revise its timetable for internal tariff reductions accordingly. The first tariff reduction of 20 per cent, designed to catch up with the EEC, was scheduled for 1 July 1960. To demonstrate EFTA's ability to act efficiently, the British government demanded that the next tariff reduction of 10 per cent, scheduled for 1 January 1962, should now also be expedited by twelve months. The British position was supported by the Swedes and the Swiss, but not by the industrially weaker EFTA countries possessing greater agricultural export interests. The Norwegians initially insisted at a meeting of senior officials of EFTA countries in July 1960 that they could not support acceleration under any circumstances.[52] Subsequently, at the decisive EFTA Ministerial Council meeting in October 1960 the Norwegian delegation argued that a significant increase in British import quotas for Norwegian fish would be the absolute precondition for their support for acceleration.[53] The

Danes also demanded further British agricultural concessions and, moreover, refused to move on the domestically highly controversial acceleration issue before the Folketing election in November. The British government eventually managed to negotiate that the next tariff reduction of 10 per cent would be pulled forward by six months to 1 July 1961,[54] but failure to keep in step with the EEC was seen in London as a major diplomatic defeat. One important reason for this defeat was, of course, that the British were neither economically capable nor politically willing to foster the cohesion of EFTA with multilateral or bilateral concessions to the same extent as the Germans were to stabilize the EEC.

Failure to accelerate parallel to the EEC was annoying, but what really mattered for the British government was the open hostility which the United States government displayed towards EFTA and a wider economic arrangement between the Six and the Seven. With the initial FTA concept the British had hoped both to safeguard their trade interests in Western Europe and to please the Americans. Macmillan initially assumed in 1956 that Eisenhower and Dulles would appreciate the fact that the British government was now prepared to move closer to Europe, if only in trade policy. In his first assessment of the likely American reaction to Plan G, however, Roger Makins, the British Ambassador to the United States, warned as early as August 1956 that the FTA proposal definitely did not go far enough to arouse 'real enthusiasm' in Washington. On the contrary, the British might in fact be accused of trying once again to secure the best of all worlds.[55] It turned out that the British had great difficulty until well into 1957 to convince the Americans that the FTA initiative was not another attempt to sabotage the customs union negotiations nor the ratification of the Rome Treaties in the parliaments of the Six, but was instead conceived as a trade roof above the EEC.[56] The French persistently warned the United States government that they could only tolerate additional competition within the EEC, but not in a wider FTA which, they alleged, endangered the successful political development of the EEC, a fear shared by Dulles and others in the Eisenhower government. From their point of view the EEC contained at least certain supranational elements. It also established a suitable institutional framework for Franco-German *rapprochement*, if on an economic rather than a defence basis. By contrast, an industrial FTA in Western Europe would result in additional disadvantages for United States exports without the political advantage of greater political integration and cohesion, an argument that became increasingly important in the late 1950s due to mounting American balance of payments deficits.

As a result, the Eisenhower government made polite statements on the FTA initiative in 1957–8, but did not actually support the British government *vis-à-vis* the Germans or the French. According to Maudling, what amounted at best to American neutrality contributed significantly to the failure of the FTA negotiations.[57] That the forthcoming veto by de Gaulle would actually suit United States interests nicely became clear at a meeting between Lloyd and Dulles in October 1958.[58] In his usual outspoken manner Dulles declared bluntly that he was suprised to see that the British government was still hoping for a successful conclusion of the FTA negotiations. After all, de Gaulle, in talking to Dulles during their first meeting in July, had declared quite categorically that he would never accept the FTA proposal under any circumstances.

The Americans not only supported the Six during the diplomatic acceleration conflict between the EEC and EFTA, but also over the reorganization of the OEEC, which was transformed into the Organization for Economic Cooperation and Development (OECD) to include the United States, Canada, Japan, Australia and New Zealand as full members and was entrusted with new responsibilities, such as the coordination of aid to developing countries. American policy over acceleration and OEEC reform contributed significantly to a growing disillusionment within the British government. It questioned whether EFTA was in fact useful as a bridge to the EEC, or rather, only one year after its creation, already a diplomatic handicap in the attempt to come to an understanding with the EEC. Impressed by open American hostility towards EFTA, the Foreign Office grew more critical of the new organization. As early as May 1960 it stated in an internal Foreign Office comment on an interministerial report on British European policy:

Already the value of E.F.T.A. is being heavily discounted in the United Kingdom and in Europe and in America, where it is increasingly assumed that we shall sooner or later have to surrender. This belief will grow, rather than diminish, as time goes on.[59]

)ual Appeasement: Towards the EEC Application, 1960–1

The disillusionment with EFTA as a bridge to the EEC, leading to the formation of a wider West European market, considerably accelerated the reorientation of British European policy until the first EEC application of August 1961, a conditional application that for Macmillan fulfilled two main functions: first, it would help to appease the United States government into continuing special treatment of Britain, particularly in nuclear matters, and secondly, it would appease the different factions of the Conservative Party into uniting behind the Prime Minister over the divisive European issue, while at the same time deepening the ideological split in the Labour Party.

In 1960–1 Macmillan gave Britain's relationship with the EEC high priority in his foreign and domestic policies. Unlike the decision against participation in a West European customs union in 1955 or the development of Plan G within Whitehall in 1956, the policy-making process was now increasingly directed from the top. A progressive reorganization of the Whitehall committee structure reflects the growing importance of the European circle. In 1955 the Messina initiative never even reached the Cabinet and was instead only discussed in the Economic Policy Committee. The Cabinet had subsequently already debated Plan G quite extensively. An *ad hoc* committee was later created to supervise the FTA negotiations. This committee was renamed the European Economic Association Committee in October 1959 and became integrated into the permanent committee structure, thus guaranteeing continuous discussion of European integration directly below the Cabinet level. The fact that Macmillan himself assumed the chair of this committee also reflected the new priority awarded to European policy.

The Whitehall committee structure was also reorganized at the official level. In 1955 the Trend Working Group of the

108

Mutual Aid Committee considered the Messina initiative. Plan G was then debated in the Sub-Committee on United Kingdom Initiative in Europe, part of the Economic Steering Committee of senior officials. After a further change in the committee structure for the FTA negotiations, the Economic Steering Committee was divided into three committees in March 1960. Frank Lee, the new Joint Permanent Secretary of the Treasury, now chaired the Economic Steering (Europe) Committee which was exclusively responsible for matters of European integration, while the two other committees dealt with Commonwealth relations and general economic issues. Created in March 1960, the European Economic Questions (Official) Committee, which was comprised of middle-ranking officials, supported the Lee Committee. European policy was now increasingly less defined in terms of trade policy. Unlike the FTA and EFTA negotiations in 1957–9, the *rapprochement* of the outer Seven or Britain with the EEC was no longer the Board of Trade's domain. The Foreign Office now insisted once more on a leading role within Whitehall. To define Britain's future role in Europe was increasingly seen as an issue of foreign policy as well as of economics. The closer the government came to applying for EEC membership, the more political considerations overshadowed economic arguments.

After the failure of the FTA negotiations and the successful creation of EFTA the economic ministries were initially much less concerned with the dangers of exclusion from the EEC market than they had been in the internal discussions in 1955. In December 1959 Heathcoat-Amory conceded in a Cabinet memorandum that after the recent visit of the American Under-Secretary of State Douglas Dillon a wider trade arrangement between EFTA and the EEC was not likely for the forseeable future if only because of growing American hostility to such a solution. According to the Chancellor, there was nonetheless no reason to take a defeatist view of the West European trade conflict as the expected export losses in the EEC market might at least partially be replaced by additional exports in the EFTA market.[1]

In late 1959 a number of reasons were decisive as to why the internal Whitehall assessment of the consequences of contin-ued exclusion from the EEC market was temporarily some-what optimistic. To begin with, the likely adverse trade effects

were realistically assessed as more limited than had previously
been estimated. The international competitiveness of British
industry had arguably declined considerably since 1945.
During the 1950s Britain's share of world exports sank from
25.5 per cent to 16.5 per cent while that of the Federal
Republic rose from 7.3 per cent to 19.3 per cent, a development that can only partly be explained by compensatory
effects after the Second World War.[2] There were no indications, however, that the structural problems of the British
export industry would necessarily result in particularly
catastrophic losses within the EEC market. During a period
of robust world-wide trade expansion British exports to
Commonwealth countries sank from £1.26 billion to
£1.19 billion between 1956 and 1962 and the share of
Commonwealth exports fell from 47 to well under 40 per cent
in terms of overall British exports.[3] During the same period
British exports to the EEC rose from £468 million to
£762 million and exports to EFTA states increased from
£378 million to £519 million, so that by 1962 the share of
British exports to Western Europe was already higher than
that of exports to Commonwealth countries.[4] By the early
1960s the progressive Europeanization of British foreign trade
patterns, already predicted by the Board of Trade in 1955, was
progressing largely independent of the political framework.
During the 1960s the share of exports to the Commonwealth
sank further, while that of exports to Western Europe increased by another 19.6 per cent. The share of British exports
to the EEC grew from 14.6 per cent to 29.2 per cent, faster in
fact – despite rising tariff barriers – than British exports to
other EFTA states in which British industry had tariff advantages by comparison with competitors from EEC countries.
Against the backdrop of the changing British trade patterns it
is clear that the problems of British export industry were not
primarily tariff-related and that the dangers of exclusion from
the EEC market were actually smaller than the Board of Trade
and the Economic Section had anticipated in 1955.

In addition, by 1959, senior Treasury and Board of Trade
officials feared that ministers could decide in favour of EEC
membership as a politically convenient but inadequate substitute for necessary yet domestically more sensitive structural
economic reforms to increase the competitiveness of British

industry; this was a more widespread fear that was shared and publicly articulated by Harold Wilson who warned in 1961 against the EEC application as 'an exercise in economic escapism'.[5] In 1959–60 the economic ministries were preoccupied with developing a Conservative British variant of French indicative economic planning which, following a suggestion of the FBI, was eventually institutionalized with the creation of the National Economic Development Council (NEDC) in 1961. This innovation in economic policy would not furnish the hoped-for results of increased productivity, higher growth rates or greater exports.[6] That it was in fact a great political temptation to regard EEC membership as an automatic cure for Britain's economic malaise became clear later in the 1960s and in the early 1970s, a hope that would be disappointed after British accession to the EEC on 1 January 1973.

In 1959–60 officials in the Board of Trade also continued to support the initial FTA concept, which had only been realized in the smaller EFTA variant. They did not wish to give up hope for a wider association between the EEC and EFTA. The Board of Trade had traditionally supported world-wide trade liberalization, a policy which appeared to exclude membership in a tighter regional economic bloc such as the EEC. The Board of Trade also continued to fear that the EEC might develop into a partial preference zone rather than a real customs union. In accordance with GATT regulations, the Six chose the average of the national external tariffs as a common external tariff, so that on average the EEC tariff on industrial goods would be below the British tariff. In the planned agricultural policy of the EEC, however, which would obviously be geared towards agricultural self-sufficiency, Board of Trade officials detected the same protectionist attitudes which it had fought internally concerning the Commonwealth preferences. The resulting critical attitude of many officials towards the Community and possible British membership was further accentuated when after the general election in autumn 1959 Maudling became President of the Board of Trade. During the internal ministerial deliberations in 1960–1 the former British representative in the FTA negotiations was particularly sceptical regarding possible British EEC membership.[7]

The Economic Steering Committee's relatively optimistic assessment at the end of 1959 was thus motivated equally by pragmatic and dogmatic economic policy considerations. According to the Foreign Office, however, irrational factors also played a role.[8] There was first the temporarily high identification with EFTA in the Board of Trade which was not based on the economic or political merits of the new organization; rather, it was the result of a short-lived euphoria that after the agony of the FTA negotiations Britain had ultimately managed to negotiate a European treaty at all. Second, the politically manipulated economic boom of 1959–60, which was geared towards the general election, perhaps distorted the economic ministries' perspective. These ministries thus seemed to underestimate the dangers of an economic split of Western Europe.[9] The preliminary assessment of December 1959 was replaced only six months later in May 1960 with a much more critical analysis of the new Economic Steering (Europe) Committee, now chaired by Lee.[10] Just as the responses of that committee to Macmillan's list with 23 questions about the future of British European policy a short while later,[11] the Lee Report was still determined by the economic perspective, which had been so dominant since 1956, but it was already much more politicized. Within Whitehall, Lee, who in November 1955 had been the only senior official to speak out in favour of common market membership, pushed for a reorientation in British European policy.[12] His efforts were now increasingly supported by the Foreign Office whose officials began to emphasize the adverse political consequences of the economic split of Western Europe into the EEC and EFTA for Britain's ability to sustain a world power role. The changing domestic and external economic context definitely influenced the Lee Report's more critical assessment in May 1960 of Britain's position in Western Europe. When the short-lived boom of 1959–60 lost steam, it once more put in the forefront the structural economic problems as well as Britain's relative economic decline which had accelerated since the debate over Plan G in 1956. Between 1955 and 1960 average growth rates were only 2.5 per cent in Britain; however, they were 4.8 per cent in France, 5.4 per cent in Italy and 6.4 per cent in the Federal Republic. The EEC average was 5.3 per cent.[13] The alternation of short-lived booms and stagflationary periods appeared increasingly to turn into the model cycle of the British economy.[14] British officials and ministers became more and more pessimistic about the chances of economic survival from outside the apparently much more dynamic Community. Nothing was as successful as success, the Lee Report concluded with a view to the high growth rates and dynamic trade expansion within the EEC.[15] Securing a share of this success for Britain was increasingly regarded as essential, as the structural problems of the British economy became more apparent.

The Lee Report once more emphasized that a solution to the West European trade conflict should under no circumstances be regarded as a suitable substitute for the necessary modernization process within Britain. It nonetheless reflected the hope that the additional competitive pressures resulting from closer association with the Six might at least support the process of domestic modernization for which no convincing concept yet existed.[16] EEC membership, more and more Treasury officials hoped, would provide a stable political framework not only for Britain's future economic development, but now also for currency policy. This motive progressively gained in importance as a result of the worsening balance of payments situation in 1960–1, leading to renewed pressure on sterling in the currency markets. When in spring 1961 sterling could only be stabilized with the concerted support of EEC states, particularly with the help of the German Bundesbank, EEC membership was now expected to help the British government sustain the international role of sterling as a reserve currency by increasing confidence in British economic policy in the currency markets.[17]

Against this broader economic backdrop the general advantages of membership, rather than the likely trade benefits, again appeared more important in the Lee Report. It basically repeated the arguments which had been used in the internal deliberations in 1955. Unlike EFTA, the larger and rapidly expanding EEC appeared to offer all the advantages in production and commercialization of a larger internal market. As part of this market, the Lee Report argued, Britain could also hope to regain American direct investment at previous levels. For the first time in 1960 50 per cent of American foreign direct investment in Western Europe went to the EEC and only 40 per cent to Britain, a trend which Heath lamented publicly in 1961.[18] In addition, if Britain remained outside the

EEC, the government feared massive outflows of British capital to the Six which might otherwise be invested within Britain. The Lee Report's warning was clear: even if the effects of the increasing tariff disadvantages in the EEC market were limited, the general long-term economic effects of continued exclusion from the EEC market were potentially disastrous,[19] an assessment that was increasingly shared by large sections of British industry which in turn influenced the internal Whitehall decision-making process. The Lee Report emphasized, for example, that:

> There is great uneasiness, amounting almost to dismay, among leading industrialists at the prospect of our finding ourselves yoked indefinitely with the Seven and 'cut off' by a tariff barrier from the markets of the Six.[20]

The changing domestic and external economic circumstances in connection with the increasingly critical judgement of the diplomatic usefulness of EFTA contributed to the Lee Report's overall assessment that in a broader economic rather than a limited and more short-term trade perspective, EEC membership would now in fact be the best policy for the future. Due to the influence of the ministries of Commonwealth Relations and of Agriculture, Fisheries and Food, however, the Lee Report repeated that pursuing the membership option was still inadvisable for well-known political reasons. Instead the Economic Steering (Europe) Committee advocated the interministerial compromise solution of what the Lee Report called 'near-identification'. According to this concept, without actually acceding to the EEC Treaty, the EFTA countries would largely accept the regulations of the EEC in a wider economic association and agree to far-reaching tariff harmonization.[21] Near-identification, which thus effectively varied little from what might have been the result of the FTA negotiations without de Gaulle's veto, was expected to help safeguard British agricultural interests and continued Commonwealth free entry. Only in connection with a broad solution to the trade conflict between the EEC and EFTA did officials advocate British accession to the ECSC and Euratom, another option which the Economic Steering (Europe) Committee considered in early 1960.[22]

Near-identification was subsequently discussed from late autumn 1960 onwards in bilateral expert talks between British and German, French and Italian officials. In Whitehall the chances that these preliminary talks might eventually lead to negotiations over a wider economic association between the EEC and EFTA were, however, regarded as slim from the very beginning. Because of the hardening American opposition to a purely economic arrangement between the Six and the Seven, the Foreign Office in particular regarded near-identification not only as unrealistic, but also as undesirable. Near-identification seemed to involve all the possible disadvantages, such as tariff harmonization, without the essential advantage of influencing the future development of the EEC from the inside.[23]

Macmillan also saw the trade conflict between the EEC and EFTA from an essentially political perspective. He believed that with the recommendation of near-identification British European policy was heading in the wrong direction. When the Lee Report was first discussed at the ministerial level in the European Economic Association Committee on 27 May 1960, Macmillan insisted:

> that it is for consideration whether, if we are prepared to contemplate 'near-identification' with all its difficulties and dangers, we should not do better to go the whole way and secure the full advantages of membership of the Common Market. To 'go into Europe fully' would at least be a positive and an imaginative approach which might assist the government to overcome the manifest political and domestic difficulties. 'Near-identification' has less attractions, and not appreciably less dangers.[24]

To most officials in the economic ministries near-identification went far enough to minimize the negative economic consequences of exclusion from the EEC market with which they were naturally preoccupied. It is not surprising in view of the interministerial discussion on the Messina initiative in 1955 that they believed in 1960 that the economic arguments were mostly in favour of EEC membership, while the political judgement initially remained controversial. In 1955 officials from the Treasury and the Board of Trade already had been largely united in the assessment that sooner or later the British government would be forced to join a common market of the Six if formed without Britain. The creation of EFTA only meant that the Board of Trade – in its foreign trade perspective – now rightly saw the adverse trade effects of exclusion from the EEC market more relaxed. In contrast, under the leadership of Lee, the Treasury, not least because of the continuous change in the policy of the Overseas Finance Division, was more concerned with the wider economic implications than in 1955. But Britain was not Switzerland. Selling more watches and cheese was perhaps a sufficient motive for the Swiss government to seek an economic arrangement with the EEC. Apart from the general economic advantages of a larger West European market, the British government was more and more concerned with safeguarding or regaining the political leadership of Western Europe, an aim that was impossible to achieve with the concept of near-identification.

When as part of his internal questionnaire in June 1960 Macmillan asked the Economic Steering (Europe) Committee what had changed in the analysis of British European policy since 1955, officials accordingly only referred to the impact of the EEC on Britain's position in the world.[25] Whereas it has usually been assumed that between 1955 and 1961 the perception of Britain's relative economic decline changed dramatically, it is now clear that the economic analysis during this period in fact remained quite stable. At the beginning of the 1960s the change in the domestic and external economic circumstances, including the evident success of the EEC, contributed to the swiftness of the reorientation of British government policy on Europe towards EEC membership. What was more important, however, was the change in the perception of leading ministers, including Macmillan, and the Foreign Office of how Britain could in future secure the greatest possible international influence and thus retain its world power status. At the end of 1960 Macmillan wrote in a lengthy personal memorandum entitled 'Grand Design':

> However bold a face it may suit us to put on the situation, exclusion from the strongest economic group in the civilised world must injure us ... We ought therefore to make a supreme effort to reach a settlement while de Gaulle

is in power in France. If he gave the word, all the Wormsers[26] would turn at once ... Sixes and Sevens ... is now not primarily an economic but a political problem and should be dealt with as such.[27]

FROM LAGGARD TO LEADER?

It has been argued that the different policies towards European integration of Britain and the founding member states of the EEC resulted from two fundamentally different foreign policy perspectives: a British global approach – the result of Britain's world-wide economic and military responsibilities – is contrasted with a eurocentric regionalism of the Federal Republic and France. In this view the EEC application of 1961 appears as a British attempt to avoid a political split in Western Europe as a result of the trade conflict between the EEC and EFTA, in order to strengthen the free world in the global conflict with the communist bloc.[28] This interpretation of British European policy is questionable in at least two respects: first, it adopts too uncritically a myth which the British political elite created and cultivated to distract from its domestic failure to modernize the British economy and, secondly, it fails to differentiate between policy areas. In foreign economic policy, for example, the German and Dutch governments defended the principle of multilateralism and the GATT as much as the British did. Neither side was always faithful to the principle of progressive global trade liberalization. It could be argued with some justification that the British equivalent to the emerging agricultural protectionism of the EEC was comparatively high external tariffs and the policy to prolong, wherever possible, the remaining Commonwealth preferences. For the British to claim that, unlike the EEC, EFTA was an outward-looking association which would promote international trade liberalization was greatly facilitated by the membership of the low tariff countries: Sweden and Switzerland. Elements of a global perspective, in which the split in the Six and the Seven did not appear exclusively a West European issue, did influence the change in the political calculation of the British government until the first EEC application.

Macmillan continuously emphasized the need to maintain a unified front in the West against communism, which to him did seem threatened by the trade conflict between the EEC and EFTA.[29] His fears were accentuated by the foreign policy of de Gaulle who was keen to increase the independence of a French-led Western Europe from the United States as much as possible. The British government was particularly concerned with the talks among the Six from 1959 about possible closer political cooperation outside the existing treaty framework, which led to the Fouchet negotiations of 1961–2.[30] For the British to move closer to the EEC was thus increasingly seen as an important contribution to safeguarding the Atlantic security architecture. Britain, or so it seemed, would be the indispensable hinge between Western Europe and North America, holding together the Atlantic Alliance. In late 1959 the Foreign Office Planning Section, which had been created two years previously, concluded in one of its memoranda that:

> It is not inconceivable that an integrated and prosperous Western Europe might ... decide to strike out on a policy of its own at variance with that of the Americans. If it is believed that the continued cohesion of the Atlantic Alliance is essential to the free world then the greatest contribution which we can make is to act as the cement in that alliance.[31]

To strengthen the unity of the free world was in fact the only significant political argument which Macmillan used when defending the EEC application in the House of Commons on 2 August 1961,[32] a motive that played a central role in the public rhetoric of ministers. It should not, however, be taken at face value. Behind the rhetorical façade was hidden a national-egoistic perspective which was almost exclusively fixated on the internal economic problems of Britain and its continuing decline as a major international power. To many in the Macmillan government, to accede to and lead the EEC increasingly appeared the only way for Britain – as junior partner of the United States – to retain a world power role, a motive that was never explicitly mentioned in public because for domestic political reasons the government preferred not to confront the British with the harsh realities of relative international decline.[33] In the dominant perception of British decision-makers in the 1950s, four factors were essential for the maintenance of a world power status.[34] The relative weight of these factors varied according to personal priorities and changing external circumstances. They were the special role of the British government as mediator between the two superpowers, the British role at the centre of the Commonwealth, the special relationship with the United States and the British nuclear deterrent, or what Macmillan liked to call 'the bomb'.[35] Within this magic quadrangle, fundamental change occurred in the late 1950s and early 1960s which radically altered the framework for Whitehall decision-making.

In the late 1950s, Britain's special role in the troika of Yalta and Potsdam appeared increasingly threatened. Ministers and officials in London did realize that Britain was neither economically nor militarily capable of competing with the two superpowers, but the Conservative governments hoped in the long term to secure a seat at the table of the Soviet Union and the United States by mediating between the two in summit diplomacy. What Churchill had made a major priority of his foreign policy, particularly during 1953–4,[36] Macmillan took up enthusiastically when after the first Berlin crisis international diplomacy temporarily became fixated on summiteering. Macmillan was keen to promote *détente* between the blocs. In addition, his summit diplomacy fulfilled certain secondary domestic and external functions. In 1959–61 the agitation of the Campaign for Nuclear Disarmament (CND) culminated in Britain. In party political terms, CND influence was primarily a problem for the Labour Party, but Macmillan also wanted to take the wind out of the sails of the Left: his summit diplomacy was to show that he was supportive of *détente* and disarmament, but that meanwhile – while the two superpowers were still continuing to arm themselves – Britain could not do without its independent nuclear deterrent.[37] To Britain's allies, Macmillan's visit to Moscow during the Berlin ultimatum in February 1959 in particular appeared to be motivated exclusively by domestic political concerns. Both Adenauer and Eisenhower suspected electoral tactics behind this visit.[38]

At the same time, Macmillan became all wrapped up in his role as mediator between East and West. He apparently enjoyed summits as social events and liked to act as elder statesman, versed in the ways of the world.[39] To translate politically between the ageing Eisenhower and the ill-tempered and unpredictable Khrushchev and to nourish the illusion that the British Prime Minister could still influence the course of world history in a major way compensated psychologically for the loss of greater independence after the Second World War. Macmillan's summit aspirations were shattered, however, when Khrushchev abruptly broke off the Paris summit in May 1960 after an American U-2 spy plane was shot down over the Soviet Union. Subsequently the British could never resume their mediating role when after the 1962 Cuba crisis a new bilateralism began to develop between the two superpowers.

According to Macmillan's Private Secretary Philip de Zulueta, the breakdown of the Paris summit, in which the Prime Minister had invested much hope and time, contributed decisively to his European reorientation towards the 1961 EEC application. In retrospect, de Zulueta, who advised Macmillan on matters of foreign policy, has suggested that after the Paris summit Macmillan became preoccupied with the question of how Britain could in future continue to play a special international role.[40] It appears that de Zulueta's assessment is borne out by the fact that Macmillan compiled the list of questions for the Lee Committee on future British European policy and subsequently had the topic discussed in Cabinet only a few weeks after the breakdown of the Paris summit.[41] On the other hand, Macmillan had already insisted in late 1959, in an internal meeting with Foreign Secretary Lloyd, Chancellor Heathcoat-Amory and three senior officials of the Cabinet Office, the Foreign Office and the Treasury, that a new attempt would have to be made to come to an understanding with the EEC. He even mentioned for the first time the possibility of a special informal arrangement with de Gaulle, involving British nuclear assistance to France, to achieve a *rapprochement* between Britain and the EEC.[42] The abrupt end to summit diplomacy may have accelerated, but it did not spark Macmillan's reorientation towards the option of full EEC membership. Moreover, Macmillan's preoccupation with summit diplomacy was never shared widely within the government.

Long-term structural changes in Britain's foreign relations clearly played a much greater role for the decision-making process in 1960–1, for example the continuous decline in the importance of the Commonwealth as a second symbol –

alongside summit mediation – of Britain's world power role. After 1945 the leadership of the Commonwealth was initially still seen as the most important basis for Britain's claim to a world power role. By the mid-1950s the decline of the Commonwealth as a trade bloc was perceived more clearly within Whitehall, but during the internal deliberations on the Messina initiative the Conservative government still assumed that the Commonwealth would nonetheless sustain a certain amount of political cohesion. The historical and cultural bonds were still regarded as strong enough and, ultimately, more important than economic advantages or institutional structures, which the Commonwealth lacked. In the early 1960s, however, the centripetal forces had become so strong that the Commonwealth was increasingly less useful for the foreign policy strategy of a government preoccupied with the maintenance of Britain's world power status and international prestige. The economic and political interests even of the Dominions diverged so much over important issues that their governments gradually became less prepared to follow British leadership. The internal controversies over Suez in 1956–7 were already indicative of this change.

The reorientation in the foreign and foreign economic policy of Britain's main Commonwealth partners had considerably accelerated by 1960–1. Economically and politically, Canada was increasingly dependent on the United States, while Australia's primary focus was now Asia. South Africa left the Commonwealth to preempt exclusion which appeared inevitable after the government was heavily criticized for its apartheid policy at the Commonwealth Prime Minister's Conference in March 1961. The British government initially wanted to keep South Africa in the Commonwealth, but was isolated over an issue which was of great symbolic importance: the controversy made it plain to decision-makers in London how much less relevant the Commonwealth was by then to the maintenance of a world power role.

The character of the Commonwealth had already changed considerably after the first phase of decolonization during 1945–8.[43] Among the new member states, India was a particularly difficult partner for the British due to the markedly independent policy of Prime Minister Jawaharlal Nehru. In 1957 Nehru temporarily considered withdrawal from the

Commonwealth over British Middle East policy. He subsequently played a leading role in 1961 in creating the Non-
Aligned Movement. Only in the course of the second phase of
decolonization during 1957–64, however, when the 'wind of
change' blew through the rest of the Empire, did the
Commonwealth change fundamentally. Ghana and Malaya
became independent in 1957 and Nigeria in 1960. Other
African and Asian countries followed suit. As a result of the
enlargement of the Commonwealth its internal political cohesion diminished rapidly. Moreover, unlike the Labour Left, the
Conservatives felt emotionally and ideologically primarily attached to the 'white' Dominions. The Commonwealth with its
new multicultural character was no longer *their* organization
to the same extent as it had been previously.

Macmillan was primarily concerned with Britain's status and
prestige in the world. From this perspective, by 1960–1 the
Commonwealth was no longer an asset of British foreign
policy, but already a liability. In view of the seemingly un-
stoppable advance of communism in the Third World, the
Commonwealth was – in foreign policy terms – still useful as
an instrument of anti-communist containment policy in the
former colonies. With Ghana and Nigeria, Britain could not,
however, make a favourable impression at the table of the
two superpowers. As a result, in terms of its usefulness for
the maintenance of British world power ambitions the
Commonwealth only played a minor role in the internal deliberations until the EEC application, although it initially remained an important party political, domestic and diplomatic
factor of Conservative European policy.[44]

During the immediate postwar period, the Commonwealth
had helped to legitimate the third symbol of Britain's international standing, the special relationship with the United
States. Decolonization undermined the British claim to
special treatment by the United States by comparison with
other NATO allies in Western Europe, notably the Federal
Republic and France. In early 1960 the Foreign Office
Planning Section warned in a memorandum, which Lloyd
forwarded to Macmillan, that the special relationship was no
law of nature in international relations. The Planning
Section saw the acute danger that, due to its growing
economic strength and increasing military capability, the

Federal Republic could well replace Britain as the most important European ally of the United States. At the same time, the importance of the fourth symbol of Britain's international status, its formally independent nuclear deterrent, was being undermined by the French nuclear programme to which de Gaulle gave priority.[45]

The United States' position on the trade conflict between the EEC and EFTA seemed to confirm the British foreign policy elite's worst fears. The American perspective on Western Europe appeared to shift continuously at the expense of Britain. The United States had not openly opposed the creation of EFTA, but Dillon had made it abundantly clear during his visit to London in late 1959 that in the view of his government EFTA was politically irrelevant,[46] a frank statement that caused Macmillan concern. The British did not regard the EEC as the main threat to their special bilateral relationship with the United States; rather, the perceived threat was de Gaulle's plans for closer intergovernmental political cooperation among the Six which would include foreign policy and, ultimately, defence matters, measures that in de Gaulle's view would help to establish the Six as a French-led group of states with substantial international influence. Once de Gaulle had made his ideas public in the summer of 1960, leading ministers and Foreign Office officials became increasingly obsessed with the danger that the Six would soon replace Britain as the second in command in the Atlantic Alliance. De Gaulle's world power aspirations were not, of course, universally shared among the Six. The Benelux governments were particularly sceptical, but nonetheless agreed at the EEC summit in February 1961 that a commission should be entrusted with developing different options for closer political cooperation. In the end, the Dutch and Belgian governments broke off the Fouchet negotiations in April 1962, insisting on the successful conclusion of Britain's entry negotiations and British participation in any future political community as absolute preconditions for their participation. In 1960–1, however, the British could not foresee that the only concrete result of de Gaulle's initiative would be the Franco-German Elysée Treaty of 1963, a minimalist project in a wider European perspective which, from the British point of view, represented no immediate threat to the British position *vis-à-vis* the United States.

In the autumn of 1959 the Foreign Office Planning Section strongly warned for the first time against exclusion from a possible political community of the Six. The officials argued that:

> Politically, such isolation would weaken us significantly. Our exclusion from an integrated Western Europe would reduce the influence we can bring to bear on the member countries and consequently our importance in NATO and the OEEC. Emotionally the United States is attracted by the concept of a united Europe, rationally, she wishes to see a strong one: if faced with the choice between a failing United Kindom which they suspect of opposing or, at the best, remaining aloof from this ideal of unity and a resurgent Western Europe which is eagerly embracing it they will no longer regard us as their principal ally in Europe. At the best we should remain a minor power in an alliance dominated by the United States and the countries of the E.E.C.; at the worst we should sit helplessly in the middle while the two power blocs drifted gradually apart.[47]

The Planning Section still lacked an independent profile within Whitehall. It was not even headed by an Under-Secretary and had to support the other Foreign Office departments,[48] but in European policy its analysis was nonetheless influential at least within the Foreign Office. The Planning Section memoranda for once tried to take a *long-term* view of Britain's European policy. They were appreciated by other departments and by Foreign Secretary Lloyd and so accelerated the change in the dominant foreign policy calculation within the government. Against the backdrop of the latent crisis in the Commonwealth and the trade conflict in Western Europe, the Planning Section's assessment developed into the new Foreign Office orthodoxy within one year after late 1959. Supported by such politically minded senior officials in the Treasury as Lee, the Foreign Office eventually had its way in the Lee Committee's answers to Macmillan's questionnaire in mid-1960 that it was absolutely indispensable for Britain 'to be in the inner circles of the Six'.[49]

The Foreign Office was determined that Britain would have to be part of any possible political organization of the Six long before an interministerial consensus was reached in 1961 on the necessity of EEC membership. 'Near-identification' in economic terms was only acceptable to the Foreign Office if 'full-identification' could be achieved for intergovernmental political cooperation in Western Europe. In the final instance New Zealand butter and Scottish tomatoes could not be allowed to jeopardize Britain's international position. In August 1960 Assistant Under-Secretary of State Roger William Jackling confirmed the new Foreign Office doctrine in a memorandum for the new Foreign Secretary Home:

> While our immediate task must be to find solutions for the complex economic difficulties, we must not lose sight of our political objectives ... It seems clear that General de Gaulle is thinking in terms of a wide intergovernmental structure for the Six covering defence, political, economic, social and cultural questions. This degree of integration among the Six would probably constitute a far graver threat than the E.E.C., not only to European unity but also to Atlantic solidarity. Our interests would presumably be seriously prejudiced if we did not participate fully in whatever new organisation emerged ... From the political standpoint [it is] more than ever essential that we should not be fobbed off with some purely economic solution which leaves us outside the inner councils.[50]

When the Planning Section presented its memorandum on future British European policy in late 1959, Macmillan had already arrived at very similar conclusions.[51] At this stage, he was not yet personally committed to the aim of full EEC membership, but in the internal meeting with Lloyd and Heathcoat-Amory in November 1959 he emphasized that the yardstick for any change in policy would have to be whether it helped Britain sustain the status of world power with world-wide responsibilities. It was extremely doubtful, the Prime Minister argued, whether the special relationship could continue and Britain's status be maintained if Britain remained outside the organizations of the Six.[52] In view of the answers of the Lee Committee and of the informal alliance between the EEC and the United States over tariff acceleration and OEEC reform, Macmillan subsequently noted in his diary in mid-1960:

Shall we be caught between a hostile ... America and a
boastful, powerful 'Empire of Charlemagne' – now under
French but later bound to come under German control? Is
this the real reason for 'joining' the Common Market (if we
are acceptable) ...? It's a grim choice.[53]

The degree of continuity in Macmillan's perception of the
dangers of exclusion from a continental bloc, ultimately led
by the Germans, becomes clear when his views on Europe in
1960 are compared with those in the early 1950s. Early in 1952
Macmillan, who was then Housing Minister in Churchill's government, had written in a personal memorandum on Europe:

If ... we are to see Western Europe and its colonial posses-
sions pass into a German-dominated customs union and our
own overseas markets threatened, the outlook will be dark
indeed ... Instead of playing merely second fiddle to the
United States, we might have to descend to third fiddle,
while the ... Continentals took the second place.[54]

In the early 1960s the fourth symbol of Britain's world
power status, its national nuclear deterrent, depended increasingly on American assistance, so that the maintenance of a
special British role *vis-à-vis* the United States became even
more important than it had been previously.[55] In 1946 the
American Congress had unilaterally terminated the bilateral
nuclear cooperation with Britain in the Manhattan project, established during the Second World War. The McMahon legislation forbade the American government to pass on any
nuclear know-how to other states, so that Britain subsequently
had to develop its national nuclear deterrent independently.
By the mid-1950s, however, Britain was being shaken off in the
nuclear race by the two superpowers. For economic reasons
the Eden and Macmillan governments decided in 1955–7 to
reduce substantially British defence spending, a policy that
was put into effect with the Sandys White Paper of 1957. It was
now increasingly doubtful whether Britain would actually be
able to finance the enormous research and development costs
of an independent national nuclear force. Moreover, at the
start of the missile age, it was not guaranteed that Britain
would possess the necessary technological know-how to
develop an effective replacement for its ageing bomber fleet

which, due to improved air defence, would be obsolete by the early 1970s. When under the impression of Soviet technological advances Eisenhower offered Macmillan the resumption of bilateral nuclear cooperation at their Bermuda meeting in March 1957, the British Prime Minister was relieved and eagerly accepted, an agreement that was legalized in 1958 when Congress amended the McMahon legislation accordingly.

The British initially continued the development of the surface-to-surface missile Blue Streak, for which the Americans now supplied the guidance system.[56] It soon became clear, however, that this new weapon would be outdated by the time it became operational, so that the project was eventually cancelled in February 1960. The British subsequently accepted an offer by Eisenhower in April 1960 to supply them with the air-to-surface missile Skybolt, which the United States was then developing, a weapon that would prolong the readiness for action of the British bomber fleet. In return the British would leave Holy Loch on the Scottish West coast to the Americans as a base for their nuclear submarines.[57] This Anglo-American agreement initially appeared to guarantee that at least during the 1960s Britain would retain a credible nuclear deterrent, although it was now entirely dependent on American goodwill. It soon turned out, however, that despite this agreement with the outgoing Eisenhower government the British national nuclear deterrent was increasingly called into question in the United States, and particularly after Kennedy's assumption of office in January 1961. From then onwards it was increasingly doubtful whether the Americans would actually finish the Skybolt project which was riddled with technical problems. When the United States Secretary of State for Defence, Robert McNamara, publicly announced the cancellation of the Skybolt project in the autumn of 1962, it no longer came as a surprise to the British.

At this point, however, it was not at all certain and, indeed, perhaps not even likely that the Kennedy government would offer the British a replacement weapon, such as Polaris. By comparison with the Eisenhower period the so-called Europeans and the multilateralists had gained influence in Washington.[58] For different reasons both groups strongly opposed continued special treatment of Britain in nuclear matters. The Europeans around the influential Under-Secretary of State for Economic Affairs, George Ball, were not only keen to strengthen supranationalism in the EEC, but also saw the Community of the Six as the most important partner of the United States in Europe. To them bilateral nuclear co-operation with Britain was an entirely undeserved bonus for the British who – against declared American interests – had now refused for more than a decade to participate in building a United States of Europe. In the markedly military-strategic perspective of the multilateralists like McNamara, American nuclear assistance to Britain was unacceptable on principle. The multilateralists rejected the idea of formally independent national nuclear deterrents within the Atlantic Alliance other than the American, and instead supported the creation of a common nuclear force in NATO, a concept that had already been developed in 1959 by General Lauris Norstad, NATO's Supreme Commander in Europe (SACEUR), and in 1960 in the so-called Herter Plan, named after the outgoing American Foreign Secretary. Under Kennedy it was then turned into the proposal for a Multilateral Force (MLF) within NATO.[59] The multilateralists had two main objectives: to prevent the emergence of an independent French nuclear force and to guard the United States against possible nuclear aspirations of the Federal Republic and other NATO allies. In February 1962 Kennedy made it plain to Macmillan in private that the multilateral approach was being seriously undermined by British insistence on a formally independent national nuclear force.[60] The MLF concept was also linked to the continuous reorientation of American strategic thinking from massive retaliation to the concept of flexible response to a possible Soviet aggression which necessitated a centralization of nuclear decision-making. Independent centres of command – whether in London or in Paris – which were not under direct control of the United States were no longer acceptable.

It is often overlooked that the British were not suddenly confronted with the danger of being forced to relinquish their national nuclear deterrent when McNamara announced the cancellation of the Skybolt project. In 1960–1 the Macmillan government was already operating against the backdrop of speculation that American nuclear assistance might be withdrawn sooner or later. As a result of the narrow verdict of the presidential elections in November 1960 the British were spared Richard Nixon and Dillon, who were expected to follow a strongly pro-French policy. Compared with Eisenhower, however, the young and unpredictable Kennedy was only the lesser of two evils. After Kennedy's election Macmillan noted anxiously in his diary: '"Skybolt" – are the Americans going to let us down, and (if so) what can we do?'[61] If the British wanted to retain any chance of securing continued American support for a credible, formally independent national nuclear deterrent, they needed to appeal to Kennedy by diplomatically outperforming the EEC states in complying readily with American interests in Europe, as defined by the new government in Washington.[62]

British ministers thus discussed future European policy in 1960–1 against the backdrop of an acute fourfold crisis in the traditional definition of Britain's international standing which fundamentally called into question their claim to world power status. In their external crisis management, EEC entry was to be the central element. In 1955 participation in a West European common market had seemed incompatible with Britain's international role based on the three circles doctrine. By 1961 it appeared that only by joining the EEC might Britain be able to sustain its international status and prestige. Within only six years, the main argument against membership had become the decisive reason for it. When Macmillan returned from the summit with Kennedy in Washington in April 1961, the Prime Minister perceived the EEC and de Gaulle's plans for closer political cooperation among the Six more than ever as an acute danger for the cohesion of the Atlantic Alliance and for Britain's world role.[63] Shortly afterwards, in a meeting of the European Economic Association Committee of ministers, Macmillan stressed that the main argument in favour of EEC membership was the extreme danger of remaining outside. Not to have equal access to the EEC market was harmful enough for British industry. To be exluded from the 'inner circles' of the Six, which by then appeared to radiate an almost magical attraction, would inevitably lead to the collapse of the British international position.[64]

In Macmillan's view EEC entry would fulfil four main functions. Leadership of the EEC would, first, replace leadership of the Commonwealth as the main source of legitimation for Britain's claim to a special role alongside the two superpowers. In 1961 the Prime Minister still assumed that Britain, once inside the EEC, would automatically take over from the French and the Germans.[65] In Macmillan's somewhat original interpretation of Kennedy's Grand Design concept for the future transatlantic relationship, the British formed the European pillar, based on the new foundation of the EEC. The Commonwealth would of course remain important, but primarily for British national identity and within the Conservative Party to appease the Empire wing. Secondly, Macmillan intended to offer Britain as the trojan horse of the Americans within the EEC, which would guarantee that the development of political cooperation in Western Europe remained compatible with the existing security structure of the Atlantic Alliance. Kennedy did believe that Britain could play a useful role within the EEC. In April 1961 he told Macmillan that he mainly expected from British EEC membership a moderating influence on de Gaulle's much too independent-minded foreign and European policy.[66]

The leadership role in the Community did not aim exclusively at replacing the Commonwealth with a new status symbol, nor was the offer to act as assistant sheriff of the United States within the EEC exclusively directed at stabilizing the Atlantic Alliance. Both roles were corresponding to the third function of EEC entry, namely to cement the special relationship with Washington. British political leadership of the Community, in Macmillan's view, would help to compensate for the increasing economic superiority of the Federal Republic and for possibly greater French influence as a result of de Gaulle's independent-minded policy, including the *force de frappe*. Within the EEC, Britain would re-establish itself as the only reliable and thus the most important partner of the United States. The British government primarily moved nearer to Europe so that the Americans would not move further away from them. At least for Macmillan, the EEC application was in the first instance an instrument of British transatlantic policy.[67] Moreover, to stabilize the special relationship was also the only way to secure the formally independent British nuclear deterrent – the fourth foreign policy function of the EEC application. The connection

between European and nuclear policy was not direct or immediately evident. The British Prime Minister did not decide to
apply for EEC membership in 1961 so that Kennedy would
agree to sell him Polaris in December 1962; rather, by anticipating shifting American interests and adjusting British policy
accordingly, Macmillan hoped to secure the goodwill of the
Kennedy government, which would also help Britain to retain
American support for its nuclear deterrent.

American European policy in fact reduced the British
options in Western Europe to two: the status quo or full EEC
membership. Like its predecessor the Kennedy government
was unwilling to accept a trade arrangement between the EEC
and EFTA, as Ball once more made clear in a meeting with
Heath and Lee at the end of March 1961 in preparation for
the summit between Macmillan and Kennedy one week later.[68]
Quite apart from French or German interests, Lee's concept
of 'near-identification' was thus very clearly out of the question. If, however, the status quo appeared unacceptable
economically and politically, Britain had to apply for full EEC
membership. In April 1961 senior officials of the Lee
Committee concluded that United States policy was now effectively dictating the direction of British policy towards the
EEC.[69] Macmillan could not care less. After the Suez disaster
five years previously he had accepted as the guiding principle
of British foreign policy that under no circumstances could
British governments act contrary to *core* interests of the
United States, if they did not wish to risk the special relationship. This was a motive that Macmillan played down in
Cabinet discussions, as some of his colleagues regarded it as
much too defeatist, and that was of course never mentioned
in public.

During his meeting with Edward Heath, Lee and other
senior officials in March 1961, Ball made it abundantly clear
that for wider reasons of security policy his government expected the British to apply for full EEC membership soon.[70]
The exchange between Ball and Lee is particularly revealing
with respect to the transatlantic motivation of the British EEC
application and deserves to be quoted in full. After Lee's
introductory question about the American position on the
ongoing expert talks between British and German, French
and Italian officials:

Mr. Ball said that the United States deeply regretted that the United Kingdom had not yet felt able to accept the Rome Treaty commitments ... British membership of the Community would represent a contribution of great importance to the cohesion of the Free World ... He did not think that the kind of solution envisaged by H.M.G. [that is, a trade arrangement between the EEC and EFTA] would be satisfactory to the United States ... He wished to repeat that the American Administration were fully persuaded that it was a misfortune that the United Kingdom was outside the Community. Sir F. Lee said that he would be grateful for any further indications as to the direction in which the United States would like to see United Kingdom policy evolve. Was Mr. Ball suggesting that the United Kingdom should join E.E.C.? ... Mr. Ball said that the United States would certainly like to see the United Kingdom join E.E.C.[71]

On other occasions Ball expressed the American desire in less diplomatic language. In early March 1961 Caccia, British Ambassador to Washington, reported, for example, that Ball had told him in an aggressive tone that Britain must join the EEC within the next five years.[72] United States hostility towards EFTA had not escaped the British media. Not surprisingly, British newspapers thus speculated after the summit between Macmillan and Kennedy whether the new government was now going further in trying to force the British to apply for EEC membership.[73] Thereafter, the Americans endeavoured to give the impression of neutrality in relation to British European policy in order not to compromise Macmillan domestically or *vis-à-vis* de Gaulle. In private meetings with British ministers and officials Ball pretended that he had not intended to pressurize the British into applying for EEC membership.[74]

For the Kennedy government British EEC entry was only one element among others in its developing foreign policy strategy which eventually led to the Grand Design concept.[75] The acute crises in Berlin, Cuba and Vietnam as well as other domestic and foreign policy considerations were given much greater attention. For the time being, Britain remained a reliable partner of the United States and to this extent was still its most important though not formally privileged ally. In contrast, leading figures in the British government believed by then that EEC membership was – in the words of Eccles – a question of death or resurrection. Despite the protestations of the Americans that they did not wish to exert any pressure, Kennedy's intended friendly encouragement appeared to Macmillan like a command with which it was inadvisable not to comply. In so far as the British acted under American pressure, it was the obligation they themselves felt not to act against American core interests in Europe.

For Macmillan EEC entry progressively developed into the cement of his foreign policy with which the fragile construction of the three circles could be held together and with which Britain's world power role could be prolonged. EEC membership would be the bitter economic and political pill which Britain had to swallow if it still wanted to be counted in the world even after the disintegration of the Empire. Just as the FTA concept five years previously, the first British EEC application had little to do with the future of Western Europe. Before the application, ministers or senior officials never even once discussed how the expected leadership role in the Community would manifest itself or to what effect the British government would want to use it.

Reluctance to think about life after entry cannot be attributed to the alleged difference between British pragmatism and continental European idealism. Unlike the British, de Gaulle, who also did not wish to build the United States of Europe, had comparatively precise ideas about the direction in which he wanted Western Europe to develop. The French President, like Macmillan, treated European policy largely as an extension of national foreign policy. But whereas French European policy was dynamic, the British were entirely fixated on Britain's decline. Macmillan's sole aim was to prevent Britain's relegation in the international system into the second league of medium-sized powers. This central motive behind the British EEC application was excellently described once by the late Lord Inchyra. From 1957 to 1961 Hoyer Millar – as he then was called – was Permanent Under-Secretary of State in the Foreign Office and one of the senior officials within Whitehall who actively promoted the reorientation towards the EEC application:

One had to find another focus, but I would not like to say that we had any clear, defined objectives there – except to get closer to Europe ... Everybody complains that they're not getting something out [of membership]. We never went in to get something out. We went in to prevent our being kicked down really to a lower league ... One did not realise at the time what a momentous decision it was and all the implications of it. One merely thought that, from a political point of view, here was a chance of saving a little of the position we've lost. And if we don't take this opportunity we shall be of no more account than a small peripheral European country – and you've got to hop on the band-wagon while you can.[76]

Macmillan's conservative perspective on Britain's role in Europe was not of course shared by all advocates of EEC entry within the government. Some saw EEC entry primarily as an instrument for domestic economic modernization. Others were long since convinced that Britain's natural place was in Western Europe. These were mostly the younger ministers and officials. Their European orientation in many cases resulted from their war experience, which led them to emphasize the pacifying effect of European integration on the postwar development of Western Europe. A growing minority within the Conservative Party, this group included for example Thorneycroft, who after his resignation as Chancellor in January 1958 returned to the government in mid-1960 as Minister of Aviation. Macmillan's traditional foreign policy perspective nonetheless dominated policy-making in 1960–1 because it was widely shared among the older generation of Conservative politicians whose perception of the world had been formed before the First World War or in the early inter-war period. Home is a typical example of the change in their view of Britain and Europe which occurred in the late 1950s and early 1960s. As Commonwealth Secretary, Home was one of the most ardent opponents of Plan G in 1956 because he expected negative consequences for the Commonwealth which he still saw as the main foundation of Britain's world power role. By mid-1960, however, he strongly believed that it was now necessary to join the EEC to strengthen the transatlantic relationship with the United States and so to retain the greatest possible international influence and prestige.[77]

The EEC application was thus never intended as a radical change in British foreign policy.[78] It did not represent an imaginative leap into the future. There simply seemed to be no alternative course of action. The analysis of the main motives behind the application reveals the conservative character of the British decision to apply for full EEC membership. It was a final and desperate attempt by the British government to support its mediating role in the three circles by pragmatically adjusting to the increased economic and political importance of Western Europe which manifested itself in the evident success of the EEC. The 1961 EEC application was a tactical change to secure the same strategic objectives that had determined British foreign policy since 1945. Only a very few leading Conservative politicians were actually searching for a new British role in the world. The clear majority simply intended to put on a new mask which would enable them to play the traditional world power role.

It has been argued that, independent of the declared aims of the decision-makers at the time, the two British EEC applications of 1961 and 1967 were the inevitable reaction of a political system trying to adapt to changing economic realities.[79] This interpretation reflects an economic determinism that does not do justice to the much more complex historical genesis of the first, or indeed the second, British EEC application. Long-term economic trends, in particular the Europeanization of British trade patterns, were no doubt of great importance. It can be argued with some justification that these structural changes made an EEC application highly likely in the long term, although not inevitable. The one-sided economic view does not, however, explain why Britain applied for EEC membership for the first time in 1961, and not in 1959 or indeed after de Gaulle's retirement from French politics. Against the backdrop of a rapidly changing perception of Britain's international decline, it is now clear that foreign policy arguments were much more influential than economic considerations in the run-up to the 1961 decision. In talking to de Gaulle in December 1959, Macmillan in fact confessed to a strong personal belief in the primacy of foreign policy.[80]

At the political level the Prime Minister also hoped to come more easily to an informal understanding with the French President, particularly over nuclear matters.[81]

The reorientation towards the EEC application was of course not undisputed within the government or the Conservative Party. To test out opinion among his colleagues, Macmillan had the Cabinet discuss the answers of the Lee Committee to his questionnaire on 13 July 1960. At this point, Macmillan had not yet decided in favour of full EEC membership. He did believe, however, that it was essential to find a suitable solution to the problem of Sixes and Sevens quickly. It was clear that substantial British concessions, for example over agriculture or tariff harmonization, for which he needed the support of the Cabinet, would be inevitable. In a major reshuffle shortly after the internal discussion, Macmillan promoted several pro-European ministers to key positions. Home, who shared Macmillan's transatlantic perspective entirely, became Foreign Secretary. Heath was promoted to Lord Privy Seal. He was co-opted into the Foreign Office and became responsible for European affairs. Sandys became Commonwealth Secretary, and Christopher Soames moved to the politically highly sensitive agriculture portfolio.

The Cabinet discussion showed that Macmillan still had to reckon with resistance against any substantial shift in British European policy. Among the colleagues concerned with matters of European policy, however, only Maudling advanced fundamental objections. The President of the Board of Trade was concerned about possible negative effects on the Commonwealth. He also did not like the customs union concept for dogmatic reasons and wished the government to adhere to the original FTA concept.[82] Compared with Maudling, the pronounced scepticism of Butler, who was the leading representative of the agricultural lobby within the party, was of much greater significance. As Home Secretary, Butler was not directly concerned with European policy. The Prime Minister was nonetheless keen from the very beginning to include Butler fully in the internal deliberations. As he was looking for the greatest possible consensus within the party on the lowest common denominator, he needed a cooperative attitude on the part of Butler in the run-up to the EEC application. Macmillan subsequently even asked Butler to chair the

Cabinet committee which overlooked the Brussels entry negotiations, in order to commit him loyally to support government policy over Europe. After the Cabinet meeting in mid-July 1960 Lloyd, who was about to move to the Treasury, once more confirmed the established European policy in a speech delivered in the House of Commons.[83] Only five months previously the Foreign Secretary had intimated in the Parliamentary Assembly of the Council of Europe that Britain should have participated fully in the creation of the ECSC ten years previously.[84] In June 1960 in a speech to the WEU Assembly, the Foreign Office Minister John Profumo had then appeared to suggest the possibility of Britain joining the ECSC and Euratom as a first step towards a new relationship with the Six.[85] Although it now seemed that British policy towards the EEC remained unchanged, Macmillan began to prepare the sceptics for a reorientation in European policy, particularly from late 1960 on when he finally made up his mind in favour of full EEC membership.

In February 1961 Heath warned Macmillan that opposition within the Cabinet against a major reorientation in European policy had still been pronounced in July 1960 because the Prime Minister had allowed a free debate. Instead he should now organize the policy-making process in such a way as to lead to the conclusion that the EEC application was perhaps not necessarily desirable, but inevitable.[86] Accordingly Macmillan subsequently arranged for the Lee Committee to prepare a study of the likely consequences of EEC membership.[87] He enjoyed working through Whitehall committees as long as he could rely on the loyal support of senior officials, such as Lee, who could guarantee the desired outcome. Interministerial reports gave the impression of objectivity. They helped the Prime Minister to diffuse more fundamental ideological criticism of the desired policy change and permitted him to declare himself openly only at the very last moment.

The Lee Committee was now asked to analyse how the domestic and external problems of accession to the EEC could be overcome. The new study was an entirely different exercise from the questionnaire of mid-1960 that had allowed sectoral interests to prevent clear-cut policy advice. When the Lee Committee presented its final report in late April 1961, most of the arguments against membership advanced previously seemed of only minor importance or were even presented as completely irrelevant in view of the overriding objective of securing a place for Britain in the 'inner circles' of the Six.[88] One such irrelevance, it turned out, was the inevitable loss of national sovereignty. In late 1960 Heath had already asked the Lord Chancellor, Lord Kilmuir, to consider the constitutional implications of EEC membership.[89] The topic was subsequently analysed in greater detail in a special study of the Lee Committee which focused on the effects of the integration of trade policy within the EEC, of majority voting in the Council of Ministers and of the controversial constitutional question of the supremacy of Community law over national law. These three aspects of the sovereignty issue were considered from a dogmatic constitutional and from a pragmatic political perspective.[90] The Lee Committee study argued that after accession to the EEC the British government would be expected to follow a constructive Community approach. In some cases, it would have to accept and support majority decisions that might be at variance with British interests. The Lee Committee believed, however, that because of the expected parallel accession of at least two other EFTA states the British would not be isolated on too many occasions, so that the effects of qualified majority voting would probably be relatively limited.[91] It is interesting to see that the officials did appreciate – at least in theory – the implications of common decision-making and qualified majority voting. In a sense they displayed more *esprit communautaire* in 1961 than de Gaulle did in 1965–6 during the constitutional crisis of the EEC which led to the informal Luxembourg compromise; this compromise allowed member states to exercise a veto whenever fundamental national interests were at stake.

Senior Foreign Office officials no longer regarded, as they had in 1955, the partial transfer of sovereignty to a semi-supranational organization such as the EEC as a problem. Stimulated by the Suez shock, which had dramatically exposed the narrow limits of Britain's independent ability to project power, the understanding of sovereignty had changed fundamentally within the British executive. Sovereignty was now no longer understood as an absolute concept of independence from external forces, but rather as a relative concept of the greatest possible international influence. In a sense, as EEC entry was expected to lead to an increase in British influence world-wide, the new policy actually promised to enhance executive sovereignty. Parliamentary sovereignty, on the other hand, no longer mattered much to the foreign policy elite and was reduced to a question of skilful intra-party and domestic political management. In 1961 the Lee Committee considered in detail only the Commonwealth and British agriculture as highly sensitive domestic political issues. It treated these in special reports which by Macmillan's order were top secret.[92] For the Commonwealth British EEC entry meant the end of free entry for its agricultural products as well as the introduction of negative preferences in the British market for industrial goods.[93] Officials hoped, however, that the adverse effects on Commonwealth exports to Britain could be limited by negotiating transitional periods and by achieving further reductions in the EEC's external tariff. The greatest problems for other Commonwealth states would be caused by British participation in a common European agricultural policy, and primarily in temperate foodstuffs such as cereals. Although the EEC's agricultural policy was not yet finalized, it was already clear that it would be based on a system of managed markets and essentially geared towards self-sufficiency.

British participation in the EEC's agricultural policy would particularly affect New Zealand which was still very dependent on its agricultural exports to Britain.[94] To safeguard at least the core agricultural interests of the Commonwealth, the Lee Committee concluded in its study, the British government would have to concentrate on negotiating with the EEC special arrangements for a few essential commodities, such as soft wheat from Australia and butter from New Zealand.[95] Special attention needed to be given to such core Commonwealth interests not least in order to avoid a split in the Conservative Party.[96] Beyond those core interests the British government would at least have to give the impression of negotiating on behalf of other Commonwealth states in so far as their interests were compatible with those of Britain in Western Europe. This was primarily a presentational problem. Even though the basic decision in favour of the EEC application had already been made at this point, British ministers thus demonstratively visited the capitals of all Commonwealth states in late June 1961 for consultative meetings over future British European policy.[97]

Finally, in agriculture EEC entry would necessitate a change in the British subsidy system. Unlike most continental European systems, the British subsidy system was based, in most commodities, on deficiency payments to farmers, state subsidies that supplemented the farmers' income, by making up the difference between the low British market price and the much higher producer price which was negotiated annually between the Ministry of Agriculture and the National Farmers Union. At the time of the Cabinet meeting in July 1960 representatives of the Ministry of Agriculture still took the line that such a change was out of the question because of the political obligations to farmers in the 1957 Agriculture Act.[98] Under the energetic leadership of Soames, however, the ministry's policy changed rapidly in 1960–1. In spring 1961 it already argued that the switch could probably be made without adverse effects on farmers' incomes. Whereas British producers were expected to do badly in some commodities, particularly horticultural products, pork and milk, they were likely to profit in others, such as cereals.[99]

The about-face in the policy of the Ministry of Agriculture was due to a number of factors. By 1961 the compatibility between British economic interests and those of the other Commonwealth states had decreased further. The British government was in fact keen to use EEC membership as a smoke-screen for putting up tariffs in certain sectors, such as textiles, in order to reduce imports from the Commonwealth and Empire, particularly from Asia. To safeguard its declining textile industry the British had already induced Hong Kong, India and Pakistan in 1958–9 voluntarily to limit their textile exports to Britain. The Europeanization of British protectionist interests was not, however, restricted to certain industrial commodities. The British also wished to prevent the continued use of the British market for dumping Commonwealth excess production in foodstuffs. The continued expansion of domestic agricultural production behind the shield of a common European agricultural policy was to be achieved primarily at the expense of third countries, such as Poland, Argentina and the United States. The Ministry of Agriculture was, however, also determined to reduce the agricultural imports from the Commonwealth.[100] Outside Whitehall, the growing British interest in West European agricultural protection of course needed to be framed in diplomatic language as it stood in sharp contrast not only to the economic interests of the Commonwealth, but also to the foreign economic rhetoric of the government. Moreover, to admit such an interest would have undermined the British negotiating position *vis-à-vis* the Six. At the end of July 1961 Soames wrote to Butler that 'we do not want the Six to know that some of their proposals [for a common agricultural policy] are really quite attractive to us.'[101]

In 1960–1 the Ministry of Agriculture was also put under pressure from the Treasury to consider a fundamental change in the subsidy system independent of whether Britain was to accede to the Community or not. In the Lee Committee's answers to Macmillan's questionnaire in July 1960 the Treasury had already calculated that a tariff-based agricultural policy, such as was planned by the EEC, could result in savings in the British budget of up to £220 million annually.[102] This financial argument continuously gained in importance because government expenditure under the established system increased quite dramatically while at the same time the domestic economic situation worsened after the short-lived election boom of 1959–60.[103] The Treasury also hoped that a substantial overall reduction of agricultural imports would improve the British balance of payments position – deeply in the red in 1960 – and so help stabilize sterling. One important side-effect of a switch in the agricultural subsidy system was of course an inevitable increase in food prices as a result of the artificial lifting of prices to and above world market levels. In their report officials speculated that EEC entry might result in an overall increase in the level of consumer prices in Britain of 1.5 per cent.[104] The prices for bread and eggs were likely to rise particularly sharply. Prices for basic foodstuffs were, however, a sensitive political issue since at least the repeal of the Corn Laws in 1846, a fact that the Labour Party later tried to instrumentalize during the entry negotiations. In 1961 the government nonetheless opted for budget consolidation and against consumer interests. Of course, Macmillan would choose a continued world power role for Britain over cheap eggs for breakfast.

Finally, the Ministry of Agriculture hoped that in negotiations over full EEC membership Britain would actually get
away with fewer concessions over agriculture than by following the policy of 'near-identification'. During the bilateral
expert talks since the autumn of 1960 it became clear that if a
trade arrangement between the EEC and EFTA could be
achieved at all, the Treasury and the Commonwealth
Secretary would ensure that it was negotiated at the expense
of British agriculture. Already in late summer of 1960 Soames
was told that 'all Whitehall is terribly keen on making concessions at our expense'.[105] Continued Commonwealth free entry
and substantial agricultural concessions to the EEC to pay for
a trade agreement, however, were seen as catastrophic for
British agriculture and unacceptable to any Conservative government.[106] If therefore, EEC membership was preferable to
any other solution, the Ministry of Agriculture argued, it
should come as soon as possible, so that the British could still
influence the structure of the common agricultural policy
which was still highly controversial among the Six in 1961 and
as yet unresolved. In the end, the sum of these arguments
even convinced Butler whom Macmillan for some time had
had canvassed by colleagues and senior officals close to the
farming community.[107]

In the Cabinet Macmillan raised the question of a reorientation of British European policy for the first time after his
return from the summit with Kennedy in April 1961.[108] There
was some speculation in the British press at that stage that the
government had already decided or was about to decide in
favour of the EEC application.[109] A clear majority of ministers
was long since of the opinion that EEC entry was either desirable or necessary. The Prime Minister nonetheless decided to
move slowly. He suggested further internal discussions about
the Lee Committee reports on the Commonwealth and British
agriculture to diffuse the remaining opposition to EEC entry.
In the end, the decision to apply for EEC membership had
already been made when leading ministers met at Chequers
on 18 June 1961 for a special meeting on European policy.[110]
It was formally confirmed by the Cabinet after the
Commonwealth tour of British ministers on 21 July.[111] Support
of the new European policy was made easier for the sceptics
such as Maudling and Butler, the latter finally assuring

Macmillan personally of his full support for EEC entry at a private dinner in August 1962,[112] because Macmillan opted for a conditional application to the effect that, according to the government motion in the House of Commons, negotiations with the EEC should be initiated 'to see if satisfactory arrangements can be made to meet the special interests of the United Kingdom, of the Commonwealth and of the European Free Trade Association'. The motion went on to assure Conservative MPs that the government 'further accepts the undertaking ... that no agreement affecting these special interests or involving British sovereignty will be entered into until it has been approved by this House after full consultation with other Commonwealth countries ...'[113] In the end, only one Conservative backbencher voted against the motion and 22 abstained, eight fewer than the party leadership had expected.

The governmental decision-making process had not, of course, taken place in a domestic political vacuum. Unlike in the latter half of the 1950s, European policy was no longer a depoliticized matter of trade relations. In 1960–1 the question of Britain's future role in Western Europe was heatedly discussed in public. In 1960 two cross-party organizations, the Common Market Campaign and the Anti-Common Market League, were formed, which campaigned for and against EEC entry. The rising domestic political importance of European policy is also reflected in the fact that it was now debated much more intensively in the House of Commons than at any time previously since the Marshall Plan. Between the first major debate on Europe in July 1960 and the announcement by the government that it would apply for EEC membership, European policy took up 1.5 per cent of debating time, twice as much as at the time of the Schuman Plan and twenty times as much as during the first few years of the ECSC.[114]

Within the Conservative Party, the influence of those who – for whatever reason – supported an upgrading of the European circle in British foreign relations grew steadily. Time clearly seemed to be on their side and not on that of the traditionalists who lamented the disintegration of the Empire and still hoped to rely exclusively on the British leadership role in the Commonwealth. At the time of the application the vast majority of MPs were fully behind the new government

policy.[115] Support for EEC entry was most pronounced among
the 1955 and 1959 intake of young Conservative MPs.[116] The
generational change is also reflected in the fact that the
Conservative school and student associations both passed reso-
lutions in favour of EEC membership in the spring of 1961
without waiting for Central Office guidance.[117] Even when in
1962 the possible conditions for accession turned out to be
much less advantageous than the government had hoped in
1961, the opponents of EEC entry in the Conservative
Parliamentary Party never numbered more than 40, just as in
the case of the Maastricht Treaty thirty years later.[118] Moreover,
strong opposition came primarily from the nationalist Right
who undermined their own position within the party with
chauvinistic remarks about the continental Europeans and
with personal attacks on Macmillan.[119] As a result, the Prime
Minister was no longer too concerned about internal opposition to his new EEC entry strategy after the House of
Commons debate at the beginning of August 1961. On
5 August he noted in his diary:

> The Conservative abstainers are of two kinds – earnest im-
> perialists, like Biggs-Davidson, Russell and others. The dis-
> gusted group (who oppose the government in every
> trouble, whatever the subject) led by three ex-Ministers.
> Two of these I had to dismiss for incompetence or idleness –
> Turton and Walker-Smith. One was dropped by either
> Churchill or Eden – Grimston – and he is angry with me for
> not having made him Speaker, a post held by a former
> Grimston in the Seventeenth or Eighteenth Century. The
> others [are] the usual grumblers, like Paul Williams, Jenkins
> etc.

At a time when after ten years of Conservative rule the
popularity of his government began to fall rapidly, Macmillan
foresaw no serious challenge of his authority. Referring to the
fall of Peel, he added in his diary: 'I see no Disraeli among
them; not even a Lord George Bentinck.'[120] The extent to
which Conservative opinion had shifted in favour of EEC
entry by the summer of 1961 becomes particularly clear in
connection with the internal debate on British participation in
a common European system of agricultural protection, a
debate that took place mainly in the party's new Agricultural

Policy Committee, founded in March 1960. Its Secretary Peter Minoprio emphasized as early as spring 1960 the potential advantages of a common European agricultural policy for British farmers and tried to convince the committee to recommend the membership option at the earliest possible moment.[121] Because of the staunch resistance of some members, Minoprio did not in fact succeed until June 1961. Even then the committee could only agree on a limited list of necessary safeguards for domestic agriculture as the lowest common denominator. The list was forwarded to Butler as the most prominent representative of the agricultural lobby in the Cabinet.[122] The committee debate nonetheless demonstrates very clearly that by mid-1961 support among the agricultural experts of the Conservative Party for participation in a common European agricultural policy and the necessary switch at the expense of consumers to a different system of agricultural subsidies was very much greater than the over-cautious Macmillan had dared to hope.[123] Equally, support for EEC entry was also more pronounced already among the party rank-and-file than Macmillan had perhaps expected; this became clear in six meetings at the regional party level of representatives of Conservative Central Office with functionaries to explain the new policy.[124]

Without the full support of the Prime Minister, the EEC application could not have come so early. At the same time, the new European policy largely reflected a change of mood within the Conservative Party in favour of the idea that Britain needed to play a more prominent role in Western Europe. In 1961 Macmillan no longer encountered serious organized opposition within the Parliamentary Party. Apart from the core of the nationalist Right, the sceptics could be appeased with the defensive justification of the EEC application in the House of Commons and in public, which illustrates very well the compromise character of the EEC application. To make a conditional application was in fact the best way for Macmillan to keep his party together over Europe. Those who supported EEC membership retained a vague hope that despite the dubious prospects of the application, negotiations with the EEC might lead to British entry. On the other hand, the opponents and sceptics could argue that the government had merely decided to start negotiations with the EEC, a step that

did not prejudice the final decision on EEC membership. At a
time when Macmillan was confronted with manifold economic
and domestic political problems, he gained precious time with
his move on the chessboard of Conservative party politics in
favour of the ambivalently worded government motion. To
achieve this short-term tactical aim of intra-party appeasement
the Prime Minister was prepared to ignore the clear warning
by the Foreign Office that such a non-committal and defensive presentation of the application in Parliament would seriously undermine the British position *vis-à-vis* the Six even
before negotiations began. Senior Foreign Office officials had
in fact prepared an alternative draft that frankly stated some
of the real motives behind the application.[125]

Macmillan also hoped that in the long term the new EEC
entry policy would contribute to the programmatic modernization of the Conservative Party which after ten years in office
was running out of ideas and appeared increasingly worn out,
a fact that was not even concealed by the bitter trench war in
the Labour Party in 1960–1 over unilateral disarmament and
Clause Four. Macmillan was keen on developing a modern
image for the Tories which would help to attract young voters
and the upwardly mobile middle class. In delimitation from
the Socialists, who still appeared fixated on old-fashioned class
ideology, the Tories would retain their conservative identity in
matters of home affairs, for example, but otherwise present
themselves as the dynamic force in British politics addressing
the central issues of the future. Macmillan was determined to
claim for the Tories the competence for the necessary
economic modernization of Britain and for the revitalization
of the British world role. His entry policy would contribute to
both.

Moreover, the EEC application would also help to deepen
the existing split in the Labour Party over Europe and give the
Conservatives a propaganda advantage in the run-up to the
next parliamentary election.[126] Until 1961 the Labour leadership, in accordance with TUC policy, followed a pragmatic line
over Europe.[127] It had supported the government over
the FTA plan and the creation of EFTA. As long as the
Conservatives treated European policy as a depoliticized
matter of trade policy, the attitude of the Labour leadership
was very cooperative. As late as May 1961, for example, Wilson

approached Lloyd to enquire how he should explain and
justify British European policy at a forthcoming meeting of
European Socialist leaders.[128] Within the party Europe initially
remained a minor issue by comparison with Clause Four
and unilateral disarmament. Once Macmillan turned the
European question into a matter of party politics, however, the
bitter infighting within the Labour Party between left-wing
fundamentalists and reforming revisionists over what it should
stand for immediately extended to the European question.[129]
In the end, Hugh Gaitskell, the party leader, chose the
European question to appease the Left in the hope that this
would help him to achieve an internal truce over the other
highly divisive issues and thus to keep the party together.

The widespread opposition to EEC membership within the
Labour Party had different reasons. The Left was still
fascinated with the leadership role of Britain in the
Commonwealth which, they hoped, would help to overcome
the North–South conflict by facilitating the export of Socialist
ideology to the newly independent former colonies. What Roy
Jenkins termed 'the new imperialism' of the Left in his speech
in the House of Commons on 2 August 1961[130] was the counterpart to the English sentimental nationalism of the political
Right. Membership in a regional West European organization
which, moreover, was dominated politically by Christian
Democrat and Conservative parties, seemed incompatible with
such a special missionary role of Britain as a bridge between
the industrialized and the developing countries. On the
Labour Left the belief was also widespread that the
Community deepened the division in Europe and that it was
an additional obstacle on the way to the desired political and
ideological *rapprochement* between the superpowers.[131] In contrast, many MPs in the centre of the party still believed that
the leadership role in the Commonwealth was the only
effective guarantee that Britain could retain a world power
status. Unlike the Foreign Office, they did not accept that
leadership of the EEC would be a suitable replacement.
Within the party as a whole the belief was also still widespread
that the British nation-state could on its own overcome the
already manifest economic problems and manage social
change. In the Labour Party internationalist political rhetoric
and nationalist economic policy formed an ambivalent

relationship which left little room for the idea of a new inter-dependence in Western Europe. The European question had been debated in various Labour Party committees since November 1960.[132] A group of strongly pro-European MPs, approximately one-third of Labour MPs, advocated EEC membership and played a leading role in the Common Market Campaign, of which Jenkins was deputy chairman. Early on it became abundantly clear, however, that support for EEC entry was unacceptable to the majority of their colleagues. In the House of Commons debate on the government motion at the beginning of August 1961 Gaitskell already distanced himself from the new government policy.[133] Subsequently at the annual Labour Party conference in October, delegates passed a resolution against EEC entry, unless a number of conditions were fulfilled, including the retention of total national independence in questions of economic and social policy, conditions that were clearly non-negotiable. Gaitskell's policy of 'no, unless' to British EEC membership was the equivalent to Macmillan's 'yes, if' approach. To the Labour leader it seemed the only way to paper over temporarily the deep divisions within the party over Europe. When during 1962 the possible terms of entry became clearer, Gaitskell eventually rejected EEC entry outright at the Labour Party conference in October. He even claimed that EEC membership amounted to a betrayal of 'a thousand years of history'. Gaitskell's notorious anti-EEC speech was directed at least as much at the Left within the Labour Party as at the general public. It could easily be portrayed by the Conservatives as backward-looking and characteristic of a party incapable of innovation. In contrast to Gaitskell, the Prime Minister now presented his decision to apply for EEC membership for the first time in more positive terms at the subsequent Conservative Party conference in October. In an open debate, which was not orchestrated by the party leadership, and in the subsequent vote an over-whelming majority of delegates opted in principle for British membership in the EEC despite the fact that the terms of entry were likely to be worse than anticipated and that the Commonwealth Prime Ministers had just issued critical statements on the state of the negotiations in Brussels. Only 50 out of 4000 delegates voted for an anti-EEC motion. So, shortly after several by-election defeats, including Orpington, and the major Cabinet reshuffle in the 'Night of the Long Knives' in July, the European issue and Gaitskell's polemic attack helped to unite the Conservative Party.

In 1961 Macmillan not only hoped that the EEC application would deepen the split in the Labour Party, but that it would also – according to a senior party official – 'dish the Liberals by stealing their clothes'.[134] In the 1950s the Liberal Party, at that stage an insignificant electoral force, had already supported closer British involvement in European integration. After 1960 the Liberals advocated EEC entry. Since the 1959 general election the Liberals' fortunes in the polls had revived largely at the expense of the Conservatives. Macmillan believed that he needed to take the Liberal challenge seriously also in programmatic terms. In his view the Liberal Party should not be allowed to occupy policy issues which were important for the development of a modern party political image for the Tories, an additional incentive for Macmillan in 1961 not to delay the decision in favour of the EEC application for too long. The Prime Minister's domestic political strategy in the European question entirely bears out Jenkins's judgement in his memoirs, intended – it seems – as flattery, that in contrast to the later 'Heathian honesty', Macmillan's 'devious cast of mind' in party politics was much more dangerous for the Labour Party.[135] Macmillan could indeed have chosen in 1961 at least to try to search for common ground with sections of the Labour Party and with its leadership over future British European policy, as he had in fact done in 1956 and again in 1959. Instead, he deliberately decided to intensify the internal crisis of the Labour Party. Macmillan knew very well that his new entry policy would not be supported by everyone in the Conservative Party. Someone like Beaverbrook would never support British EEC membership under any circumstances. What mattered to Macmillan was the *relative* cohesion of the two parties and that Labour could be relied upon absolutely to be much more deeply split over Europe than the Conservatives. This was so because the issue of EEC entry fitted so neatly into the existing ideological faultlines, and also because Labour MPs, opponents of membership as well as the staunch supporters like Jenkins, were so much less prepared to follow their party leadership.

What is more, while public opinion over Europe remained extremely volatile throughout the negotiations, two trends can be identified in the opinion polls which were entirely in line with the Prime Minister's party political calculation. First, while many voters were admittedly undecided, more supported the government line than were opposed.[136] Secondly, the degree of support was to some extent at least correlated with party preference. Among Conservative voters, the lead of supporters over opponents of EEC entry was consistently greater than the lead among Labour voters of opponents over supporters. As a result, it was highly unlikely from the very beginning that, even if the Labour Party could unite behind an anti-EEC policy – and Macmillan knew that it would not – it would be able to use the European question to its advantage. Otherwise, the Conservatives did not care much about public opinion. They reckoned that the British would ultimately be prepared to follow the lead of the government of the day, an expectation that is entirely borne out by contemporary comparative research on the 'system effect', that is the preparedness at times of economic stress or external challenges to declare one's solidarity with the political system in general and the government of the day in particular.[137] The pronounced willingness of the British to follow leadership, particularly in foreign policy, corresponded with the expectation of the Macmillan government that it could surely convince the population that EEC entry was now necessary, although it had argued only a short while earlier that for a whole number of reasons it was quite impossible. It is perhaps typical of the highly patriarchal attitude of the Conservative leadership that Macmillan and Heath believed that the government would simply have to 're-educate' the British in order to turn them into 'good Europeans' – almost as they had tried to re-educate the Germans 15 years previously in the hope that this would make them good democrats.[138]

As a result of the deliberate party political polarization over Europe in the early 1960s, Britain lacked a minimum national consensus and degree of continuity in European policy from the beginning, a phenomenon that since British entry into the EEC in 1972–3 has contributed significantly to the image of the British government as a particularly difficult partner within what is now the European Union. The structural reason

for the lack of consensus and continuity is arguably the confrontational character of the British political system, which in
1961 appeared to put such a high premium on the party political exploitation of the comparatively deeper split of the
Labour Party over Europe, but it also belongs to Macmillan's
political legacy.

THE BOMB AND EUROPE

The shrewd party politician that he was, Macmillan carefully
devised what he believed were the best domestic political
tactics over Europe, but he also spent much time thinking
about the best diplomatic approach to the Six, and particularly to de Gaulle. The central question here was whether and
under what conditions Britain would actually be allowed to
join the EEC. Only after de Gaulle's rejection of the British
FTA plan in December 1958 had British ministers begun fully
to appreciate the importance of the evolving partnership
between France and the Federal Republic for any future
attempt to secure British economic and political interests in
Western Europe. At the end of 1959 Macmillan wrote to
Foreign Secretary Lloyd that it was the governments of these
two countries that had to be influenced to reach an economic
settlement between the two groups, the EEC and EFTA, which
at that stage was still British policy.[139]

One exceptionally important continuity in Macmillan's
thinking on Europe is the very close link he felt existed
between matters of European integration and security policy, a
belief that began to influence British diplomacy in Western
Europe in 1958 when Macmillan suggested internally that
Britain would have to retaliate in the field of defence and
security policy if the FTA negotiations were to break down. In
June 1958 he wrote to Lloyd and Heathcoat-Amory:

> I feel we ought to make it quite clear to our European
> friends that if little Europe is formed without a parallel de-
> velopment of a Free Trade Area we shall have to reconsider
> the whole of our political and economic attitude towards
> Europe ... We should not allow ourselves to be destroyed
> little by little. We would fight back with every weapon in our

armoury. We would take our troops out of Europe. We would withdraw from NATO. We would adopt a policy of isolationism. We would surround ourselves with rockets and would say to the Germans, the French and all the rest of them: 'Look after yourselves with your own forces. Look after yourselves when the Russians overrun your countries.' I would be inclined to make this position quite clear to both de Gaulle and to Adenauer, so that they may be under no illusion.'[140]

It soon became clear, however, that such threats did little to impress de Gaulle who was aiming at a more independent French policy within the Atlantic Alliance. In dealing with the French President Macmillan therefore restricted himself to broad hints at possible adverse consequences of the economic division of Western Europe into Sixes and Sevens for Western security. On the other hand, Macmillan believed that he could pressurize Adenauer into supporting Britain first over the FTA negotiations and later over Sixes and Sevens and British EEC entry. After the first Berlin crisis, which had exposed once more the precarious German security situation on the iron curtain, the Prime Minister wrote to Lloyd in October 1959 that 'the Germans are not in a strong political position, and I should have thought that there was some chance of bullying them'.[141] Macmillan had already told Adenauer at their meeting in August 1958 in the context of the FTA negotiations that Britain could hardly be expected to help defend a continent which 'declared economic war upon her'.[142] Shortly afterwards the Prime Minister warned Adenauer in writing that if the Paris negotiations were broken off by the French, it might well lead to the break-up of NATO.[143] These and other such threats continued to set the tone of Macmillan's approach to Adenauer. Even when in August 1960 he wished to enlist German support for a wider economic arrangement between the EEC and EFTA, he came back to his beloved idea of retaliation. During his meeting with Adenauer in Bonn he even warned for the first time in such concrete terms that he might have to withdraw the entire British Army of the Rhine (BAOR), if no solution to the problem of Sixes and Sevens was found.[144]

The Prime Minister never coordinated his German-bashing with the Foreign Office. The diplomats in fact thought that Macmillan's threats were foolish and counterproductive. Already in late October 1958 the Assistant Under-Secretary of State Anthony Rumbold, for example, wrote on the margins of one of Macmillan's novel-like internal memoranda on possible political sanctions against the nasty continental Europeans: 'The reason why we keep four divisions on the continent is because it is in our interest. We are defending ourselves. It is not a favour that we are conferring on other countries.'[145] After the meeting between Macmillan and Adenauer in August 1960 Hoyer Millar remarked on the margins of another such memorandum that he could simply no longer follow the Prime Minister's chain of reasoning.[146] Evelyn Shuckburgh, Deputy Under-Secretary of State in the Foreign Office, added that the Prime Minister apparently believed that he could manipulate NATO to force a political solution to the problem of Sixes and Sevens. If that was so, it was advisable to remind him of the basics of British foreign policy. Shuckburgh explained to Home:

> No NATO, no American participation in our defence ... No American participation, no defence (This is true however many bombs we and the French might succeed in making). Consequently, the need to preserve NATO and the principle of integrated forces, which alone guarantees us the American contribution, overrides any considerations of tactics *vis-à-vis* France and Germany.[147]

In the end, Macmillan's threats were surely a bluff to intimidate Adenauer into changing his European policy which aimed primarily at strengthening the new Franco-German alliance. The Prime Minister was not really prepared to consider such far-reaching steps as the complete withdrawal of British troops from the Federal Republic or British withdrawal from NATO, policies that would have antagonized the United States and contradicted established British foreign policy priorities. Not surprisingly, the bluff was called. Adenauer was not terribly impressed. On the contrary, the repeated threats only reinforced his deep-seated mistrust of the Prime Minister. Eden later recalled that even at the time of late 1957

Adenauer had complained to him 'that during Churchill's time and mine he had known exactly where he was, but now he could not feel the same confidence in our leadership nor obtain any clear indication of our intentions'.[148] In April 1960 Adenauer wrote to the German President Theodor Heuss that he felt Macmillan's threats were simply embarrassing.[149] At their subsequent encounter in Bonn in August 1960 Adenauer confronted Macmillan head-on and told him, almost in Foreign Office diction, that he knew very well that the British troops were stationed on the Rhine not primarily to protect the Federal Republic, but Britain.[150] It was altogether too obvious that Macmillan was not prepared to let drastic measures follow his violent rhetoric. Moreover the potential effect of any such political sanctions would have been limited. In the final instance, the external security of the Federal Republic depended not on British, but American willingness to help defend it. Instead, it might have made more sense for the British to think about possible political incentives to whet Adenauer's appetite for a solution to the division of Western Europe into Sixes and Sevens. This, however, the British never did between 1958 and 1961. Instead Macmillan continuously gave priority to other domestic and foreign policy interests over the cultivation of good Anglo-German relations.[151]

Adenauer was particularly angry about Macmillan's Berlin policy. De Gaulle at least followed a hard line *vis-à-vis* the Soviets in public, although he did of course have his own *détente* ambitions. In contrast Macmillan seemed to demonstrate openly that he was happy to make concessions to the Soviets at the expense of the Germans when he went to Moscow in February 1959 without prior consultation with the Bonn government. On his return Macmillan told Adenauer that for him the decisive question was whether the West was prepared to go to war over the Soviet demands.[152] He implied that he was certainly not, and that he would try to defuse the situation, if necessary with concessions to the Soviets. Previously, Adenauer had been annoyed with the Prime Minister over his decision in 1957 to reduce the strength of British troops in the Federal Republic in steps from 77 000 to 55 000.[153] The German Chancellor showed very little understanding for the severe budgetary and balance of payments pressures under which the British attempted to reduce their defence spending. Since 1955 the Anglo-German relationship had already suffered as a result of an endless quarrel about German compensation payments for British stationing costs in German marks for BAOR troops.[154]

That the British were not prepared to put aside some of their domestic or foreign policy interests to cultivate the bilateral relationship with the Germans was not even primarily because they underestimated the growing influence of the Federal Republic within the West. At least in the case of Macmillan it was also the result of his intense anti-German gut feelings. In his memoirs he quotes freely from his diaries that he believed that the Germans were all 'rich and selfish'.[155] The Prime Minister stuck much more to the image of the ugly and loathsome German than de Gaulle who accepted the need for close cooperation with the Federal Republic. Macmillan's particular dislike of Adenauer, whom he thought 'vain, suspicious, and grasping',[156] was mutual. Christopher Steel, the British Ambassador to Bonn, once informed Macmillan that the German Chancellor was reported to have said that he had only three enemies, the Communists, the British and his own Foreign Ministry.[157]

However ill-conceived British policy *vis-à-vis* the Germans may have been, de Gaulle's veto against the creation of an industrial FTA in December 1958 had illustrated that the key to a satisfactory settlement in Europe lay in Paris.[158] Macmillan and the Foreign Office rightly thought that, contrary to Adenauer, de Gaulle would be able to negotiate from a position of strength essentially for three reasons. First, his domestic political position was considered to be increasingly secure. In 1958 France had appeared to be on the brink of civil war. Despite the explosive Algerian question, which was only resolved in 1962 with the Evian agreement, by 1960–1 the Fifth Republic had already enjoyed a comparatively high degree of internal stability following the introduction of the new constitution in October 1958. This in turn allowed the ever more self-assertive de Gaulle to shift his attention to foreign policy issues, particularly to the idea of a reorganization of the Atlantic Alliance, which he began to develop with his 1958 memorandum on tripartism, and to the political cooperation of the Six, whose foreign ministers began to meet regularly at the end of 1959. On both issues, the British were in a very awkward position as they expected to lose much of their influence both in Europe as well as *vis-à-vis* the United States as a result of any change in the status quo.

Secondly, by 1959 France had experienced several years of comparatively strong economic expansion. The introduction of full convertibility of the franc at the end of 1958, combined with a substantial devaluation, created positive conditions for the programme of internal economic modernization. Moreover, the EEC's development was beginning to be perceived as an unparalleled success story and French membership as the key to continued economic progress. The arrangements of the Rome Treaties could hardly have been more favourable. Not only had the French secured substantial financial support for their agriculture and overseas territories, the small customs union also provided an apparently ideal route to modernization through limited competition, which was practically largely restricted to Germany and the Benelux countries and would only increase gradually. As a result the economic status quo in Western Europe seemed entirely satisfactory to the French, particularly after the 1962 agreement on important aspects of the Common Agricultural Policy (CAP). The British government, on the other hand, felt pressed for time, as Britain's meagre economic performance during the 1950s was increasingly beginning to be perceived as the result of deeper structural problems and as a sign of long-term relative decline.

The third reason why Macmillan believed that de Gaulle was in a very strong political position over Sixes and Sevens was that within the EEC French interests were also ideally secured in institutional terms. The Free Trade Area negotiations had already vividly illustrated the extent to which the EEC's institutional arrangements encouraged the progressive development of a new *esprit communautaire* with a high premium on internal consensus in external affairs. As the other Five, but particularly the government in Bonn, would not allow the marginalization of France, it was obvious that neither an economic arrangement between the EEC and EFTA nor British EEC membership could be achieved without explicit French consent.

Macmillan believed that with his veto against the FTA plan, de Gaulle had not in fact shut the door on a West European settlement in principle. He was also convinced throughout that for de Gaulle any economic benefits which the French might be able to negotiate in connection with British entry to the EEC would not suffice. In order to bring the General around to accepting British membership of an enlarged Community, which could be expected to be substantially less French in character, political incentives were needed. From the beginning, as long as solutions to the economic issues could be found, the decisive question was whether Britain and France would be able to reach an informal understanding about a mutually advantageous division of political leadership within Western Europe as well as about the future direction of European integration and the Community's role in the world.

Most interpretations of de Gaulle's foreign and European policy which emphasize its ideological nature[159] have stressed the basic incompatibility between British membership of the EEC and de Gaulle's strategic aim; this goal was to establish the Community, strengthened by the envisaged political co-operation between its members, as an economically and politically cohesive organization led by France which would eventually be capable of acting as a third force on the same level as the United States and the Soviet Union. This would suggest that the successful conclusion of the entry negotiations between 1961 and 1963 was at least unlikely, but perhaps even impossible, whatever concessions the British decided to make. More recently, however, it has been argued that while de Gaulle's policies may have been influenced to some extent by *une certaine idée* not just of France but also of Europe's role in world affairs, the French President was essentially pragmatic and may have been prepared to contemplate British membership of the EEC in exchange for a British offer for Anglo-French cooperation in security matters, particularly nuclear weapons.[160]

As early as October 1959 Macmillan did in fact come to the conclusion that if Britain wanted to secure its economic and political interests in Europe de Gaulle would have to be bribed into accepting a European settlement.[161] The Prime Minister became increasingly preoccupied with the idea of a strategic trade-off between Britain's European interests and France's ambitions in the field of defence and security. If unwelcome from the point of view of Britain's NATO policy, de Gaulle's

memorandum on tripartism at least seemed to leave open this
diplomatic avenue to a mutually advantageous overall solution. Initially, Macmillan hoped that to offer somewhat closer
trilateral cooperation among France, the United States and
Britain could suffice. More formal mechanisms for consultation, the Foreign Office agreed, would not do much harm if
the Americans could be brought to accept the idea.[162] The
much treasured special relationship with the Americans would
continue unimpaired because it was primarily based on the
habit of continuous *informal* bilateral consultation on the
political and administrative levels.

When in February 1960 Macmillan appealed to Eisenhower
in a personal letter to agree to the introduction of formalized
trilateral talks, his request was flatly rejected.[163] It was still regarded by the Americans as incompatible with their wider
policy for NATO which did not provide for a special formal
status for any partner, including Britain. The Prime Minister
later brought up the idea once more in his first talks with
President Kennedy in April 1961. By then, however, he had
long come to the conclusion that what was really necessary to
persuade de Gaulle to accept a European settlement was a substantial nuclear offer which would sharply accelerate the
development of the *force de frappe*. Within the British government the idea of a nuclear quid pro quo for a European solution had been brought up for the first time in December 1958
by Julian Amery, Under-Secretary of State in the Colonial
Office. Amery hoped to reconcile British interests in the
Commonwealth and in Western Europe with a nuclear offer to
de Gaulle which might still rescue the FTA negotiations.[164]
One year later, Macmillan took up the idea in his meeting with
Lloyd and Heathcoat-Amory who, however, both advised
against any offer at that stage.[165]

The French nuclear programme, dating back to the early
1950s, had almost immediately been given top priority by de
Gaulle when he came to power in 1958, and the French successfully exploded their first nuclear bomb in February
1960.[166] By that time French interest in nuclear cooperation
had shifted to the long-term aim of acquiring a missile capability that would eventually replace the planned Mirage IV
bombers. These could not reach their targets without refu-
elling and would be increasingly vulnerable to modern systems

of air defence. The missile development, however, presented considerable technical problems. A national programme would also be very costly. The initial French approach to the United States for technical assistance had already been turned down when de Gaulle met Macmillan at Rambouillet in March 1960. This was the first and only occasion until the breakdown of the EEC entry negotiations in January 1963 on which de Gaulle asked Macmillan head-on whether he was interested in a joint Anglo-French missile project.[167] Thereafter the French chose a more low-key approach. In early 1961, for example, British and French experts discussed whether to resume the Blue Streak missile project which the British government had abandoned in 1960 and which was now envisaged for use as a satellite launcher. During these talks the French left the British in no doubt that they were primarily interested in its potential military use, and more particularly in the American guidance system.[168]

At Rambouillet in March 1960 Macmillan politely declined, referring to the restrictions on bilateral cooperation with third countries under the contractual obligations of the Anglo-American nuclear partnership re-established in 1957–8. The same line was taken by the British experts at Strasbourg in early 1961. Macmillan was not interested in Anglo-French nuclear cooperation as such, as long as the bilateral arrangements with the United States seemed satisfactory. It was true, of course, that after the cancellation of Blue Streak and the subsequent American promise to supply them with Skybolt air-to-surface missiles for their Vulcan bombers, the British were totally dependent on the United States for modern means of delivery, but at least it still seemed justified to speak of an independent deterrent in the sense of national control over its use, and it was also by far the least expensive option available. Macmillan was only prepared to consider a nuclear offer as a clear quid pro quo for French concessions over Europe, but until the spring of 1961 he was not entirely sure what to ask for, as his government had no agreed European policy. At the time of the Rambouillet meeting of March 1960 and thereafter a new initiative to overcome the economic division into Sixes and Sevens had seemed inadvisable because of the developing confrontation between the EEC and EFTA over the acceleration of tariff reductions. When the two leaders next met for bilateral talks in January 1961 the Prime Minister was still waiting for the outcome of the expert discussions between British and German, Italian and French officials which, he expected, would show that a purely economic arrangement was now neither available nor desirable and that Britain had to apply for full EEC membership.

Neither de Gaulle nor any French government minister or official, it seems, ever confirmed explicitly before or after the British EEC application that a nexus existed between Europe and 'the bomb'. Nonetheless, Macmillan firmly believed that although British cooperation on nuclear matters would perhaps not of itself bring about a satisfactory European settlement, it was clearly the indispensable precondition for it.[169] At the turn of the year 1960–1, having himself decided in favour of EEC membership, he wrote in his Grand Design memorandum on Britain's future role in the world:

> De Gaulle's second – and to him vital – ambition is the nuclear weapon. Can we give him our techniques, or our bombs, or any share of our nuclear power on any terms which i) ... are publicly defensible ... and ii) the United States will agree to? At first this seems hopeless. But since I think it is *the one thing* which will persuade de Gaulle to accept a European settlement ... – I think it is worth serious examination.[170]

Immediately after the summit meeting with de Gaulle four weeks later he noted in his diary that 'everything' now depended on whether a nuclear deal could be struck.[171]

Sometime later, after the Kennedy government had expressed its own interest in Britain joining the Community to offset the eccentricities of Adenauer and de Gaulle, Macmillan concentrated on organizing a trilateral package deal.[172] Perhaps Kennedy could be brought to accept de Gaulle's nuclear ambitions and to elevate France to a status *vis-à-vis* the United States similar to that enjoyed by Britain. Although he certainly could not expect the Americans to be enthusiastic about assistance to de Gaulle, Macmillan, as always in Anglo-American relations, hoped that his personal influence might make the decisive difference. In this spirit he approached Kennedy during their summit meeting in April 1961, explaining the perceived link between European and nuclear matters.[173] Macmillan asked Kennedy 'to study whether he had the power, as President, to allow the British to give either warheads or nuclear information to the French'.[174] Although at that stage Macmillan had no idea what would satisfy de Gaulle, he made it plain to Kennedy that if the Americans decided to help with nuclear know-how or weapons systems, this ought not to be made dependent on any conditions, such as the assignment of the French deterrent to NATO. The Prime Minister rightly believed that such an offer would be refused outright by de Gaulle who, as Macmillan explained to Kennedy, wanted a national nuclear force which enjoyed at least the same degree of independence as the British government had over its force.

There was probably never much chance that the Americans would be willing to cooperate. Almost immediately after Kennedy's inauguration Dean Rusk, the new Secretary of State, had already indicated to Caccia that the British government might feel the need 'to appease' de Gaulle over Sixes and Sevens, but that his government was under no such pressure.[175] By the time Macmillan received Kennedy's official response to his proposals which, on the President's request, he had put down in a personal memorandum, nothing much had changed.[176] The Americans were prepared to make some highly symbolic gestures, such as to concede the position of SACEUR to a French general, if only in return for a more cooperative French NATO policy, but they rejected any assistance whatsoever for the French nuclear programme. This would have flatly contradicted American non-proliferation policy and appeared as an undeserved reward for de Gaulle's obstruction policy within NATO; the French lobby, on which the Prime Minister paradoxically had to rely over his plan for a trilateral nuclear deal with de Gaulle, remained a splinter group in the new government. Kennedy also feared that it could entail an increased German desire for nuclear weapons. Finally, there was one very important domestic political reason. As Kennedy's national security adviser McGeorge Bundy explained to Caccia, because of the strongly anti-Gaullist mood there, the President could not expect to attain the necessary consent of Congress,[177] a problem that Macmillan had completely overlooked despite the fact that the cooperation of Congress had also been constitutionally indispensable for the resumption of Anglo-American nuclear cooperation in 1957–8. After Kennedy's initial negative reply Macmillan decided to make a final effort. Although Caccia had reported that the Americans had made it absolutely plain to him that nothing could alter their position,[178] the Prime Minister wrote a second personal letter, almost begging the President to help him out with de Gaulle.[179] Predictably, Kennedy merely reiterated his arguments.[180]

Even if the United States had been prepared to cooperate in 1961, however, it is highly questionable whether this could have enabled the successful conclusion of the EEC entry negotiations in 1962–3 because the British and French leaders had two entirely different concepts of what constituted an 'independent' national deterrent. The most Macmillan could ever hope to get from the Americans was the offer which Kennedy finally made after the Anglo-American summit at Nassau in December 1962, namely also to sell Polaris missiles to the French provided that once operational, their *force de frappe* would be fully integrated into a multilateral NATO nuclear force and only withdrawn and used independently when 'supreme national interests' were at stake, as it was put in the Anglo-American agreement. Macmillan was content with theoretical sovereignty over the use of the British deterrent. As a status symbol, it was primarily intended for domestic political consumption, or, as Kennedy once remarked to Bundy, 'a political necessity but a piece of military foolishness'.[181] Only in the wake of McNamara's speech of June 1962, in which the Defense Secretary appeared to condemn the existence of any non-American independent nuclear force within the Atlantic Alliance, did Macmillan find out that even though he was legally entitled under the bilateral arrangements with the United States to press the button, no operational plans whatsoever existed for a possible independent use of the British deterrent.[182] This was more than five years into Macmillan's premiership, and it was highly typical of the British approach.[183]

De Gaulle, on the other hand, was increasingly aiming at full independence not just over the use of the future French deterrent, but also over its technical development and production. The 'qualified independence' which the British enjoyed *vis-à-vis* the Americans was not acceptable to France,

as the French Armed Forces Minister Pierre Messmer explained to the British Defence Secretary Thorneycroft in
October 1962.[184] Although this did not exclude the possibility
of cooperation with the Americans and the British on target-
ing or early warning systems, for example, the *force de frappe*
had to be 'fully independent for all time', meaning that it
should never be dependent on any other government's strategic planning or goodwill to provide successor weapons
systems.[185] In this respect at least the French made their position very clear during numerous bilateral Anglo-French meetings at ministerial and official level in 1961–2. When he left
for his Nassau talks with Kennedy, hoping to secure the survival of the British deterrent, Macmillan knew that the solution he sought for Britain would be rejected by de Gaulle if it
was offered to him by the Americans. In fact, the French did
not even have the warheads or the submarines to launch the
Polaris missiles. To fight for the missiles being offered also to
France merely helped the Prime Minister to deceive Kennedy
into believing that the bilateral Polaris agreement with Britain
would not shut the door on the enlargement of the
Community.

A second reason why it was unlikely that American concessions on the nuclear front would have enabled Britain to join
the EEC is that from the British perspective, support for
assistance to the French within the Kennedy administration
came from the wrong side for the wrong reasons. While the
State Department was strictly opposed and had basically determined the line taken by Kennedy in May 1961, the Pentagon,
rightly believing that the French would acquire a nuclear deterrent anyway, came out more and more in favour of cooperation during 1962–3.[186] What they were primarily looking for as
a suitable quid pro quo from de Gaulle, however, was not
British EEC membership, but a more constructive French
defence and security policy within NATO. Accordingly,
Kennedy explained to the new British Ambassador to
Washington, David Ormsby-Gore, that if his government was
to assist the French 'something really spectacular' had to be
obtained in return, not just British EEC membership.[187]

American economic self-interest was another problem. If
there was going to be cooperation with the French, then the
Americans would of course prefer to deal with de Gaulle

directly in order to sell their own weapons. This became abundantly clear in 1962 when the French government placed an order for a heat exchanger for use in a future French nuclear submarine with the British firm Foster Wheeler. Even though this device did not even contain classified information under the Anglo-American nuclear agreement, the British government still preferred to obtain American consent before allowing the sale to go through which, however, was not forthcoming during the summer.[188] At that stage de Zulueta bitterly complained to the Prime Minister that 'there is a marked contrast between the high principles which the Americans express when they are dealing with our interests and the brutal self-interest with which they deal with their own.'[189] Then, only one month after the Americans had declared the planned Foster Wheeler sale undesirable, the British heard rumours, later confirmed to Thorneycroft by Messmer,[190] that the Americans were now themselves offering not just a heat exchanger, but complete nuclear hunter submarines of the Nautilus class to the French, and had of course decided to do so without consulting the British.[191]

Macmillan's top secret negotiations with Kennedy in the spring of 1961 and his response to the American counter-proposals illustrate very well the limits to which he was prepared to go in defence matters. To get EEC membership, the Prime Minister would accept the formal equality of France in relation to the United States in nuclear matters, but not a privileged French role, if only in symbolic terms. Macmillan intensely disliked the proposal, made by Kennedy during their meeting in April, that the United States cede the position of SACEUR to the French on a permanent basis.[192] Macmillan argued that such a decision might be interpreted by the Soviets as a first step towards an American withdrawal from Western Europe. In fact, he was anxious that it would amount to the symbolic degradation of Britain to third rank in the Atlantic Alliance. The Prime Minister was even less prepared to relinquish existing British privileges, particularly formal independent national control over the use of the British nuclear deterrent. This became immediately clear when the multilateralists in the Kennedy government took the opportunity of Macmillan's request to go for the nuclear castration of Britain by revitalizing previous plans for a NATO nuclear force. Kennedy now actually proposed to Macmillan that the Americans should subordinate part of their nuclear deterrent and the British *all* their weapons to a strategic NATO command to induce de Gaulle to do the same.[193] Some support for such a solution in fact existed in the British government.[194] The idea that Britain could be forced to relinquish its national nuclear deterrent, however, led de Zulueta to the ironic commentary that in that case he was inclined to emigrate, a notion entirely shared by Macmillan.[195]

The negative American response to his request for support for a trilateral nuclear deal meant, in Macmillan's own logic, that the EEC application, which at that stage had not yet even been agreed upon by the Cabinet, was already practically dead. Even though Macmillan had a marked weakness for wishful thinking, there are clear signs that he was fully aware of this. After Kennedy's first letter he told Caccia that:

> in order to bring the General around, the President may be able to offer something on tripartism and some review of N.A.T.O. This may be enough [but] he may well make his general cooperation conditional on some satisfaction for his nuclear ambitions. I should be very glad if I were wrong about this, *but I do not think that I am.*[196]

Very shortly after Kennedy's second letter Macmillan even referred to the European question as 'obviously insoluble' in his diaries.[197] He now deliberately ignored the option, contemplated one year earlier in anticipation of a possible Nixon–Dillon government, of a direct bilateral offer to de Gaulle for closer Franco-British nuclear cooperation. Macmillan also decided against another personal approach to de Gaulle to test his willingness to negotiate in earnest, that is with the clear aim of British entry to the EEC.[198]

After the Prime Minister's return from Washington in April 1961 the Cabinet had at first agreed to the compromise formula that no new approach should be made to the Six unless a clear signal could be obtained from de Gaulle in advance that Britain was actually welcome.[199] This was entirely in line with the conclusion in the Lee Committee's answers to Macmillan's questionnaire in July 1960 that 'to launch another initiative and receive a second rebuff would be disastrous'.[200] It was hoped in London that Kennedy could perhaps elicit a clear signal either way from de Gaulle during his state visit to France at the beginning of June. The result of Kennedy's approach was discouraging. In a very matter-of-fact tone he reported back that apparently de Gaulle still 'had no particular wish to see the United Kingdom join the Six'.[201] After Kennedy's visit to London Macmillan noted in his diary:

> Nor did Kennedy have anything very good to say about his French visit ... It was clear that the President (with the exception of the actual delivery of nuclear information or nuclear weapons) carried out most loyally our arrangements and really did do everything I had asked him to do both in Washington and in the memorandum which we sent him recently. De Gaulle was very avuncular, very gracious, very oracular, and very unyielding. He would take all the plums – tripartism, new arrangements in N.A.T.O., and help with the technique of missiles and bombs (other than the actual nuclear content) with Cavalier profligacy. But when it came to giving anything in return – e.g. Britain's desire to enter Europe on reasonable terms, having regard to Commonwealth and British agricultural structures – then the General was in his most austere and Puritan mood. So far as I can see (unless the General was just playing the hand very close to his chest) *my great plan has failed* – or, at least, failed up to now.[202]

The British Ambassador to France, Pierson Dixon, reported a short while later that de Gaulle had told him that British EEC membership was perhaps desirable in principle, but that it would take 'a very long time'.[203] At that stage the French President still seems to have hoped that a British application for full membership, because of the political problems over domestic agriculture and the Commonwealth, would not be forthcoming for some time. After he had been informed of the British decision to apply only two weeks later, he let it be known to Macmillan through Jean Chauvel, the French Ambassador to London, that it came as 'an unpleasant surprise'.[204] In view of Macmillan's top secret nuclear diplomacy and these reports, it is no longer sufficient to discuss why the British came to the conclusion in 1961 that EEC membership was now necessary at the earliest possible junction. Instead one must ask why the application was actually launched in such unfavourable circumstances when according to Macmillan himself there was little or no chance for negotiations to succeed.

Macmillan's decision to ignore the adverse international circumstances and the sound warning of Maudling, among others, against an untimely move on the European front[205] and to proceed with the EEC application regardless resulted from a combination of different factors. While at one moment Macmillan was certain that there was no chance at all for the negotiations to succeed, at others he appears to have hoped that solutions could be found to the economic questions and, more particularly, to the thorny political issues which he believed were, in the end, decisive. In Macmillan's view there was always the possibility of another El Alamein, a sudden turn of events which might still enable Britain to join the EEC. Perhaps Kennedy could be brought around eventually to assisting the French over the *force de frappe,* or Macmillan might manage to convince de Gaulle that British EEC membership was also in the French interest. The Prime Minister was slightly more optimistic, for example, after de Gaulle's private visit to Birch Grove in November 1961. At that stage it seemed to him that de Gaulle had perhaps not yet decided against British EEC entry.[206] Other reasons why the British EEC application was launched regardless of the adverse international circumstances included a distinctive British interest in the negotiations as such, independent of the outcome, as well as structural factors. These factors produced a situation in the summer of 1961 where the European debate within the government and in public had developed such dynamism that it is difficult to see how Macmillan could have stopped the process which he himself had encouraged so much, even if he had believed that it was the most prudent course to take.

The most important reason of all was perhaps that even simply to apply for EEC membership helped to appease the Kennedy government. Macmillan thought that to take this step would at least prove to the Americans that Britain was finally prepared to play a full and constructive role in European integration. If the British EEC application was vetoed by de Gaulle, it would be abundantly clear that the French were to be blamed exclusively for the economic division of Western Europe and the resulting lack of political cohesion. At a time when an extremely unpredictable American government was reconsidering its foreign policy options, every effort had to be made to present Britain as the most reliable and valuable NATO ally to save as much as possible of what the Conservative government still regarded as a bilateral special relationship.

The British application did have the desired effect. On 11 June 1961, after Kennedy's visit to London, Macmillan already noted with evident satisfaction in his diary that while the EEC application was doomed:

> we have at least got a completely new American attitude to our efforts and a new understanding. So Dillon (as a leading Democrat Minister) is hardly on speaking terms with that Dillon (who was a leading Republican Minister a few months ago and treated me so badly in Washington by giving our private talks almost verbatim to the Press).[207]

Macmillan also seems to have believed that even a failed application would serve a useful party political purpose. He hoped that EEC entry on acceptable terms might win the Conservatives the next general election, probably wrongly as this considerably exaggerated the salience of foreign policy issues in British politics. By comparison an application that was vetoed by de Gaulle would at least be the best way to keep his party together over Europe. To the pro-Europeans it demonstrated that he was prepared to go in, while the opponents and sceptics would not actually need to be asked to follow anywhere. Even simply to apply for EEC membership would also force the Labour Party to take a stand and thus help to split the main opposition.

Of the two structural reasons, the first had characterized British European policy ever since Messina. It was the belief, widely shared among ministers and civil servants, that there was no alternative course of action, in this case to the EEC application. All other options short of full EEC membership were neither politically satisfactory nor diplomatically feasible because of either American or French opposition. On the other hand, the status quo was deemed intolerable for economic and political reasons, so to do nothing at all in this by now highly politicized matter was not acceptable either. Whatever the merits of any particular course of action, the

Prime Minister was always keen to give the impression of acting decisively. Indecision was incompatible with his 'Supermac' image which had originally developed out of the mockery of a 'Vicky' cartoon in the *Evening Standard* and which was so useful in domestic politics. At least the EEC application would help clarify the situation in Western Europe after the long drawn out expert talks at the official level which, if anything, had obscured the actual intentions and interests of the key players, a motive that Macmillan conceded in the House of Commons on 31 July 1961 when asked by the Liberal Party Leader Jo Grimond and a backbencher whether the EEC application meant that the Prime Minister actually believed that the negotiations would be concluded successfully. Not surprisingly Macmillan replied evasively, but he then added:

> I felt certain that it would be far better for everybody to bring this matter to an issue and not to allow it to drag on indefinitely … I am sure that we have now reached a point where merely going on with uncertainty would injure rather than benefit the life and strength of the free world.[208]

The second structural reason why the application was launched despite the adverse international circumstances was that by July 1961 the debate about Britain's future role in Europe within the Cabinet, the Conservative Party and the public had moved forward so dynamically that the application only seemed a question of time. While mass opinion remained volatile, opinion among the political and economic elite in politics, administration, the media, banking and industry had shifted dramatically in favour of British EEC membership. In the category of 'informed opinion' – the people that really mattered in Macmillan's Edwardian perspective on politics – 70 per cent were in favour, only 20 per cent against and 10 per cent undecided.[209] Among the smaller foreign policy elite, including politicians, diplomats and international managers, an even greater majority was in favour.[210] This sea-change in elite opinion manifested itself in the changing attitude of the media, at that time primarily the press. As early as December 1958 the influential weekly journal *The Economist* supported British EEC membership. Until the summer of 1961 the vast majority of quality and tabloid newspapers advocated EEC entry, including the *Daily Mirror* which was otherwise close to the Labour Party. Predictably, only the Express Group, which was owned by Beaverbrook, opposed EEC entry.[211]

To understand the full extent of the pressure for change in European policy in the early 1960s, it is also necessary to know that by the summer of 1961 British entry to the EEC was also supported by the vast majority of bankers in the City. They hoped that EEC membership would help to secure British exports to the Six, improve the balance of payments situation, stabilize sterling and, ultimately, safeguard the future of London as a leading financial centre. Moreover, after the latest run on sterling the decision to apply for membership was expected to lead to an increase in the confidence of the financial markets in the ability of the British government to tackle the structural economic problems within a stable external framework for economic policy-making. The views of the City had of course traditionally mattered much more to the Conservative Party than those of industry. The frequent contacts between representatives of the City and the Conservative Party are not, unfortunately, well documented because they were mostly of an informal character.[212] Wherever they are documented, however, it becomes clear that leading figures in the City impressed upon senior Conservatives the need for a reorientation in European policy. Senior representatives of Lazard, for example, told Conservative politicians and senior officials in spring 1961 that the general view of the City was that membership would be advantageous and should be sought at the earliest possible moment.[213] Heath has confirmed in retrospect that these and other such informal contacts with representatives of the City were an important additional incentive for the Conservatives to apply for EEC membership.[214]

Unlike in the case of Plan G in 1956, the government did not consult with representatives of the FBI or the TUC in any systematic way before it decided to go ahead with the EEC application. When FBI representatives asked in the Palmer Group in May and again in July 1961 whether the government intended to apply in the near future, senior officials present answered evasively. Once more the British government took the support of industry for granted. Preoccupied with the best party political tactics over Europe, the Conservative leadership followed the policy-making process within the FBI very much *en passant.* Heath, who after all was responsible for European questions, enquired for the first time in June 1961 about the likely FBI reaction to the envisaged application.[215]

In the early 1960s the FBI was once again no driving force behind British European policy, not only because of its non-interventionist approach to politics, but also because the re-orientation towards EEC membership was at that stage still hotly contested. As in the past the FBI leadership gave priority to internal interest mediation. In its statement on European policy, which was published without prior consultation of the membership, the FBI leadership made its support for entry dependent on several conditions.[216] The statement empha-sized, for example, that problems related to Commonwealth trade, domestic agriculture and the future relationships of the other EFTA states with the EEC should be solved before the start of negotiations. The government was surprised at the am-bivalence of the FBI statement and criticized the FBI leader-ship so heavily over its allegedly disloyal behaviour that Norman Kipping, the Director General of the FBI, immedi-ately began to interpret the statement in a way compatible with the membership option which the government now appeared to pursue.[217] The comparatively negative tone of the FBI statement was due to the opposition of the Commonwealth Industries Association and the more sceptical attitude of a large proportion of members from small and medium-sized firms. These firms originally were agnostic and uninformed about European integration in the 1950s, but became more vociferous in their concerns about membership as they became more informed of its implications for them in terms of much greater competitive pressures in the home market.

The leadership of the National Farmers Union, led by its President, Harold Wooley, was also strongly opposed. The farmers themselves were not actually united against EEC mem-bership and the resulting change in the subsidy system. According to one opinion poll during the negotiations, the farmers were approximately equally divided over the issue.[218] Some sections of British agriculture expected that they would profit from British participation in a common European agricultural policy. As early as June 1960, for example, repre-sentatives of the food processing industry, which was part of the NFU, strongly supported EEC membership.[219] Apart from the economic implications of EEC membership, however, the NFU leadership wished to safeguard its domestic political influence. According to Soames, the NFU functionaries did not want to lose the place in the sun from where they could put the government under pressure in connection with the annual price review,[220] an additional incentive for Soames to support EEC entry which would externalize this political inconvenience.

By 1961 British business views on European integration were still highly diverse and complex. A main factor for this was the uneven impact of European integration on different sectors, and within each sector on different firms. What mattered most to the government, however, was that the more export-oriented big firms such as General Electric or Imperial Chemical Industries were strongly in favour of EEC entry. As a result of the tendency towards informal consultation with leading industrialists, these large firms were much better placed to present their views to the government than small firms. As in the case of the FTA plan five years previously, the degree of support was greater in the ABCC where an internal questionnaire in June 1961 showed that 30 out of 36 trade associations were in favour of EEC entry if certain conditions could be fulfilled, while only two were against.[221] The prevailing mood here as well as in the FBI was that in the end it was a matter for the government to decide and to give a political lead. The economic interest groups were primarily interested in an early decision on which their members could then base their business decisions.[222]

While the government paid little attention to industry, it largely ignored the trade unions, even though they were open-minded about the possibility of British EEC entry. As early as July 1960, representatives of the TUC had in fact suggested British entry to the EEC in a meeting of the Economic Planning Board.[223] Since August 1960 more and more individual unions came out in favour of EEC membership.[224] At the annual conference of the TUC in September 1961 a clear majority voted for EEC membership under certain conditions, which resembled much more the government position than Labour Party policy. Apart from pragmatic economic considerations, which were paramount, the trade unions were increasingly convinced by the early 1960s that the social standards within the EEC were probably at least as high as those in Britain and that any harmonization would now be increased towards continental European standards. The unions also realized that their sister organizations in the EEC had much better access to their respective governments and greater influence on policy-making within the EEC than they had within Britain and EFTA. In the early 1960s the TUC was not yet a forum for fierce ideological debate. Despite the close organizational and financial links with the Labour Party, TUC policy remained essentially pragmatic in 1961–2, even after Gaitskell's aggressive attack on the government in the autumn of 1962. It did not matter very much to the Conservatives though. If anything, the pragmatic approach of the TUC in connection with the increasingly pro-European attitudes in business contributed to the development of a political climate among the political and economic elite which strongly favoured a reorientation in British European policy.

By the summer of 1961 elite opinion had in fact shifted so dramatically that the EEC application seemed only a question of time. At some point Macmillan would thus have had to explain a decision to defer a decision on Europe. He could not, however, refer to the negative American response to his proposal for a trilateral package deal with de Gaulle, which he had treated as top secret. The matter had never been properly discussed in the Cabinet, not even after the Prime Minister's return from Washington, even though in Macmillan's view it was of such crucial importance. It is clear that only a very few leading ministers and senior civil servants were informed about Macmillan's ideas for a strategic trade-off between Britain's European interests and de Gaulle's nuclear ambitions and were involved in preparing Macmillan's top secret letters to Kennedy.[225] Any public debate about the package deal which he had envisaged would have seriously damaged his government not only within Britain, but also in relation to the other Five. In a domestic situation that was so favourable to a reorientation of British European policy, it was clearly out of the question for Macmillan to put the brakes on his own policy initiative by pointing to the negative result of his entirely secret contacts with the American President to find a suitable nuclear bribe for de Gaulle.

6 Failure, Yet Success: The EEC Entry Negotiations, 1961–3

The entry negotiations opened in October 1961 with a statement on British European policy by Heath, who led the British team, at a WEU ministerial meeting in Paris. They were continued in Brussels. The negotiations were conducted through a series of ministerial meetings, supported by meetings at the official level which mainly dealt with technical issues. The Community decided that the national governments would conduct the negotiations, supported by the Commission.[1] The Six agreed that before a particular issue was tackled or compromises offered to the British, they first had to find a common negotiating position among themselves. This was not surprising, as the Six had already begun to act as a unit towards the end of the FTA negotiations in 1958. It nonetheless made the negotiating process difficult to manage for the British.

In his speech before the House of Commons at the beginning of August, Macmillan had emphasized three main problems for which adequate solutions needed to be found in the negotiations: the future relations of the other EFTA states with the Community, Commonwealth agricultural exports to Britain and domestic agriculture. Of the three, the EFTA states presented the fewest problems until de Gaulle's veto. It soon became clear that no serious, detailed negotiations would take place about EEC membership for Denmark and Norway – according to Article 237 of the EEC Treaty – or association of the other EFTA states – according to Article 238 of the EEC Treaty – before the negotiations with Britian had progressed to the point at which success was in sight.

The diversity of the economic and – even more so – the political interests of the EFTA states had already become clear in 1960–1 over the issue of tariff acceleration. The internal faultlines within EFTA were exposed even more drastically in April 1961 when Macmillan, having just returned from his talks with

Kennedy, informed the EFTA Ambassadors to Britain of the possibility of a British EEC appliation in the near future.[2] Due to their neutrality, which appeared to them incompatible with membership in a regional economic bloc with a common trade policy and ambitions for closer political cooperation, Sweden, Switzerland and Austria regarded EEC entry as an unacceptable alternative to a purely economic arrangement between the EEC and EFTA. As a result, their governments initially clung to the idea of a deal between the two groups and pressed the British government to do the same. To the intense dismay of Macmillan, who aimed to appease the Kennedy government by adapting British policy to American long-term strategic interests in Europe, the Swedish and Swiss governments protested in Washington in harsh terms against American opposition to a purely economic arrangement in Western Europe, one which the Foreign Office had for some time regarded as neither possible nor desirable.

The relationship between neutrality and European policy was never discussed within the British government at the ministerial level. It was hardly mentioned even at the official level. The special problems that a British application for EEC membership would cause to the neutral EFTA states played no role at all in the decision-making process up to the British application. At no point were the British interested in the consequences of neutrality on the neutrals' European policy. They cared only about neutrality's impact on the British diplomatic position in Europe. Depending on British aims in Western Europe, the neutrality status of some EFTA states was either useful or else presented an additional obstacle to British European policy. When the British government tried to keep the outer Seven together, such as in 1959–60 and once again after de Gaulle's veto in January 1963, neutrality was helpful because it limited the neutrals' European options and excluded the possibility of a separate deal with the Community without consideration of the needs of the British. It was inconvenient, however, in connection with the British EEC application, first because the Six were reluctant to grant the neutrals equal access to their market if they did not share the economic and political costs of membership, and secondly because the Americans were opposed to bilateral arrangements between the EEC and the neutrals.

While in the spring of 1961 the neutrals pushed the British to continue to work for a purely economic arrangement between the EEC and EFTA regardless of the American attitude, Denmark and Norway – both NATO member states – were open-minded about the possibility of EEC entry together with Britain. The Danish government actually pressed the British to apply at the earliest possible moment. In April 1961 the Danish Foreign Minister Jens Otto Krag asked Home, his British counterpart, to give advance warning of a forthcoming British application, so that his government could announce its intention to apply at the same time.[3] At the NATO Ministerial Council meeting in May, Krag declared that in the Danish view British EEC entry was now highly desirable in that it would increase the political cohesion of Western Europe.[4] During his subsequent visit to London Krag emphasized once more Danish interest in EEC entry alongside Britain.[5] The government in Copenhagen primarily believed that this was now the best way to safeguard Danish agricultural interests. If Denmark remained in EFTA, its agricultural exports to the Federal Republic would be threatened by the CAP. Losses in that market could not be compensated by greater British imports, as the British refusal to pay a price in agriculture for the acceleration of tariff reductions had made plain. As a result, the Danish coalition government, led by the Social Democrats, had increasingly come under fire from the influential agricultural lobby, which in view of the evolving CAP argued forcefully that Denmark's joining of EFTA rather than the EEC had been the wrong decision in the first place.[6]

The conflicting economic interests and political demands of the EFTA states complicated British entry diplomacy even more. At least temporarily, EFTA proved another burden on British European policy in 1961–3, alongside the Commonwealth. Unlike the Commonwealth, however, which had grown historically and which at least fostered the romantic memory of former colonial greatness, EFTA neither contributed to British national identity nor had any significant lobby in Britain. In domestic political terms, the organization was therefore largely irrelevant to British policy-making – not only in the run-up to the EEC application, but also during the negotiations themselves. Under intense pressure from its partners in EFTA, particularly the Swedes and the Swiss, the

British government eventually agreed in July 1961 not to enter the EEC before the question of EEC membership or association of the other EFTA states was resolved. The British were extremely reluctant to accede to this promise. They only agreed to do so because they did not want to overburden their European policy in advance of the application and the negotiations. Moreover, it appeared useful to maintain a good political climate within EFTA in case the EEC entry negotiations failed and Britain was forced to continue to live with its EFTA partners. It is highly doubtful, however, that the British would actually have kept their promise had British EEC membership proved possible, but no solution had been found to the economic problems of the neutral EFTA states.

With regard to the negotiations, those countries which planned to join the EEC along with Britain were likely to prove the smaller problem. After Denmark, Norway eventually also decided to apply for membership in 1962. More problematic was the Irish case, which was given only scant attention within Whitehall before the British application. The Republic of Ireland had not joined EFTA primarily because its small, highly protected industrial sector was not up to the competitive pressures of a free trade area. But Ireland was still highly dependent on its agricultural exports to Britain. These exports were unaffected by the creation of EFTA, but would have been badly damaged as a result of a unilateral British accession to the EEC, so the Dublin government decided also to apply for EEC membership.[7] In contrast to Denmark and Norway, however, Ireland was neutral, and it was initially unclear how this might affect the reaction of the Six or of the Americans to the Irish application. The Irish government thus insisted that their neutral status was fully compatible with all obligations that EEC membership involved at the time or, indeed, in the future.[8] Seán Lemass, the Irish Taoiseach, explained to Heath at a meeting in Brussels in February 1962:

> that Eire's present neutrality was not of the sort which would prevent them taking a full part in all the political activities of the Community. The only reason Eire had not joined N.A.T.O. is because it would have meant guaranteeing the border between Northern and Southern Ireland. This was politically impossible for any Eire

Government at the moment ... The Eire Government would be able to take part in any foreign policy or defence activity provided it did not involve actually signing the North Atlantic Treaty.[9]

This degree of flexibility as well as continued Irish dependence on the British market should have ensured Irish EEC entry together with Britain, as it was achieved ten years later. Unlike the Swedes or the Swiss, the Irish of course had a strong domestic lobby in the United States, so that the support of the Kennedy government was also likely to be forthcoming.

By far the most serious political problem was presented by the neutral EFTA states Sweden, Switzerland and Austria. The first practical obstacle was that when Britain applied in 1961, the Six were generally of the opinion that association according to Article 238 of the EEC Treaty should only be a temporary arrangement on the way to full membership, which, however, the neutrals did not want. More fundamentally, because of French and American policy on association, it was highly unlikely that the British – had they been allowed to join the EEC – would actually have delayed accession until the future economic relations of the EFTA neutrals with the EEC were also defined. In this case, a face-saving exercise for the British might have included a statement by the EEC or the French that they intended to deal with this question in due course.

De Gaulle had let it be known all along that it was not in the economic interest of France to support a purely economic association – in particular of the two wealthy neutrals Sweden and Switzerland – without the compensatory price the industrial exporters had to pay within the EEC. Moreover, the British had to acknowledge that the Kennedy government, in line with its established policy on a possible trade arrangement between the EEC and EFTA, was also strictly opposed to the bilateral economic association of the EFTA neutrals with the EEC. In early 1961 Ball handed Caccia a memorandum in which the Kennedy government made plain that 'it would not be prepared to see substantial derogations from the principle of the Rome Treaty in order to accommodate third countries which can negotiate their commercial problems in the G.A.T.T. and the Trade Committee of the Twenty-one just as

the U.S. Government is prepared to do.'[10] Shortly afterwards
in a letter to Macmillan, President Kennedy restated in slightly
more diplomatic language:

> For similar reasons we have hoped that perhaps the
> problem of your relation to EFTA might be handled in
> stages, always of course with full responsibility to your part-
> ners in EFTA, so that the accession of the United Kingdom
> to the Rome Treaty might be possible without awaiting com-
> plete arrangements for everyone else. We cannot help
> thinking that if you are safely and strongly in the Common
> Market, you will be in a very good position to protect all of
> the interests which so legitimately give you concern at
> present.[11]

As British European policy at that stage was marked by a pronounced obedience to the Americans, British statements
before and during the negotiations to the effect that it was
essential to safeguard the interests of the other EFTA states, including those of the neutrals, should not be taken at face
value. They were in fact largely declamatory.

While the question of the future relations of the other EFTA
states with the Community never became acute before de
Gaulle's veto, those of Commonwealth agricultural exports to
Britain and of domestic agriculture did.[12] Early on, the British
government had to acknowledge that two of its most important hopes in connection with the application proved illusory,
namely that Britain might still be able to enter the EEC early
enough to influence the CAP and that EEC entry could be negotiated largely at the expense of third countries, including
the Commonwealth.

Stimulated by speculation that the British wanted to join the
EEC to shape the CAP in accordance with their interests, the
CAP negotiations among the Six in fact made much faster
progress in 1961–2 than Soames had initially hoped. In May
1961 the French Foreign Minister Maurice Couve de Murville
indicated for the first time that France would not agree to the
opening of negotiations with Britain before the CAP negotiations among the Six were concluded. The French feared that
after British accession the governments in London and Bonn
might combine to undermine what they saw as a central part

of the package deal among the Six over the creation of the
EEC. The Six finally reached agreement on the future structure of roughly 40 per cent of the CAP in early 1962, an agreement that was very different from what the British might have
hoped for. The crucial problem for the government in
London was that the financing of the CAP, as agreed by the
Six, would disadvantage Britain after accession and that, as a
result, British EEC membership would be very costly to the
Exchequer, as was to be the case after British entry to the EEC
in 1973. According to the 1962 CAP agreement, all proceeds
from import levies would go towards the Community budget.
As Britain imported more food from third countries than the
Six did put together, it would have to pay much more into the
budget than it would receive in the form of EEC agricultural
or other funds. Hence, in their opening bid on agriculture the
British insisted that they required several changes in the CAP
before they could enter the EEC, a demand that, not surprisingly, was rejected outright by the French.

The British government also failed to connect the agricultural issues. The problem here was that the EEC wanted to differentiate between the export interests of the Commonwealth
and British agriculture. The Six did, in fact, accept in principle the need for protection of the core agricultural export interests of the Dominions, particularly of New Zealand, and for
transitional periods.[13] In contrast, they did not see the need
for special arrangements for British farmers. The Six acknowledged that the CAP agreement might be costly to the British
Exchequer, but as a major industrial export nation and a late-
comer to the EEC, Britain had to pay a price for membership.
It was not evident to the Six, however, that the CAP agreement
would have any particularly negative effects on British farmers
who needed primarily to get used to a different subsidy
system. As a result, the Six insisted that the two agricultural
issues, Commonwealth exports and British agriculture, be negotiated separately. While Commonwealth agricultural exports
were to be considered straightaway, British domestic agriculture would be left for later.

When the British decided to apply for full membership of
the EEC, whose agricultural policy was now obviously geared
towards self-sufficiency, the governments of Australia and New

Zealand were disappointed. Their earlier hopes of 1957–8, and again 1960–1, that they might be able to use trade negotiations in Europe to increase their exports to the EEC in return for further reductions in the remaining British preferences proved illusory. On the contrary, it was clear that the other Commonwealth states would suffer economically. Hence, British ministers concluded in the spring of 1961 that the new British entry policy could only be defended *vis-à-vis* Britain's partners in the Commonwealth in the broadest political terms.[14] During their tour of the Commonwealth capitals in late June and early July 1961, British ministers thus stressed that by assuming a new leadership role in Western Europe, Britain would help to strengthen the West in the global competition with the Soviet bloc, something that would also be in the interests of the Commonwealth. To the Conservatives, only the three Dominions of Canada, Australia and New Zealand mattered. Accordingly, only the Prime Ministers of these three countries received advance warning of the reorientation of British European policy. On a stop-over in Ottawa immediately after his meeting with Kennedy in April, Macmillan informed the Canadian Prime Minister John Diefenbaker of the possibility of a British EEC application in the near future. With some justification, Diefenbaker suspected an American conspiracy.[15] In mid-April Macmillan sent personal letters to Robert Menzies and Keith Holyoake, the Prime Ministers of Australia and New Zealand respectively. In the letters he emphasized that, if Britain remained outside the EEC, its economic strength and political influence would decrease further and, as a result, so would its capacity to fight for the interests of the Commonwealth states in the world.[16] The Canadian, Australian and New Zealand governments therefore had enough time until the visit of Sandys in July 1961 to study the implications of possible British EEC entry. On his return, Sandys was able to report that even the New Zealanders had put greater emphasis on the possible adverse long-term political effects on the Commonwealth than on the more immediate economic dangers.[17] Sandys admitted that the Dominions feared that the internal cohesion of the Commonwealth, already limited as a result of decolonization, would decrease further. On the other hand, the Dominions seemed to accept the argument that Britain's international influence was bound to diminish outside the Community and that this, too, might have negative repercussions for the Commonwealth.[18]

Canada, Australia and New Zealand would have been affected in different ways by British accession to the EEC. Canada was least dependent on its exports to Britain, but had long followed a policy of multilateral trade liberalization in GATT. The Canadians disliked the EEC and EFTA as regional economic blocs. British EEC entry appeared to strengthen the tendency towards a regionalization of the world economy and therefore was undesirable. Canadian attitudes were also influenced by Canada's geographical proximity to and its increasing economic dependence on the United States. Diefenbaker in particular was fixated on the dangers of Canada's further economic and cultural absorption into the orbit of the United States and still greater political dependence on it.[19] The relationship with Britain had always provided a welcome counterweight to the hegemonic influence of the United States, but after British accession to the EEC, this counterweight would hardly be meaningful any longer. For Australia, the purely economic consequences of British entry to the EEC were already much more important. The tone of Menzies' response to Macmillan's first letter was quite moderate.[20] He acknowledged that Australia could at least hope that a larger and fast-expanding West European market would, in the long term, also offer greater export opportunities for third countries. Menzies was rightly concerned, however, that a safeguarding of Australian trade interests in negotiations with the Six would not be a high priority for the British.[21] In early May 1961 the British High Commissioner in Canberra was already reporting that the Australians were fed up with general assurances by the British. Instead, they expected detailed information on the likely effects of British accession to the Community on 'wheat, sugar, butter and bananas'.[22]

In economic terms New Zealand, where the economic structure was still largely agrarian, was bound to suffer most from British participation in the CAP. In writing to the British Prime Minister in April and June 1961, Holyoake warned in the strongest terms that his country would face 'economic disaster' if it lost access to the British market for its agricultural produce.[23] In the negotiations the New Zealanders, by supporting in principle British entry to the EEC on political grounds, convinced the British and the Six that they deserved to be treated as a special case. Butter and lamb were among those commodities for which they sought special treatment for the period after British entry to the EEC.[24] In January 1963, at the time of de Gaulle's veto, New Zealand had secured important safeguards for its agricultural exports to Britain. On the other hand, due to their own economic interests and the uncompromising negotiating tactics of the French, the British had paid much less attention to the trade interests of Australia and Canada, who were much less dependent on their exports to Britain.

When British ministers visited the Commonwealth and Empire in late June and early July 1961, they did not encounter any fundamental opposition either in the new Commonwealth states or in the colonies. On his return from a tour of Asia, Thorneycroft reported that Pakistan and Malaya were actually expecting greater export opportunities in Western Europe as a whole. Sri Lanka and Singapore were mainly interested in particular commodities such as tea, textiles and jute. For the Indian government, Nehru expressed doubts about whether the political cohesion of the Commonwealth would suffer, but had no fundamental objections to British EEC entry.[25] During his tour of Africa, the Minister of Labour, John Hare, got the impression that the governments of Ghana, Nigeria, Sierra Leone and Rhodesia were already expecting British EEC entry.[26] Finally, Iain Macleod reported from his tour of the colonies that in view of the economic competition between them and the associated overseas territories of the EEC, all colonies were hoping that the British government would secure for them the same status. Only Hong Kong was resigned to the fact that it could not possibly expect such special treatment because some of its industries, particularly textiles, already constituted fierce competition for British industry.[27] Only Heath had to report a straightforward negative reply from Archbishop Makarios who feared that the agricultural exports of Cyprus to Britain would suffer as a result of British entry to the EEC.[28]

These consultations before the EEC application showed that the Commonwealth states and the colonies were already expecting a British EEC application at that stage. In the end, they also generally regarded this as a matter for the British government to decide. That some governments publicly formulated maximalist demands for the safeguarding of their trade interests before the entry negotiations even began was as much the result of domestic politics as was Macmillan's presentation of the application in Britain.[29] In Canada and Australia elections were scheduled for 1961, so that these two governments depended particularly on giving the impression in public of relentlessly defending national economic interests. Representatives of the opposition Labour Party in New Zealand even admitted to the British High Commissioner that without doubt, the British had no other option but to apply for EEC membership. Nonetheless, their party would exploit the agricultural issue to the full at the expense of the New Zealand and British governments.[30] This example very well illustrates that what was debated in the other Commonwealth states were the best means to defend the respective trade interests in the negotiations, but not British European policy. In the early 1960s British accession to a West European organization with some supranational features was no longer regarded as a revolutionary development. Even Menzies, who was a pronounced anglophile and as such was much liked in Britain, admitted the following about British EEC membership and the Commonwealth during a visit to Brussels in 1962:

> For most of its members the Commonwealth is in a sense functional and occasional. The old hopes of concerting common policies have gone. Under these circumstances, it may well prove to be the fact that even if federation could be achieved in Western Europe, the anomalous position of Great Britain in the Commonwealth which would then emerge would be regarded as no more anomalous than many other things which have been accepted, and with which we have learned to live.[31]

As the British government had expected, the negotiations with the Six about Commonwealth agricultural exports to Britain proved difficult. It was a domestically sensitive issue due to its sentimental appeal. Moreover, it was highly complicated because the concerns of the Dominions differed so greatly from those of the newly independent states in Asia or of the African colonies. The diversity of interests and the range of commodities involved and the constant demands for Commonwealth consultation ensured long drawn out negotiations. On the other hand, the diverse nature of the economic interests of the Commonwealth states prevented the emergence of any unified opposition to British EEC membership, which would have made it very difficult for Macmillan to sell any entry terms to his party or the British public. It turned out, however, that Canada, Australia and New Zealand were much more concerned with protecting their own trading interests than with promoting Commonwealth solidarity. Even Menzies, who was particularly outspoken on the alleged adverse political impact of British EEC membership on the Commonwealth, would not lead a unified protest of a multicultural Commonwealth against Britain. The New Zealanders believed anyway that they would best secure their interests by emphasizing the special nature of their economic dependency on their agricultural exports to Britain.

Judging by the state of the negotiations in early January 1963, it seems unlikely, therefore, that British entry negotiations would have foundered over the Commonwealth issue. For the British government the main political problem was that while the core trade interests – particularly of New Zealand – could have been protected through the comparatively cooperative attitude of the Six, British participation in the CAP could not be achieved on terms particularly advantageous to British agriculture at the expense of third countries, including the Dominions. During the spring and summer of 1962, the details of British participation in the CAP were relegated to a secondary position. The thorny issues were left over until the resumption of negotiations in October after the summer break. At that time the Macmillan government, having survived the Commonwealth Prime Ministers' Conference and the Conservative Party conference quite well, was under so much greater strain domestically that unlike in 1960–1, it could now no longer afford the perception of making too many concessions on the initial negotiating position. The difficulties over British agriculture were also aggravated by tensions among the Six, which were accentuated by the particularly cosy relationship between Adenauer and de Gaulle after de Gaulle's highly successful visit to the Federal

Republic in September. Subsequently, they were aggravated further by the expected Gaullist victory in the French elections on 18 November 1962, which gave de Gaulle a free hand over Europe.

In the end, deadlock over British agriculture was only avoided by a procedural innovation, the creation of the Mansholt Committee. The purpose of this committee was to examine the merits of the British and Community arguments in greater technical detail.[32] The new procedure allowed both sides to discuss important issues, such as the transitional periods for British agriculture, more freely. It also lowered the temperature of the talks. The final report of the Mansholt Committee was issued on 15 January 1963. At last, progress became possible. Much ground remained to be covered, but the prospects for a successful conclusion of the agricultural negotiations no longer looked hopeless when de Gaulle vetoed the British application.[33]

Without doubt, the agricultural questions were central to the entry negotiations. They were of great domestic political significance for the Conservative Party and of equally great economic importance for the French, who had a strong interest in the CAP. More generally, France was interested in safeguarding the economic equilibrium established within the Community between industrial and agricultural interests. But as long as the economic package was saleable to the Conservative Party and to the public, the British government was prepared to pay a price to gain equal access to the EEC market for British industrial exports and to achieve the wider political objective of getting into the 'inner circles' of the Six. The British negotiating team certainly believed until de Gaulle's veto that solutions to the agricultural problems could be found.[34] The negotiations were thus only superficially about special arrangements for New Zealand butter and transitional periods for British horticulture. The economic talks were constantly overshadowed by the crucial issue, which Macmillan regarded as the key to a successful conclusion of the negotiations, whether Britain and France would come to an understanding about the wider political questions involved in the British EEC application. As part of a package deal, the economic problems might well have been overcome.

At first, Macmillan continued to flirt with the plan for a trilateral nuclear deal in an effort to bring de Gaulle to accept
British EEC membership, and in the further hope that a fundamental change in the American attitude might yet occur. It
became progressively more clear during 1961–2, however, that
this preferred option could never form a suitable basis for the
successful conclusion of the entry negotiations, if only because
of de Gaulle's resolute determination to increase French independence from the United States. This still left the obvious
alternative strategy to be explored, that is the pooling of
British and French resources in order to develop some kind of
common deterrent, or a Franco-British 'nuclear condo-
minium'. It has been argued that such an offer, representing a
substantial 'reorientation of British security policy towards
Europe', was what de Gaulle was waiting for and might have
accepted as the British contribution to a package deal over
Europe.[35] Much has been made in this context of the failure
by Macmillan and de Gaulle to come to an agreement during
their encounter at Rambouillet in December 1962 and of the
subsequent Anglo-American summit meeting at Nassau.

Anglo-French consultations during 1961–2 provide ample
evidence of the fact that de Gaulle was definitely interested in
establishing a bilateral nuclear partnership with the British. In
this context the meeting between Macmillan and de Gaulle at
Champs in June 1962 turns out to have been much more important than their subsequent encounter at Rambouillet in
December. In April the British Prime Minister sent up a *ballon
d'essai*. In speaking about the topic of Britain and Europe to
the departing French Ambassador to London, Chauvel, he
suggested that in his opinion 'the best solution would be for
France and England to reach an understanding with a view to
making the nuclear armament'.[36] Very shortly afterwards, in a
meeting with the new French Ambassador Geoffroy de
Courcel, the former secretary general of the Elysée, he again
stressed the need to develop 'some political and even defence
aspects' for the EEC, and that Britain and France ought 'to
hold their nuclear power as trustees for Europe'.[37] No concrete offer was made, but Macmillan's comments led to a re-
markably more forthcoming attitude by de Gaulle at Champs
than he admits in his memoirs. During one of the meetings de

Gaulle suggested that 'an Anglo-French plan agreed with others' could perhaps be developed to form the basis for what he rather loosely described as 'a European deterrent'.[38]

At this stage the French President would not define his ideas more precisely than that. He merely tested the ground, as he had done so often before since 1958, without having any long-term plan. However, the French did approach the British later with a very concrete proposal for bilateral collaboration in the nuclear field. Only one month afterwards, during a meeting with the British Defence Secretary Harold Watkinson, who was then about to be replaced by Thorneycroft, Messmer enquired whether the British would be interested in the joint development of an underwater missile deterrent for the 1970s, a kind of Anglo-French Polaris. The French would develop the missile system. The British, who had considerable technical expertise in this particular field, would construct the nuclear submarine.[39] Such a proposal for bilateral nuclear collaboration could never have been made without de Gaulle's explicit consent, if not, as seems more likely, at his own initiative.

The French proposal was entirely in line with all of the previous overtures de Gaulle had made to the Americans and the British since 1958, which were primarily aimed at receiving advanced scientific know-how in order to technically and financially facilitate the development of the *force de frappe*. As de Gaulle's offer to the British in 1962 was strictly limited to the joint development of a modern nuclear weapons system, it is difficult to see how this could possibly have been presented as a project for a 'European' deterrent. After all, as long as both partners separately retained full control over the use of the weapons, the envisaged bilateral cooperation would have left two independent national deterrents intact. It would not in the least have affected the national French nuclear doctrine as explained to Thorneycroft by Messmer. De Gaulle seems to have believed that any deterrent which was not under direct or indirect American control would automatically be 'European' at least in purpose, even if France or Britain exercised control over its use. But from the German point of view, for example, an American nuclear force designed to deter the Russians from crossing the Elbe qualified more easily for the strained 'European' label than a French *force de frappe* with the operational task of deterring the Russians from crossing the Rhine, which de Gaulle privately defined as constituting an attack on France justifying the use of nuclear weapons.[40]

The possible establishment of a Franco-British nuclear partnership, as suggested by de Gaulle after the Champs summit, had been discussed on and off within the British government. In the wake of the Suez débâcle, which had shown the full extent of British dependence on the United States, Foreign Secretary Lloyd had first suggested close Anglo-French collaboration in nuclear matters in January 1957,[41] an option that was, however, immediately rejected by the Cabinet in favour of restoring good relations with the Americans. The overall assessment had not changed much when the question of a bribe for de Gaulle began to be discussed within a small circle of a few ministers and senior officials from November 1959 onwards. On the one hand, there was some support within Whitehall for Anglo-French cooperation on the basis that both forces should be assigned to the multilateral NATO nuclear force envisaged by the Americans. On the other hand, there was also some support for replacing the close cooperation with the United States in nuclear matters with a new 'special relationship' with France. Thorneycroft was one senior minister who advocated such a fundamental reorientation of British policy at the time of the entry negotiations. It is clear that the Defence Secretary would have executed the final break with the Americans over Skybolt and Polaris during the tense Nassau summit in favour of Anglo-French collaboration, had it not been for Macmillan.[42]

By 1962 a greater degree of independence from the United States also seemed desirable to many British defence experts who were becoming increasingly anxious about the future direction of American strategic thinking. The concept of flexible response would involve higher expenditure on conventional forces which the British government desperately wished to avoid. It also indicated that the American government, because of the new threat of retaliation against American cities, could no longer be relied upon to the same extent as in the past. The United States might no longer be prepared, if necessary, to respond to a limited Soviet agression in Western Europe with nuclear weapons.[43] As de Gaulle put it to Macmillan at Champs, nobody could possibly know how the Americans would react in the event of a Soviet nuclear attack on, for example, Hamburg (or, for that matter, Birmingham or Marseille), in order to blackmail Western Europe.[44] Nonetheless, the advocates within the government of a reorientation of British defence and nuclear policy towards Europe and, more particularly towards France, remained in a clear minority in 1960–3. For most ministers, including Macmillan and Home, and for the majority of senior officials it was never more than the option of last resort should the Americans decide to put an end to their existing bilateral nuclear partnership with Britain. Macmillan's tentative advances to de Gaulle in 1962 should be seen primarily against the backdrop of an increasing insecurity about continued American support for a formally independent British nuclear deterrent. A decision by the British government to gain entry to the EEC by replacing the Anglo-American nuclear partnership with close Anglo-French cooperation was out of the question. It would have flatly contradicted the dominant objective of the British decision of 1961 to seek membership, namely the objective of rescuing the bilateral special relationship between Britain and the United States. This relationship still seemed to guarantee the British a disproportionately influential role in world affairs, even though the nation's economic and military strength was in sharp decline. It has been argued that the British were not prepared during the EEC entry negotiations to exchange 'more Europe' for 'less America'.[45] In fact, a majority within the British government, including Macmillan, wanted more Europe mainly in order to have *more* America. It is not surprising, therefore, that the British themselves never made a concrete proposal for bilateral Anglo-French nuclear cooperation during 1961–2 which would have put an end to the existing arrangements with the United States. Nor is it difficult to understand why Britain did not respond in a constructive way to de Gaulle's approach through Messmer in July 1962.

The option of a direct offer to the French regardless of the American attitude, having been considered within the government, had already been deliberately ignored by Macmillan after Kennedy's initial refusal to cooperate.[46] In his consultations with de Gaulle at Champs in June 1962, Macmillan's elliptical allusions to the possibility of an Anglo-French nuclear deal were a curiously ineffective diplomatic bait, as it had to be withdrawn whenever the General approached it too closely; or, as the Prime Minister put it to Kennedy in April 1962, he was prepared to leave the 'carrot' of Anglo-French nuclear co-operation 'dangling in front of de Gaulle',[47] but would not let him have a bite. Unless, that is, the Americans suddenly decided to support a solution by which an Anglo-French force would form the European pillar within NATO and it was guaranteed that the Anglo-American nuclear partnership could continue unimpaired. For Macmillan this was the *absolute* precondition for any cooperation with the French ever since he had brought up the idea of a nuclear bribe.

Even if such a constellation had materialized by December 1962, however, Macmillan would still not have made any substantial offer to de Gaulle at Rambouillet, as he had altogether dropped the idea of a package deal involving a nuclear offer to France even before the Champs summit with de Gaulle. Macmillan began to doubt whether, if de Gaulle got what he wanted in terms of nuclear assistance or cooperation, he would then deliver over Europe – or, in other words, whether British EEC entry on reasonable terms would be *guaranteed*. Initially, Macmillan may have been influenced by Kennedy who told him at their meeting in April that the State Department had always believed that de Gaulle would grab whatever he possibly could without making the slightest move over Europe or NATO in return.[48] More important, however, even when pressed hard, neither de Gaulle nor any French government minister or senior official ever admitted that a direct link existed between Europe and the bomb. Prime Minister Michel Debré, for example, indicated to Heath that de Gaulle would certainly 'want to take a broader view which would involve questions of European defence, a common policy in Africa etc.'. When he was then asked bluntly by Shuckburgh whether this meant that Anglo-French nuclear cooperation would form part of the 'final bargaining' in the Brussels negotiations, Debré answered evasively.[49] Despite his evident interest in Anglo-French nuclear cooperation to speed up the development of the *force de frappe*, nothing on the British side suggests that de Gaulle was prepared to accept British EEC membership as the inevitable quid pro quo. On the contrary, on several occasions during 1962 the General actually indicated to Macmillan through Dixon that the best solution would be for the British to withdraw their application.[50] This does not exclude the possibility that de Gaulle may eventually have *granted* EEC membership under certain conditions, but he never gave the British the impression that he would ever feel under any *obligation* to do so.

Political consideration for the other five members of the Community would certainly have made any open negotiation of a bilateral package deal a very awkward balancing act for the French government, but it would by no means have been impossible. Instead, talking to Dixon less than a fortnight before the Champs summit and responding to newspaper reports, de Gaulle actually took the step of positively denying the existence of a nexus between the European and nuclear questions.[51] On becoming British Ambassador to France in 1960, Dixon had been surprisingly confident of being able to read de Gaulle diplomatically. By the time of this meeting with the General, however, he was at a loss as to how to interpret his utterances. In writing to Home and Macmillan, he admitted that there was always the possibility that de Gaulle had meant the exact opposite of what he had said. In the end though, Dixon, the Foreign Office and Macmillan concluded that the General was really not prepared to accept British EEC membership as the agreed quid pro quo for a nuclear offer and that as a result, none should be made before the entry negotiations were successfully brought to an end.[52] Shortly before Macmillan left for Rambouillet six months later, however, a small group of senior officials finally concluded that even in the case of British entry to the EEC, Anglo-French nuclear cooperation, particularly in the development of a delivery system for the post-bomber period, would be undesirable. The massive extra costs did not justifiy the 'theoretically greater degree of independence which we should secure for the British deterrent'.[53]

Even if de Gaulle was prepared to accept a trade-off between the British government's European interests and his nuclear ambitions, it is now clear that no basis for such a package deal ever existed either before or during the negotiations. Whatever de Gaulle's intentions, the conclusion is inevitable that, because of its intrinsic transatlantic character, the British EEC application was doomed to failure from the very beginning. The Rambouillet meeting between Macmillan and de Gaulle and the Nassau talks between Macmillan and Kennedy were largely irrelevant to the outcome of the negotiations. Macmillan's decision to accept the American Polaris offer merely confirmed for de Gaulle that the primary interest of the British was to foster their bilateral relationship with the Americans, an objective for which they would willingly subordinate themselves to American hegemony within the West at almost any price.

By the end of 1962 the British could not anticipate how de Gaulle would stage the breakdown of the negotiations. Some in the British negotiating team in Brussels believed that the French would continue their blocking policy through formal negotiating channels and insist on terms which would force the British government to withdraw. In that case, the British thought, they would have to convince the Americans and the British public that the failure of the negotiations was due to French intransigence and not to British inflexibility. Heath believed that it was impossible to draw the line at British agricultural interests. After all, it was generally expected that the British would have to pay a price for securing equal access for their industrial exports and for the wider political benefits of membership. If the French obstructionist policy forced the British to break off the negotiations themselves, it would probably have to be done over the interests of the Commonwealth.

It turned out that the Nassau agreement between Macmillan and Kennedy provided the ideal opportunity for de Gaulle to break off the negotiations himself. He issued his harshly-worded veto on 14 January 1963 during a press conference at the Elysée. Answering a question from a journalist, the French President suggested that Britain was not yet fit to join the Community, because her political interests, economic needs and cultural traditions were still incompatible with those of the core continental European countries. 'It is predictable', the French President concluded with a view to an enlarged Community:

> that the cohesion of all its members ... would not last for very long and that, in fact, it would seem like a colossal Atlantic community under American dependence and direction, and that is not at all what France wanted to do and is doing, which is a strictly European construction.[54]

De Gaulle's veto put an end to any residual British hopes that entry to the EEC might be achieved without an attractive offer to the French. The British government now had to decide how to retire from the negotiations with the most advantageous publicity. The Cabinet allowed Heath to continue with the ongoing ministerial meetings and to lean on the Germans to isolate de Gaulle diplomatically. Despite diplomatic pressure by the governments of the other five member states, the French team in Brussels, referring to de Gaulle's statement, finally declared on 28 January that it would no longer negotiate. For some time thereafter the British seem to have entertained residual hopes that negotiations might be resumed as a result of German pressure on de Gaulle. The half-hearted efforts of the German Atlanticists around Foreign Minister Gerhard Schröder, however, came to nothing. Despite de Gaulle's unilateral veto, they were not prepared to risk a serious rupture in Franco-German relations over British entry to the EEC.

Throughout the negotiations Macmillan and others in the government perhaps underestimated that de Gaulle, unlike the British, did have a particular vision of Western Europe. De Gaulle's Europe would be more independent of the Western hegemon, the United States, and Britain did not fit easily into his design. 'He is part visionary, part calculator,' Dixon characterized de Gaulle in an internal memorandum for the Prime Minister and the Foreign Office in November 1961. He warned that 'people often see one side of his personality and neglect the other. But both are important.'[55] Among others, Macmillan made this very mistake. Initially he had thought of de Gaulle as more of a pragmatist who would welcome any attractive opportunity for a trade-off of interests than perhaps the French President actually was. As the bitterness within the British government over French obstruction in the negotiations increased, de Gaulle was increasingly regarded as a much more stubborn dogmatist, determined from the very beginning to exclude Britain from the process of European integration. But after de Gaulle's remarks at Champs, ministers and officials in London at least began to understand the underlying ideological reasons for de Gaulle's scepticism towards British membership of the EEC, reasons that had been previously neglected.

Three possible results of EEC enlargement particularly worried de Gaulle: that the EEC might become 'spiritually diluted',[56] that French political leadership within the EEC could be weakened, and that a larger, less tightly-knit Community would be too closely linked to the United States. De Gaulle put much emphasis on the first of these arguments in his press conference. He portrayed Britain as insufficiently 'European' in political, economic and cultural terms to join the Community. This might perhaps have been dismissed as a convenient public excuse to distract from the real reasons for his veto, such as the lack of an attractive nuclear offer. But at Champs de Gaulle had already spoken about Britain and Europe along the same lines, using the same arguments and sometimes even identical phrases, indicating that they reflected more deeply rooted convictions. 'Was it possible for Britain to adopt a genuinely European approach?' the French President asked Macmillan, or was Britain not psychologically separated from the continental countries by the Channel? Did it not have many world-wide interests? And was it not much too closely linked by political and cultural ties with America to join a Community which, in de Gaulle's view, had to keep and further develop a separate European identity? 'Europe must be Europe,' de Gaulle insisted more forcefully at Champs than he could ever convincingly explain.[57] The General was also afraid that enlargement would take the remaining dynamism out of the integration process and render the EEC ineffective. At Champs he complained to Macmillan that without a Franco-German-British directorate – which was impossible to bring about – an enlarged EEC would inevitably degenerate into 'a new United Nations'. And this was not what he had in mind.[58]

The second reason for de Gaulle's scepticism in relation to British membership of the EEC was, of course, never explicitly touched upon in Anglo-French discussions. The French President feared that enlargement would result in an erosion of France's influence within the Community relative to the Federal Republic and Britain, and this fact was compounded for the British by what they believed to be his deep anti-British feelings. After his meeting with de Gaulle in November 1961 the Prime Minister noted in his diary:

His pride, his inherited hatred of England (since Joan of Arc), his bitter memories of the last war; above all his intense 'vanity' for France – she must dominate – make him half welcome, half repel us, with a strange 'love-hate' complex. Sometimes, when I am with him, I feel I have overcome it. But he goes back to his distrust and dislike, like a dog to his vomit.[59]

Six months later, in a preparatory meeting for the Champs summit at Chequers, Macmillan, Home and Heath came to the conclusion that British membership of the EEC was perhaps altogether incompatible with de Gaulle's 'dream of domination'.[60]

The more difficult the French President seemed to be, the more the British perhaps underestimated his flexibility. After all, the partnership between Paris and Bonn was built on a mutually lucrative *division of leadership* into the political and economic spheres. But the British government never gave any attention to the crucial question of whether and how a comparable Anglo-French arrangement could be devised. There were two main reasons for this: first, the foreign policy process was still dominated by a deeply rooted aversion to entering into any long-term bilateral relationships in Europe. Such a relationship would have put an abrupt end to the traditional British balance of power policy, which under the conditions of the postwar bipolar world had ceased to be a global strategy and was now limited to Western Europe. Secondly, the transatlantic logic of the British EEC application necessitated the acquisition of more than just an equal share of political leadership of the Community, as this could hardly justify the continuation of a special role *vis-à-vis* the United States. Between their EEC application and de Gaulle's veto the British never thought about where they wanted to lead Europe, but lead they certainly would. The ambitions of both the French and the British to lead Europe guaranteed the Anglo-French confrontation which culminated in de Gaulle's veto. Besides, the belief in a natural British leadership role was characteristic of a foreign policy which was based largely on unquestioned historical assumptions and did not take sufficient account of the harsh economic and political realities of the postwar world.

Probably as important as this bilateral leadership conflict was de Gaulle's third fear which he later stressed in his memoirs, namely that an enlarged EEC could easily develop into a 'système atlantique' as opposed to his plan for an 'Europe européenne'.[61] The transatlantic motivation of the British EEC application had not escaped the French. It was altogether too obvious that the British government had acted, if not under pressure from the United States, then at least with the Americans' strong encouragement.[62] And once inside the EEC, Britain could 'draw Europe closer to America', as Macmillan himself once put it to Kennedy.[63] This clearly annoyed de Gaulle greatly, as he was aiming at the greatest possible independence from America within the limits imposed by the East–West conflict. He frequently indicated to the British that, if they really wished to be part of the Community, they would have to make their choice: it had to be Europe or America, not both. But 'Britain does not yet seem ready politically speaking to prefer Europe to the United States,' he bluntly told Macmillan during their meeting at Champs.[64]

The French President was right in the sense that the British government did not want to make this choice and, if forced, would have still preferred the United States. This much had been shown symbolically at the Nassau summit in the politically highly sensitive nuclear field. There was also considerably more truth in de Gaulle's critical assessment of Macmillan's belief in his 'power of leadership with the Americans' than the British dared to admit.[65] On the other hand, he underestimated the extent to which the British transatlantic perspective, instead of being regarded as awkward, was widely shared among his partners within the EEC, who saw no inconsistency between the development of a West European identity and a very close defence and security relationship with the United States. The breakdown of the Fouchet negotiations over intergovernmental political cooperation among the Six outside the EEC structure and the Bundestag preamble to the Elysée Treaty, which emphasized the continued importance of German-American relations and of NATO and was forced upon Adenauer by the German parliament, provided ample evidence of this. Perhaps de Gaulle's 'European Europe' was 'a splendid plan', but, as Lacouture has rightly added in his biography of the French President:

> Its major fault was to presuppose that France was the heart, the soul, the kernel of Europe; that the shared hope of Europeans, French and non-French, lay in independence rather than in security; and that the influence of France seemed less of a threat to their liberty than the hegemony of the United States.[66]

In addition, it also grossly overestimated the degree of autonomy the West Europeans could possibly acquire even after the beginning of *détente* which would see the replacement of the former confrontation between the two superpowers with a new American-Soviet bilateralism. What really stood in the way of greater political independence of Western Europe from America was not Britain or the Cold War, but the division of the continent. Somewhat ironically, since 1989 this division has been shown to have been the very basis of French political leadership of the Community.

In the early 1960s Anglo-French differences over the future direction of European integration were often played up for domestic political reasons. The economic interests and the foreign policy concepts of both countries varied considerably, but so did those of the Federal Republic and France. Otherwise, British and French views on European integration issues were in many respects actually similar. This is certainly true for the question of the EEC's future institutional development. 'Federalist ideas', de Gaulle told Dixon before the meeting at Champs, 'do not correspond to reality and are fit only for schoolboys and political theorists.'[67] Macmillan could easily subscribe to this view, which de Gaulle frequently repeated between 1961 and 1963. After they had resolutely thrown the traditional constitutional definition of sovereignty overboard in the spring of 1961, the British were, if anything, more flexible in institutional matters than de Gaulle.

What is perhaps somewhat more surprising is the degree of British interest in 1961 in participating in a European system of agricultural protection. The British hope that entry to the EEC could be achieved with concessions to the agricultural exporters in Western Europe at the expense of third countries outside and inside the Commonwealth later proved unrealistic. The shift in British thinking on agriculture does, however, exemplify that the British government, far from following a coherent *global* approach, was definitely beginning to think and act *communautaire* in a way largely compatible with the evolving, sometimes rather narrow West European regionalism. Thus the Anglo-French conflict in the early 1960s was primarily a reflection of a national rivalry about the political leadership of Western Europe, which by then seemed to both sides to be the most suitable institutional vehicle for securing a prominent role in world affairs. The decisive difference was that France was safely inside the Community, which provided considerable economic benefits and was potentially useful for political cooperation, while Britain was outside.

On the day of the last ministerial meeting in Brussels Macmillan wrote in his diary: 'De Gaulle is trying to dominate Europe. It is the end – or at least a temporary bar – to everything for which I have worked for many years ... All our policies at home and abroad are in ruins.'[68] The impression conveyed here of de Gaulle's veto as a major catastrophe for Britain was due to a sense of deep frustration which the Prime Minister must have felt when his residual hopes for a European El Alamein were finally dashed, but it is highly misleading. Without doubt, Macmillan was disappointed because he wanted Britain to join the EEC. Moreover, the veto came after a bad year for his government with by-election defeats followed by a highly controversial Cabinet reshuffle compounded by worsening opinion polls, all of which gave the impression of a government adrift, led by an ageing Prime Minister. But Macmillan's melancholy mood after de Gaulle's veto should not deflect from the instrumental character of the British application. In 1961 Macmillan could not precisely foresee the developments of 1961–3. He had no detailed master plan for manipulating American nuclear policy or for destroying the political cohesion of the Six. He rightly reckoned, however, that if membership was impossible to achieve, a British application and failed negotiations were definitely the second best option. Indeed, if measured against the main objectives of the British EEC application, the failed negotiations were at least a half success. In economic terms Britain failed to secure equal access to the EEC for its industrial exports. It would also have to survive without the greater

competitive pressures which some had expected to stimulate
the process of domestic economic restructuring. On the other
hand, the tariff barriers were much less significant than they
had been in the interwar period; they were being negotiated
downwards within GATT and, if anything, were only a minor
impediment to British exports to the Community. Instead,
exports to the Community expanded dynamically during the
1960s. Moreover, the hope that EEC membership would
cure the British economic disease was much exaggerated, as
became abundantly clear in the context of Britain's actual
accession to the EEC in the early 1970s.

De Gaulle's veto also meant that the Conservatives were
unable to use EEC entry as a propaganda tool at the next
general election. But the political salience of what was still regarded exclusively as a matter of foreign policy was low and
Macmillan's hopes much exaggerated.[69] Moreover, the British
government easily convinced the public after the veto that the
failure of the negotiations was entirely de Gaulle's fault.
Macmillan believed that de Gaulle had vetoed the British application because the negotiations were too near to success.
This belief was later corroborated to some extent by the
findings of the European Commission who judged that it
would ultimately have been possible to resolve the outstanding
technical issues.[70] While the Conservatives could make
no electoral use of the European issue, the veto did them no
harm in the 1964 election in which Europe played no
significant role. At least, the EEC application had split the
Labour Party on an issue of great importance for future
British politics and had helped to unite the Conservatives
behind an increasingly weak Prime Minister. Moreover,
Macmillan rightly believed that de Gaulle's veto greatly
strengthened his personal position at Westminster and in the
country generally.[71]

Ultimately, however, the effect of the veto needs to be measured against the main foreign policy objective of the EEC application, which was to safeguard a special international role
for Britain over and above France and the Federal Republic.
In this respect the British government's policy of applying for
membership regardless of the adverse international circumstances and of declaring its readiness to participate fully in
political cooperation among the Six was, in fact, highly

successful. The British reaped the first major benefit of their new strategy in April 1962 when the Dutch and Belgian governments refused to discuss political cooperation any further without British participation or before British entry to the EEC. Thereafter, de Gaulle's project for a wider intergovernmental structure for the Six, which might have included foreign policy and defence matters, was practically dead. After de Gaulle's veto it was replaced by the more limited and essentially consultative Franco-German Elysée Treaty. This development removed the most important threat that the British perceived to their world power role, that is that the Six, initially led by France, would replace Britain as the key partner of the United States.

Moreover, Macmillan successfully appeased the Americans by indicating his readiness to play a full and constructive role in European integration. This readiness also helped Macmillan to induce Kennedy to supply Britain with Polaris missiles, despite the wider objectives of the Kennedy government, and secured the formally independent British nuclear deterrent at the cheapest possible price. The total British dependence on American goodwill to supply them with successor weapons did not bother Macmillan. Militarily, the British nuclear force was insignificant. Strategically, it helped to deceive the Soviets by suggesting that a second centre of command existed within the West, although the British force actually had no practical consequence whatsoever for NATO strategy. To Macmillan the British nuclear deterrent mattered only as a symbol of Britain's privileged status as a world power, despite its relative economic and political decline. The EEC application and de Gaulle's subsequent veto also allowed the British to demonstrate to the Americans that the blame for the economic division of Western Europe and the resulting lack of political cohesion lay squarely with France.

At a more general level, the British application, by provoking another French veto, plunged the EEC into a major crisis. British readiness to enter the EEC already laid bare the full extent of disagreement among the Six over the institutional development of the Community and its future role in the world. It exposed, for example, how isolated de Gaulle was with his confrontational approach to the transatlantic relationship. De Gaulle's veto then caused a major upheaval in the

EEC. The Six eventually managed to settle the most crucial economic issue in late 1963 when the French agreed to support a common negotiating position with respect to tariff reductions in GATT, in return for continued progress in the CAP along the lines of the 1962 agreement. In terms of the institutional development of the EEC or of political cooperation among the Six, however, the veto led to a complete standstill that culminated in the constitutional crisis of 1965–6. Substantial progress in European integration no longer seemed possible before de Gaulle left French politics.

At the same time, while de Gaulle's veto undermined the internal solidarity of the Six, it coerced the EFTA member states at least temporarily into a new enthusiasm for the European counter-alliance that the British had discounted before their EEC application. With great relief the neutral states Sweden, Switzerland and Austria registered that British solidarity with their EFTA partners, over which there had been much speculation during the entry negotiations, would now not be tested. It was turned by de Gaulle into 'an academic question', as the Swedish national daily newspaper *Svenska Dagbladet* noted in March 1963.[72] While the Six were still trying to come to terms with the political fall-out of de Gaulle's veto, the British government now got all the EFTA states to support a new accelerated timetable for the abolition of internal tariffs by 1 January 1967. The Austrian government, which decided to pursue the association option with the EEC, independent of the fate of the British application, initially refused to agree at the EFTA Ministerial Council meeting in Geneva in March 1963.[73] When it became obvious that they would be completely isolated over the issue, however, the Austrians finally gave in and at the subsequent EFTA Ministerial Council meeting in Lisbon in May 1963 accepted the new timetable.[74]

Britain had failed to secure EEC membership. This was not surprising in view of the lack of an attractive British offer to the French and of the more fundamental objections of de Gaulle to enlargement. But by mid-1963 the failed EEC application had removed the greatest threat to a special British role *vis-à-vis* the United States; it had helped Macmillan to save the formally independent national nuclear deterrent at a cheap price and thus – in the British view – continued world power status; at least temporarily it had also increased the internal cohesion of and improved the international image of the European counter-alliance EFTA in contrast to the Community of the Six. At the diplomatic level, therefore, the failed application was a full success for the British government.

7 Epilogue: Britain and European Integration, 1963–96

A great deal of scholarship on Britain and Europe after 1945 has been preoccupied with the question as to why and at which junction Britain 'missed the bus' with the destiny of ever closer political union in Western Europe. This implies that something was fundamentally wrong with British policy-making regarding Europe. If, however, the moral perspective of the politically minded pathologist is exchanged for serious historical analysis, the definition of British interests and goals in Europe during the first two decades after the Second World War turns out to be not so dysfunctional after all. It was, in fact, quite rational. That the Attlee government decided in 1950 not to join a supranational community in coal and steel should not be so surprising, for not only were the British coal and steel industries at that time competitive and thriving, but the overriding political logic behind the creation of the ECSC – namely French desire to secure access to German coal supplies and to gain political control over the German steel industry – affected Britain only marginally. Likewise, the British decision in 1955 against participating in setting up a West European customs union was also quite logical given the continued importance of Commonwealth trade ties – at least as long as the Six seemed unlikely to succeed without Britain. Moreover, until Suez it seemed that Britain still had independent international leverage, unlike France and the Federal Republic, so the political incentives for pooling Britain's resources with those of the Six were also limited.

At least the economic ministries realized the long-term dangers of British exclusion from a customs union of the Six surprisingly clearly in 1955. After the breakdown of the FTA negotiations the decision in favour of the EEC application in 1961 came quickly. It was actually based on an *exaggerated* assessment of the economic and political dangers of non-

204

participation. Britain's trade with the Six in fact flourished in the 1960s, despite rising tariff barriers between the EEC and EFTA. Moreover, the transatlantic foreign policy orientation of the other Five in the EEC made it unlikely that de Gaulle would ever be able to establish the Six as a cohesive international power under French leadership, independent of the United States and pursuing fundamentally different goals.

The crucial factor that determined British non-participation in the ECSC and EEC was not lack of far-sighted policy-making, but the time-lag in the Europeanization of Britain's trade and political interests. This time-lag was due primarily to Britain's greater extra-European trade interests, which had been artificially inflated by the 1932 Ottawa preference agreements. It was also the result both of the politically affirmative experience of the Second World War and of the pronounced and not wholly unjustified scepticism with respect to the democratic stability particularly of France and the Federal Republic. Depicting a decision by the British government in 1955 to encourage the creation of a West European customs union and to participate in such an organization as the natural response to the Messina initiative, which should be expected, would be comparable to the claim that the French government surely should have supported the creation of a customs union with West Germany in 1947.

Although British European policy-making in the 1950s was much more rational than has been suggested in the past, it was based on a *short-term* definition of Britain's economic and political interests. But the pronounced attachment of subsequent British governments to the status quo in Western Europe is understandable. Unlike the case of France or the Federal Republic, Britain's participation in closely integrated West European organizations, while possibly providing substantial long-term benefits, would have resulted in short- and medium-term economic and political disadvantages, largely as a result of an accelerated loosening of the economic and political Commonwealth ties. The more critical assessment of Britain's *long-term* interests in Europe at the official level also did not filter through to the political level mostly due to deficiencies in the administrative policy-making structure which favoured compromise formulae, and due to the historically rooted mental barriers among the political elite

against a substantial shift in British foreign policy from its traditional global orientation, which would still bring considerable prestige and superior international status, to a narrower
European orientation.

While British European policy-making during the first two
decades after 1945 was generally quite rational, British governments did run into difficulties determining an order of preference when two foreign policy goals were clearly incompatible.
The best example is the British attitude to the thus perceived
close linkage between the European and nuclear issues in the
bilateral relationship with France in the years 1957–63.
Throughout this period it was clear that Britain could not
have its European cake and eat it without substantial concessions to France, first over the FTA negotiations and later
during the EEC entry negotiations. These might have included a British decision, either in 1957 or in 1961, in favour
of a bilateral nuclear partnership with France instead of with
the United States. If Macmillan's assessment was correct and
the choice in 1961–3 was between EEC entry and continued
bilateral nuclear collaboration with the United States, the
British decision against the French option was not made explicitly, but was based on the implicit assumptions of a clear
majority of the older generation of the Conservative governing elite. An analysis of the linkage between the European and
nuclear issues during 1960–3 reveals, however, that even this
implicit choice was rational in so far as the overriding strategic
goal of the British EEC application of 1961 was in fact to stabilize Britain's bilateral special relationship with the United
States.

If British European policy after 1945 is compared to that of
other West European states – and not just to the Six – it
becomes immediately clear that the *Sonderweg* thesis exaggerates the differences between Britain and the rest of Western
Europe and ignores how many interests the British shared
with some among the Six, and with even more outside the
core Europe institutions. When the history of postwar Western
Europe is interpreted backwards, starting off with the evident
success of the Messina initiative, it ignores the fact that in the
1950s Britain was not alone in favouring trade liberalization
within loose intergovernmental institutional structures. This
concept was also supported by the other EFTA states, and not

only by the non-aligned countries who believed that closer integration was incompatible with their neutrality status. Denmark and Norway, too, were initially opposed to the community concept. These were mature democracies who had understandably little desire to merge their identities and to create new political allegiances. Studies that suggest that there was a fundamental difference between the British pragmatic, intergovernmental approach and the continental federalist approach to European integration also ignore the fact that by the mid-1950s enthusiasm among the Six for federalist institutional solutions was restricted to European pressure groups and individual politicians. The Six were in fact extremely flexible regarding the institutional arrangements for the customs union they envisaged and awarded a strong role to the Council of Ministers. On the other hand, the Commission was granted only limited rights, mainly with respect to initializing common policies. After the creation of the EEC, enthusiasm for a larger role for the Commission, which Hallstein hoped to turn into a kind of European government, was limited even in his native country, the Federal Republic. After de Gaulle's return to power in spring 1958, Adenauer, for example, increasingly saw the Commission's ambitions and its federalist integration programme as an obstacle to Franco-German partnership in leadership.

An analysis of the FTA negotiations also shows how flexible the British government was when it came to the question of majority voting, which in some cases it believed to be in Britain's best interest to prevent France from circumventing the rules of a possible FTA treaty. By the time of the first British EEC application, the British government, unlike de Gaulle, had actually come to terms with the implications of majority voting in the EEC.

The *Sonderweg* thesis overestimates the importance that the Conservatives attached to the constitutional concept of parliamentary sovereignty by the early 1960s.[1] Conservative leaders' frequent references to parliamentary sovereignty in parliamentary debates are taken for granted as a sign of its crucial role in influencing British European policy after 1945. In reality, such references were – and still are – primarily a means for the Conservative leadership to rationalize British distance from the more integrated core Europe for domestic consumption, just as neutrality has been for other European countries. Recent studies of the Conservative Party and Europe have appropriately distinguished among the various meanings of sovereignty. Moreover, a commendable attempt has been made to divide and subdivide the Conservative parliamentary party into several groups, each willing to concede various degrees of sovereignty for different economic and political reasons.[2] This has, however, obscured three characteristics of the approach to the question of surrendering powers to the Community level by the Conservative *governing elite* – a group which can usefully be defined as consisting of all present and prospective government members. This inner circle of Conservative government machinery should be distinguished from the backbenchers on the one hand, whose main party duty is to represent their constituencies and to vote reliably for their government, and from the Tory rank and file on the other.

The Conservative governing elite has, first, never cared much about public opinion on Community membership or further integration. Because they see their party as *the* party of representative government, this elite consistently opposed the idea of a referendum on membership, or, more recently, on the Maastricht Treaty. Calls by the so-called Eurosceptics in the Conservative Party for a referendum on the results of the 1996–7 IGC or on possible British participation in monetary union marked no fundamental departure in this respect. They were merely instrumental in advancing a particular view of future British European policy within the party. That the Conservative leadership adopted the demand for a referendum to ratify possible participation in monetary union in spring 1996 was simply designed to diffuse a policy controversy that had undermined the internal cohesion of the party and had reduced its electoral chances. Furthermore, the Conservative governing elite has traditionally reckoned with a highly deferential political culture among the electorate in regard to foreign policy and more particularly European matters – that the voters are generally uninterested and pre- pared to follow any lead that the goverment of the day might decide to give.[3] As a result, this elite has tended to treat the electorate with a certain degree of publicly disguised contempt over major decisions regarding Europe, including, in the first place, EEC membership. Typical of this elite's distinctly non-participatory conception of politics, Macmillan and Heath believed in 1961 that the government, after having told the British people that they did not quite belong to Europe, would simply have to 're-educate' them in order to turn them into 'good Europeans'.

Second, despite the endless public lip-service paid to parliamentary sovereignty, a large majority of the Conservative governing elite has never cared much for the concept. Indeed since at least the first application, this elite has been preoccupied with securing the greatest possible degree of executive autonomy from parliamentary and other domestic influences.[4] The transfer of powers to the European level has in practice often resulted in a welcome increase in executive autonomy. An early example is the relief with which the majority of the Conservative governing elite was looking forward in 1961 to getting rid of the politically sensitive domestic lobbying by the NFU after Britain's accession to the EEC. From this perspective one can also understand why subsequent Conservative governments have never really encouraged improved parliamentary scrutiny of their own decision-making in the Council of Ministers in Brussels. This has been the case despite the fact that the inefficiency of parliamentary scrutiny of Community legislation, a problem for every member state, has been particularly acute in Britain, where the more profound knowledge of the structure and the internal operations of the EU is largely restricted to the unelected second chamber.

Third, at least since the first British EEC application the Conservative governing elite has consistently understood executive sovereignty not as an absolute, but as a relative concept. The primary focus has been to secure the greatest degree of practical control of the British state over its own destiny. Subsequent Conservative governments have usually not only been prepared to surrender powers to the Community level, but also to accept the extension of majority voting, whenever this was expected to further British interests in Europe. This has been a constant feature of Conservative governments' European policies from the FTA negotiations through to the 1987 Single European Act, when majority voting was rightly expected to facilitate the completion of the single market programme.

It is not only with respect to British institutional conceptions of European integration, however, that the *Sonderweg* thesis exaggerates the alleged differences between an abnormal British approach and continental European support for an ever more integrated Community. The policies Britain has followed in Western Europe, too, are portrayed as diverging fundamentally from those of the Six. The analysis of the real motives behind the first British EEC application reveals, however, that by the early 1960s the British government was in fact keen to participate in the economic trade-off, which was so crucial to the early EEC, between the interests of the agricultural exporters, notably France and the Netherlands, in increasing their agricultural production and exports, and of the industrial exporters, notably the Federal Republic, in industrial free trade in a much larger domestic market. Among the Six, Britain's general preference for a liberal trading order and its interest in boosting trade in industrial products was shared by the Federal Republic and the Benelux countries. Furthermore, below the level of such general preferences, Britain became increasingly interested in the early 1960s in participating in common protectionist policies, even in certain industrial sectors. The best example of Britain's increasingly 'communautaire' attitude is its intense interest in protecting the declining British cotton industry against cheap imports from South and East Asia with import quotas and behind West European tariff walls.

But what is perhaps most striking about the economic rationale behind the first EEC application is the degree to which the majority of the Conservative governing elite was enthusiastic about participation in a common European system of agricultural protection. The Macmillan government initially had great hopes for early British entry to the EEC as a means toward influencing the structure and, most of all, the financing of the evolving CAP. What they aimed for in 1961 was an arrangement favourable to both British and continental farmers at the expense of imports from the Commonwealth and other third countries, allowing the costs of agricultural subsidies to be passed on to the consumer. This would in turn relieve the Exchequer of the ever heavier financial burden of deficiency payments, an agricultural support system the government believed it could no longer afford.

The prevailing conception of the future international role of Western Europe among British policy-makers was also very much in line with the majority view among the Six. This applies most of all to the British preference for a close transatlantic relationship with the United States. Even at the height of Franco-German bilateralism the Germans awarded the highest priority to stable relations with the Americans, although they did so for different reasons than the British, believing that only the United States could guarantee the Federal Republic's external security. For the Dutch and the Belgians, the maintenance of a close relationship between Western Europe and the United States was even decisive in breaking off the Fouchet negotiations in April 1962.

Moreover, it was not at all unusual that Macmillan treated European policy largely as an extension of British national foreign policy, hoping to prop up Britain's role in the world. For Adenauer, European integration was at first a means of achieving the re-entry of the Federal Republic into international politics, becoming later the most suitable institutional vehicle for developing the Franco-German partnership. On the other hand, de Gaulle intended to use French political leadership of the EEC and within a system of political cooperation that he hoped to create to strengthen France's international role and to increase its independence from the United States. In terms of their respective fixations on a national political leadership role in the emerging Western Europe Macmillan's and de Gaulle's concepts were in fact very similar. Macmillan's talk of a continued British world power role and de Gaulle's vision of a leadership role of the *grande nation* were in reality two sides of the same coin. The main differences were that French interests were ideally secured within the EEC and that France's close bilateral relationship with the Federal Republic provided the French with suitable means to pursue their European goals.

Unintentionally, the *Sonderweg* thesis of British postwar history adopts the myth, created by the British political elite, of British exceptionalism – only this time with negative connotations. However, its misguided criticism of British European policy-making only detracts from the real reasons why the British role in European integration has often been perceived as awkward by critics within Britain and among the Six.

One of these reasons is the lack of rational, cooperative diplomacy in pursuing British goals in Europe. British governments have taken a very long time indeed to adapt to decision-making among equal partners in a community of states. Three main factors can be identified which have aggravated the severe adjustment problems of British diplomacy in Europe. They concern, first, British reluctance to enter into a long-term commitment to close bilateral partnerships; second, lack of experience in cooperation with other states on equal terms due to a strong tradition of unequal relationships in foreign relations as well as within Britain; and third, the presence of historical misperceptions and national prejudice in the political mentality of British leaders and their impact on British diplomacy in Europe. National alliances over particular issues certainly continued to play a role in Western Europe after 1945 despite the institutionalization of transnational, partly supranational decision-making structures with the creation of the ECSC and the EEC. Only the British government, however, remained completely fixated on its traditional balance-of-power approach and thus on constantly changing alliances and partnerships to pursue British interests and counteract any hegemonic influence of continental European powers. But this has excluded the possibility of a long-term commitment to partnership with France, for example, which would have been stable enough to bridge more fundamental economic and political differences of interest. British governments have often failed to understand that such a commitment, while necessitating a greater preparedness to compromise over many issues, might yield much greater influence over the general direction of further integration. Although more recently the breakdown of the iron curtain and subsequent German unification has strained the Franco-German partnership and seems to have led to greater flexibility in the patterns of cooperation within the EU, the Major government once again did not make the most of the new opportunities in the run-up to the 1996–7 IGC. Its White Paper on EU reform, *A Partnership of Nations*, published in March 1996, aimed mainly at appeasing the different wings of the Conservative Party, said very little of significance on any of the main issues at stake and in the end pleased none of Britain's partners in Europe.

British governments after 1945 have also found it extremely difficult to adapt their European diplomacy to the ever-shrinking British economic and military power base and to accept a status of equality with the other medium-sized powers: France, the Federal Republic and Italy. The main reason for this phenomenon was – and to some extent still is – British lack of experience in foreign policy conducted on equal terms. Britain's two key external relationships after 1945 were characterized by clear hierarchies: Britain led the Commonwealth, and it was led by the United States. Moreover, the difficulty of adapting to sustained bargaining in a community of states also has a domestic component which has tended to reinforce established foreign policy habits. Unlike federal Germany, for example, the British domestic experience is one of an unequal, dependent relationship between core and periphery in a highly centralized state.[5]

Finally, even when diplomatic strategies in European matters have been based on a rational analysis of the interests of Britain as well as its partners, British leaders from Macmillan to Thatcher have too often allowed their personal diplomacy to be influenced or even determined by their own peculiar historical misperceptions and prejudices. Two good examples are Macmillan's entirely uncoordinated, continuous German-bashing and his absurd obsession with the EEC as an attempt to create a new continental blockade and exclude Britain from the benefits of economic integration. On several occasions his ideas became public, such as in the spring of 1960 when the Americans leaked his slating of the EEC. His wild comments harmed Britain's credibility in Europe considerably and provoked Wilson into making the ironic remark in the Commons that:

> We all know the Prime Minister's liking for ... historical roles. We have had him as Gladstone, Disraeli, and, last year, as Marco Polo ... This year we saw him cast himself in the role of the younger Pitt. We do not want to interfere with the Right Hon. Gentleman enjoying himself in this way, but we must ask what effect in heaven's name do utterances of this kind have on Britain's ability to get her views accepted in Europe ...?[6]

More recently, the adverse impact of the influence of personal prejudice on British diplomacy became clear in Thatcher's vehement opposition to German unification, which she has since confirmed in even clearer terms than in 1989–90;[7] it subsequently reduced British influence on the general direction of further integration.

A second important reason why the British role in European integration has often been perceived as awkward lies in the economic consequences of Britain's late accession to the Community long after the Six had determined its institutional design and key policies. The most severe disadvantage for Britain was, of course, the financing system of the CAP. Having been so keen in 1961 to join the EEC early to shape the CAP, the Macmillan government was forced to realize during the EEC entry negotiations in 1961–3 that it would have to pay a high price for membership through disproportionate contributions to the financing of the CAP. When Britain actually joined in 1973, the price had become even higher, and Britain was for a long time the only net contributor to the Community budget apart from the Federal Republic. But while the benefits from their consistent trade surplus with the other member states easily compensated for the Germans' much greater net budgetary contributions, Britain continued to decline throughout the 1970s to the status of the second poorest member state in terms of GDP per head – after the Republic of Ireland, which had also joined in 1973. Moreover, it accumulated a substantial trade deficit with the other member states.

After 1979 Thatcher vociferously fought for a substantial rebate of approximately one billion pounds annually on the British net contribution to the budget and for a reform of the CAP. After much internal and public wrangling the Community eventually agreed on a medium-term solution to the budgetary question at the Fontainebleau summit in 1984, and took a first step in the direction of a reform of the CAP in 1988. The *Sonderweg* thesis has habitually criticized Thatcher's European policy particularly harshly, but it fails to differentiate between substance and style. What caused such consternation among Britain's partners was not the British demand as such to redress the evident imbalance in the budget contributions, but that Thatcher duplicated her aggressive style in relation to Labour in the European theatre of politics. In fact, Margaret Thatcher in many ways proved to be the first Conservative and British Prime Minister to develop any practical notion of the future direction of European integration. Underneath her often violent rhetoric, Thatcher's approach to further European integration was basically constructive, at least until she realized the full extent of the unwelcome political integration dynamism set off by the Single European Act and strengthened further in connection with German unification and the two IGCs on economic and political union leading to the Maastricht Treaty. It was only Thatcher's eventual defection to the minority group of constitutional purists within the Conservative Party, opposed to any kind of surrender of 'sovereignty' to the Community level, which finally contributed to her downfall in November 1990.

The political leitmotif of the new Conservative approach to European integration under Thatcher was the extension of Thatcherism to the continent. Whereas previous party leaders had hoped that more Europe would cure Britain, she strongly believed that it was the Community that needed to be cured from its alleged corporatist and protectionist tendencies by Britain, fighting for freer markets and freer trade. This philosophy was reflected in the European policies followed by the British government during the 1980s, for example with respect to a strengthening of competition policy, but most importantly with regard to the internal market programme, which had its origins in the 1985 White Paper submitted by the British Commissioner Lord Cockfield. With minor modifications this essentially economic approach was continued by John Major after 1990, finding its expression in strong British support for global free trade in the Uruguay Round GATT negotiations and for the enlargement of the West European market to include several more EFTA states and eventually the new democracies of East-Central Europe. In addition, the Thatcher and Major governments also advocated closer cooperation on foreign policy between the member states within the intergovernmental framework of what was the European Political Cooperation and is now the Common Foreign and Security Policy. However, this never assumed a high priority, as long as the close personal rapport between Thatcher and the American President Ronald Reagan during

1980–8 and again Anglo-American cooperation during the 1991 Gulf War nourished the illusion of a transatlantic 'special relationship' that could bring Britain greater international prestige, if not necessarily influence.

The financial costs of Britain's entry have been high indeed. But in 1971–2 the Conservative government led by Edward Heath felt it had no other option, if it wanted to prevent Britain from degenerating into a far-away country of which the continental Europeans knew little and cared even less.[8] Labour Prime Minister Wilson soon came to the same conclusion after the so-called renegotiation of the entry terms during 1974–5, which he had initiated to appease the anti-EEC wing of his party, produced few substantial results. The financial price for entry and its ruthless domestic political exploitation by Labour and, after 1979, by the Conservatives always made it unlikely that the British would develop great enthusiasm for membership or for further integration. But this structural problem was exacerbated by the totally exaggerated expectations of all British governments since Macmillan, constantly conveyed to the British public, that membership would automatically deliver the political leadership of Western Europe to Britain and would spur the economic revitalization of the British economy.

In 1961, despite the evidently close Franco-German partnership, the Macmillan government assumed that once inside the EEC, Britain would automatically take over. The strong belief in a natural British leadership role continued even after de Gaulle's 1963 veto. It transcended party divisions and was eagerly embraced by the Wilson governments of 1964–70. Willy Brandt, German Foreign Minister during 1966–9, recalls, for example, that Foreign Secretary George Brown was eager to enter the Community so that Britain could take the lead.[9] In his diaries, Richard Crossman recalls an official paper on EC entry which argued that entry was desirable primarily for the opportunity it afforded Britain to be counted in the counsels of Europe and the world once more.[10] Tony Benn, in one of his diary entries, recalls that his permanent secretary assumed that Whitehall would automatically dominate the Community decision-making process because the British civil service was 'so full of experienced people'.[11] By the early 1960s, the assumption of a natural British leadership role in the Community was already an illusion, but by the time of Britain's actual entry in 1973 it was an outright absurdity. Most of all, it ignored the reality of the Franco-German partnership which was at the heart of European integration.

With Britain's relative economic decline continuing unabated throughout the 1960s, the economic rationale for entry and the related expectations became progressively more important. What Britain desperately needed, Nigel Birch had argued in the House of Commons in 1961, was 'an external stimulus. What we want here is a good shake-up.'[12] Conservative and Labour supporters of EEC membership hoped that, if exposed to the more competitive economic climate of the larger European common market, British industry would be forced to make rapid, drastic adjustments, would become more competitive again and would be able to secure a larger share of exports. Increasingly, Community membership was regarded as the key to 'whether Britain became a thrusting, modern society, rescued from complacency and decline'.[13]

As leader of the opposition and then as Prime Minister, Edward Heath saw membership as the indispensable external supplement to the domestic strategy of economic reform which he unsuccessfully attempted to implement during 1970–2. In the early 1970s, a more clearly economic motivation was apparently widely shared within the Conservative parliamentary party. During ten days' debate on Europe in July and October 1971, for example, roughly one out of two Conservative MPs named the expectation of a 'growth dividend' from membership as the main argument in favour of entry. By comparison, foreign policy arguments, such as the hope for 'greater British influence in the world', now featured less prominently.[14] The hope that membership would revitalize British industry was entirely shared by the supporters of EEC membership in the Labour Party.

In itself, the externalization of domestic problems, in which Macmillan and Heath, in particular, invested so much hope, was not peculiar to British European policy. However, nowhere else in Western Europe were the expectations so high and the chances that they would be fulfilled so low as in Britain. It was always much more likely within the Community that the Danes could secure their agricultural interests or that the Irish could reduce their economic dependence on Britain than that the

British should miraculously occupy an exclusive leadership
role and automatically be cured of their economic disease.
The first of these two assumptions was based on the grave mis-
conception that Britain was still indispensable as a mediator
between France and Germany within Western Europe. The
second assumption ignored the politically inconvenient fact
that integration into a larger European market could at best
provide a stimulus for change, but that Britain's structural
problems had to be tackled domestically.

A remarkable reduction in British expectations of membership occurred only under Thatcher. She gradually succeeded
in putting an end to the equally introspective and defensive
preoccupation with Britain's relative decline and relocated
political responsibility for the process of economic modernization in the domestic political arena. For almost twenty years
until then, a key feature of the British political elite's approach to European integration had been its essentially instrumental character. But using Europe as little else but a means
to achieve non-European foreign policy aims or as a smoke-
screen for political failure or for domestic reforms created
what might be dubbed the excessive expectations syndrome of
the British over Europe, and this led directly to the inevitable
disillusionment with the realities of membership. Perhaps with
the exception of Heath, the British political elite has done
very little indeed to redress these problematic long-term
effects by stressing the positive aspects of membership and
further integration. For them, using Europe as a smoke-screen
or a convenient scapegoat has never been a temporary tactical
move to escape domestic criticism, but rather a systematic
political approach to domestic and European politics, which
has helped to sustain this elite's political legitimacy after the
decline of the Empire.

What is arguably even more relevant to understanding
Britain's relationship with its European partners was – and is
more than ever in the 1990s – the enormous influence of
party political controversies and tactics. Seen over the entire
postwar period, these have been far more devisive than in any
other member state. Until the late 1980s – ironically in view of
that party's recent split over Europe – the terms of party political engagement in European matters were largely dictated by
the Conservatives, beginning at least with the deliberately con-

frontational first EEC application of 1961. As has been shown, Conservative governments have generally been willing to play a more constructive role within the Community and have usually been under fewer internal party or other domestic constraints in doing so than has often been suggested. At the same time, they have tended to treat the internal policy-making process over Europe on the one hand and domestic politics on the other as unrelated. Thus, the actual policy followed has, with the partial exception of Heath's leadership during 1965–75, stood in sharp contrast to the Conservative governing elite's domestic presentational tactics. These in turn have been determined by the calculated political strategy, initiated by Macmillan, of positioning the Conservatives as the 'party of Europe' in relation to Labour and the Liberals, while at the same time continuing carefully to cultivate the image of the only truly 'patriotic party' in relation to the wider electorate.

For almost thirty years after 1961 this policy, although highly ambivalent, in fact worked very well for the Tories. The 'party of Europe' ideology was developed by Macmillan in connection with the first EEC application, although he could pick up the thread of Churchill's public support for the idea of European integration, if not British membership in core Europe institutions. Macmillan had previously treated the FTA negotiations in 1957–8 and the creation of EFTA in 1959–60 in the same bipartisan way that, irrespective of Churchill's rhetoric, had been characteristic of the semi-detached approach to European integration by all Labour and Conservative governments during 1945–56. By 1960–1, however, the EEC entry option appeared to offer a distinct party political advantage.

Even in the event of a successful conclusion of the Brussels negotiations it seems more than doubtful whether this alone would have saved the Douglas-Home government in the 1964 general election. The Conservative strategy was nonetheless highly successful in another respect. Macmillan counted on two developments that had become evident in the public debate over membership during 1960–1. First, the hard core of entry supporters within the Labour Party would easily outnumber the Conservative opponents. The Labour supporters mostly regarded the issue as a matter of principle and played a leading role in the inter-party Common Market Campaign. Second, as a result of his government's decision to open entry negotiations with the EEC, the Labour Party would become much more deeply split than the Conservatives because the issue fitted so neatly into the existing patterns of violent internal strife between the socialist left and the moderates over unilateral disarmament and Clause Four. Indeed, the resulting Conservative strategy of a flexible escalation of the process of party political polarization over Europe had the desired effect. Gaitskell's increasingly hostile statements allowed the Tories to portray Labour as unfit to govern. At the Conservative Party conference in Llandudno in October 1962 Butler characteristically responded to Gaitskell's '1000 years' speech by summing up 'that truly remarkable oration in these words, that the Socialists have decided to look backwards and to leave the future to us. For them 1,000 years of history books. For us the future.'[15]

In the early 1960s Macmillan was preoccupied with the short-term political effect of his 'party of Europe' strategy. However, it turned out to be highly successful in the longer term, too. Wilson's 1967 EEC application could only briefly disguise the fundamental divisions within Labour over Europe. The internal controversy turned once more into open warfare during the debate in 1971–2 over the terms of entry negotiated by the Heath government, and again in connection with the 1975 referendum. Subsequently, the temporary takeover of the Labour Party by the socialist left in 1979–80 led to the decision to demand immediate withdrawal from the Community without another referendum. As a consequence, the European question contributed significantly to the defection of key reformers, led by Jenkins, who founded the Social Democratic Party in 1981, and indirectly to the Conservative election victories of 1983 and 1987. When the Labour Party dropped the demand for withdrawal under the new leadership of Neil Kinnock, this marked the fifth fundamental change in its position on Europe since Macmillan's application. Only the recent transformation into a technocratic reform party finally made the new Labour leadership discover after the 1992 general election that it could use European policy to cause party political and parliamentary difficulties for a Conservative government with a majority of 21 and decreasing rapidly.[16]

Britain and European Integration, 1963–96   221

As opposed to the 'party of Europe' ideology, the 'patriotic party' image, which the Conservatives have traditionally promoted of themselves, has its much older historical roots in late nineteenth-century and early twentieth-century British imperialism and unionism, and is primarily directed at the general public. Whatever the actual European policies followed between the first EEC application and the Maastricht Treaty, flying the Union Jack at party conferences and on the return from negotiations in Brussels has been a major preoccupation of almost all Conservative leaders; this has been particularly at times when they were in a weak political position within their party and in the country. The differences between leaders have been in style, not substance. The gentlemanly Macmillan emphasized frequently, for example, that the British people would, if necessary, fight the EEC to the bitter end, as they had previously fought continental leaders from Philip II to Hitler.[17] Allegedly banging her handbag on the negotiating table, Thatcher demanded 'our money back' during the budgetary dispute in the early 1980s.[18] Finally, in one of his preferred sporting analogies, Major publicly claimed after the conclusion of the Maastricht negotiations that the result was 'game, set and match to Britain'. In reality, he had failed to influence the general thrust of the Maastricht Treaty. All he had in fact achieved was permission not to play the decisive set by securing the two opt-outs on the social chapter and monetary union to safeguard the internal unity of his party.

In the domestic political context, Conservative leaders and ministers have regularly employed distorted images of three alleged public enemies: the French, the Germans and the Commission. Whom they abused depended on the respective foreign policy and domestic circumstances. The French were a particularly useful target during the 1960s when de Gaulle, after already having broken off the FTA negotiations, twice vetoed British EEC applications – in 1967 even more predictably than in 1963. The Conservative governing elite has, however, generally preferred public attacks on the Germans, which have usually promised considerably greater domestic political benefits. In this respect, despite the far-reaching differences in political style and policies followed, there is a striking continuity among Conservative leaders, only briefly interrupted by Heath, from Macmillan to Thatcher and beyond. They have been united, first, in a distinct aversion to what they see as the dangers of *the* German national character. Secondly, they have generally felt extremely uneasy about a possible German domination of European institutions. And finally, they have shown great unwillingness to make concessions to German political interests in order to establish a more stable long-term bilateral relationship.

To illustrate this point, the attitudes of Macmillan and Thatcher can be compared. Culminating in 1958–9, Macmillan frequently made disparaging remarks about the Germans in connection with his permanent warnings against a revival of Nazism. The image of a 'Fourth Reich' to some extent reflected real anxieties, but it also served the domestic political purpose of cultivating the collective memory of and pride in Britain's heroic fight against the 'Third Reich'. This rather conveniently deflected attention – particularly in an election period – from the domestic economic and political problems of the present. In 1952 and again in 1956, Macmillan also suggested – initially in internal memoranda – that a common market in Europe, in any case without British participation, would necessarily result in a revival of German power through economic means. As he later freely quoted in his memoirs, it 'is really giving them on a plate what we fought two wars to prevent'.[19] This is already the distorted image of European integration as a subtle German device to establish hegemony in Europe, and it has reappeared ever since, not least in connection with the Maastricht Treaty and monetary union. And finally, Macmillan demonstratively never made any diplomatic effort to be on good terms with the Adenauer government – not even during 1960–3 when close cooperation with the Germans over Europe might have been helpful in persuading de Gaulle to accept British EEC membership.

Nearly thirty years later, virtually nothing had changed. Thatcher still believed in *the* German national character as it was analysed at the notorious Chequers meeting with close advisers in 1990. This is confirmed by her memoirs, in which she goes to some length to discuss the psychological roots of 'the German problem'.[20] Moreover, even more drastically than Macmillan, the Secretary of State for Industry Nicholas Ridley provocatively claimed in relation to the two IGCs on economic and political union that if the British agreed to further

European integration, they could just as well have surrendered to Hitler in the first place. Although Thatcher never publicly put it in quite the same way and was eventually even forced to fire him, Ridley's derogatory remarks about the Germans as well as the French and the Commission clearly reflected her own gut instincts at that stage. Finally, Thatcher also never cared much about the impression her nationalist rhetoric would create in Germany, such as in the context of her short-lived attempt to prevent German unification. When Major subsequently attempted to improve relations with the Kohl government this was soon frustrated when for party political as well as personal reasons Chancellor Norman Lamont became involved in bitter public exchanges with representatives of the Bundesbank after the ERM crisis in September 1992.

The Commission, finally, was a particularly useful public enemy while the ambitious and energetic Jacques Delors was its president. The Thatcher and Major governments have continuously portrayed the Commission as 'unelected Brussels bureaucrats' who are allegedly the driving force behind a conspiracy to create a European 'super-state', constantly trying to 'introduce Socialism through the back door'.[21] To some extent these allegations have been designed to deflect attention from the fact that decisions within the EU are actually made by the Council of Ministers in which the British government commands ten votes whenever decisions are made by majority vote. But it is not Thatcher who invented the regular abuse of the Commission as another useful scapegoat. Macmillan and several colleagues, such as Eccles, had already made the odd derisory public comment about the institution whose members were understandably suspicious of the motives behind British European policy. They did not wish to endanger the deepening of the Community and thus generally opposed the FTA proposal in the late 1950s and British EEC membership in the early 1960s. Internally, Macmillan made some particularly chauvinistic remarks about the Commissioners. In November 1959, for example, he commented that the real trouble with the Commission was that it was run by 'the Jews, the Planners and the old cosmopolitan element'.[22] More recently, the disparaging of the Commission has been supplemented by increasingly aggressive attacks on another institution, the European Court of Justice, for its allegedly illegitimate intrusion into the British legal system, attacks that highlight the incompatibility of the constitutional traditions of Britain and all other EU member states which have written constitutions and – in most cases – independent constitutional courts.[23]

The hostile nationalist rhetoric at the same time echoes prejudices of the British electorate and strongly reinforces them. It is of course still to be seen in the historical context of the Second World War which in Britain resulted in a strengthening of nationalism as a legitimating and unifying ideology. Dunkirk and subsequent events appeared to be an intellectually satisfactory justification for the continuation of a special British role not just in Western Europe, but in the world. In the 1990s it still helps to sustain the myth of a positive British political and cultural uniqueness. This finds its expression in Conservative ministers' habitual assertions in both the Commons and the media that British is best – even in relation to such issues as education or vocational training where in a comparative European perspective this sounds implausible.

Three main reasons can be identified for the frequent, sometimes spontaneous, sometimes carefully calculated nationalist outbursts of leading Conservatives who are cultivating the 'patriotic party' image. First, they have generally reflected their gut feelings as well as a distinct inability and sometimes also unwillingness to understand the positions and political style of the other member states. In her memoirs Thatcher typically confesses that after 1979 she was intensely surprised by 'the quintessentially un-*English* outlook' of the other leaders in the Community,[24] which implies that she expected not just the Scots and the Welsh, but also the Italians or Belgians to share 'the English', that is *her* point of view. Much more importantly, however, the nationalist-populist line has traditionally been extremely popular among large sections of the Conservative Party, as the euphoric reception of Michael Portillo's Euro-bashing speech at the 1995 Conservative Party conference once more confirmed.[25] Moreover, it is rightly regarded as a formidable source of electoral strength for them.[26] Running down the French, the Germans and the Commission has played a prominent role in any Conservative *panis et circenses* policy. The worse the party's results in local elections, by-elections and opinion polls in recent years, the more vehement the attacks became, not least because opinion polls showed that the only issue on which the Conservatives were not massively behind Labour was Europe. Although the attacks came primarily from the nationalist far right of the party, they were not only tolerated, but effectively encouraged by leading moderates with their own less vicious broadsides against the other Europeans.

To promote the party interest, Conservative leaders have therefore traditionally spoken with two completely different voices in Europe and in Britain. What they have largely ignored is the extent to which the careful cultivation of the 'patriotic party' image at home, often accompanied by aggressive nationalist rhetoric, has very significantly contributed to the relative failure of successive British governments to implement their views in Europe. This is exemplified by Britain's inability to influence the general thrust of the Maastricht Treaty. It was evident early on, for example, that American and Soviet policy would not allow Thatcher to prevent or even simply to delay German unification. With her openly displayed anti-Germanism she merely succeeded in burdening the bilateral relationship with the united Germany which is arguably the key to greater British influence in the EU. More recently, the negative effects of the Conservatives' aggressive rhetoric on British influence in Europe could also be observed in the context of the internal EU dispute in 1993–4 over the adaptation of majority voting after enlargement. This controversy was first provoked and then prolonged by the Major government purely for internal party political reasons. The final so-called compromise reached with Britain's EU partners in spring 1994, which introduced an extra period of reflection before following the established majority voting procedures, entailed no significant concession to the official British position. It was another badly disguised face-saving exercise for a government under attack from what at that time had already developed into a party within the party. But by risking enlargement through linking the issue of majority voting with British ratification of the accession treaties of Austria, Finland, Sweden and Norway, the Major government left the worst possible impression of British European policy on Britain's former EFTA partners, whom the British regarded as their natural allies within the EU.

Over the past 15 years the EU has actually become more 'British' in the Conservative sense of the word. For example, the general bias towards deregulation and reduction of trade union influence throughout Europe since at least the mid-1980s, as well as the agreement which the member states eventually reached on the 1993 GATT deal, indicate a strengthening within the EU of the Conservative notion of freer markets and freer trade. The recent enlargement by Austria, Finland and Sweden on 1 January 1995, moreover, has accelerated the shift from institutional deepening to faster widening of the EU to include East-Central European and Baltic countries. By early 1996, it also seemed likely that the 1996–7 IGC on EU reform would produce no very far-reaching results, for example in strengthening the powers of the European Parliament. These developments ought to make the so-called Eurosceptics in the Conservative Party feel more relaxed both about Britain's position in the EU and further integration.[27] It is also still the case, of course, that key domestic supporters of the party, above all the City and the Confederation of British Industries, expect the continuation of a policy aimed at avoiding the emergence of an economic two- or multi-tier Europe with Britain on the fringe. If there were to be a Conservative government by 1998 or later, it was still difficult to see in early 1996 how it could simply reject participation in monetary union if Britain fulfilled the convergence criteria.

On the other hand, the one-sided strengthening of the 'patriotic party' image, which has been forced upon the Conservative leadership in recent years and which is continuously being reinforced by the ill-informed and deliberately misleading reporting on EU matters by the British tabloid press, does not merely reflect the decline in electoral support for the Tories. This decline was in fact unrelated to the European issue. Rather, this strengthening mirrors a deeply felt anxiety that while Europe may become more 'British', Britain may also become more European in a way English nationalists do not approve of. On the right of the Conservative Party it is increasingly felt, and rightly so, that integration in the EU is having a creeping effect on the British constitution in the broadest sense, and on what this constituent believes to be the British – or rather English – identity. The perceived

dangers include, for example, the impact of the decisions of
the European Court of Justice on the British legal system or
the potential effects of an independent European central
bank on government autonomy in economic policy. Similarly,
the right wing of the Conservative Party also fears that the subsidiarity concept and the 'Europe of the Regions' could have
serious repercussions for the increasingly fragmented nature
of the United Kingdom, which anyway seemed to be approach-
ing fundamental reform in its governance, and could even
eventually lead to its break-up.[28]

In the mid-1990s, both electoral decline and the anxieties
about the future of a Conservative English Britain made it
look no longer impossible that the next Conservative leader
after Major might be Enoch Powell reincarnated and that the
Tories would degenerate into a party of English nationalism.[29] Such a development would amount to a dramatic
break with the established strategy of presenting the Conservatives simultaneously as the 'party of Europe' and the 'patriotic party'. This would be highly ironic in view of its
invention by Macmillan, who wanted Britain to lead Europe.
It is of course doubtful whether such a shift in the identity of
the Conservative Party would actually produce the desired
electoral benefits. It probably overestimates both the electoral salience of Europe and the anti-European feelings of
the British, which both larger parties have done their utmost
to encourage in the past, whether intentionally or not.

The Labour Party, on the other hand, has a long-standing
tradition of disorientation over Europe. The Conservatives at
least mostly share a particular vision of the EU's future
development. They generally favour a less integrated *Europe
des patries* involving a degree of variable geometry in a widened
Community. In contrast, the Labour Party still has no distin-
guishable concept for the EU's future development. Moreover,
the opposition to membership and further integration within
the Labour Party is probably still more pronounced than in
the Conservative Party. As a result, it is as yet unclear as to
whether a future non-Conservative government would in fact
break with the long-established British tradition of using
Europe and abusing the Europeans.

Notes

INTRODUCTION

1. On the Conservative divisions over the ratification of the Maastricht Treaty see David Baker et al., 'The parliamentary siege of Maastricht 1993: Conservative divisions and British ratification', *Parliamentary Affairs*, Vol. 47, No. 1 (1994), pp. 37–60.
2. See in particular Stephen George, *An Awkward Partner. Britain and the European Community* (Oxford: Clarendon Press, 1990).
3. William Paterson, 'Britain and the European Union revisited: some unanswered questions', *Scottish Affairs*, No. 9 (1994), pp. 1–12 (1–2).

CHAPTER 1 BUILDING AND DEFENDING A BRITISH EUROPE, 1945–55

1. Quoted in Alan S. Milward, *The Reconstruction of Western Europe 1945–51* (London: Methuen, 1984), p. 62.
2. Alec Cairncross, *The British Economy since 1945* (Oxford: Blackwell, 1992), p. 47.
3. Roger Makins, 'Some notes on British foreign policy': PRO FO 371/124968/24 (11 August 1951).
4. *House of Commons Debates*, vol. 494, col. 237, 20 November 1951.
5. Harold Macmillan, *Riding the Storm 1956–1959* (London: Macmillan, 1971), p. 65.
6. The continued imperial orientation of British foreign policy is stressed in John Kent, *British Imperial Strategy and the Origins of the Cold War* (Leicester: University Press, 1994).
7. David Reynolds, 'A "special relationship"? America, Britain and the international order since the Second World War', *International Affairs*, Vol. 62, No. 1 (1985), pp. 1–20 (7).
8. The United States of Europe (15 February 1930), quoted in Michael Wolff (ed.), *The Collected Essays of Sir Winston Churchill, Vol. II* (London: Buckram, 1976), pp. 185–6.
9. John W. Young, *Britain and European Unity, 1945–1992* (London: Macmillan, 1993), p. 12.
10. Cf. Ritchie Ovendale, *The English-Speaking Alliance: Great Britain, the US, the Dominions and the Cold War* (London: Allen & Unwin, 1985), p. 45.
11. See, for example, Geoffrey Warner, 'The Labour governments and the unity of Western Europe', in Ritchie Ovendale (ed.), *The Foreign Policy of the British Labour Governments 1945–51* (Leicester: University Press, 1984), pp. 64–5/79–80.

12. Wilfried Loth, *Der Weg nach Europa. Geschichte der europäischen Integration 1939–1957* (Göttingen: Vandenhoeck & Ruprecht, 1991), pp. 69–76.
13. Cf. Loth, *Weg*, pp. 97–105.
14. Cf. Loth, *Weg*, pp. 92–100.
15. The degree of continuity is rightly stressed in John W. Young, 'Churchill's "No" to Europe: The "rejection" of European Union by Churchill's post-war government, 1951–2', *The Historical Journal*, Vol. 28, No. 4 (1985), pp. 923–37.
16. Saki Dockrill, *Britain's Policy for West German Rearmament, 1950–1955* (Cambridge: University Press, 1991), pp. 80–8.
17. See also John W. Young, 'German rearmament and the European Defence Community', in John W. Young (ed.), *The Foreign Policy of Churchill's Peacetime Administration 1951–1955* (Leicester: University Press, 1988), pp. 81–107.
18. Milward, *Reconstruction*, p. 464.
19. Milward, *Reconstruction*, pp. 56–89.
20. On United States policy towards Western Europe after 1945 see Michael J. Hogan, *The Marshall Plan: America, Britain, and the Reconstruction of Western Europe, 1947–1952* (Cambridge: University Press, 1987).
21. On the British reaction to the Schuman Plan see in greater detail Edmund Dell, *The Schuman Plan and the British Abdication of Leadership in Europe* (Oxford: University Press, 1995).
22. For the role of the ECSC High Authority see the comprehensive study by Dirk Spierenburg and Raymond Poidevin, *The History of the High Authority of the European Coal and Steel Community. Supranationality in Operation* (London: Weidenfeld & Nicolson, 1994).
23. On Britain's association with the ECSC see John W. Young, 'The Schuman Plan and British association', John W. Young (ed.), *The Foreign Policy* in pp. 109–34.
24. The only comprehensive account of the diplomacy of the creation of the EEC is still Hanns Jürgen Küsters, *Die Gründung der Europäischen Wirtschaftsgemeinschaft* (Baden-Baden: NOMOS, 1982).
25. Alan S. Milward, *The European Rescue of the Nation-State* (London: Routledge, 1994), pp. 119–20.
26. Cf. John W. Young, *Britain, France and the Unity of Europe, 1945–51* (Leicester: University Press, 1984), pp. 68–70.
27. Young, *European Unity*, p. 17.
28. On the Beyen plan and Dutch European policy in 1952–5, see Milward, *European Rescue*, pp. 185–96.
29. Denkschrift der Bundesregierung (1 June 1955), Bulletin des Presse- und Informationsamtes der Bundesregierung 106 (11 June 1955), p. 880. See also John Gillingham, *Coal, Steel and the Rebirth of Europe, 1945–1955. The Germans and French from Ruhr Conflict to Economic Community* (Cambridge: University Press, 1991), p. 363.
30. The only account of the creation of Euratom remains Peter Weilemann, *Die Anfänge der Europäischen Atomgemeinschaft. Zur*

Gründungsgeschichte von Euratom 1955–1957 (Baden-Baden: NOMOS, 1983).

31. For the work of the Spaak Committee see Michel Dumoulin, 'Les travaux du Comité Spaak (juillet 1955 – avril 1956)', in Enrico Serra (ed.), *Il rilancio dell'Europa e i trattati di Roma* (Baden-Baden: NOMOS, 1989), pp. 195–210.
32. Comité Intergouvernemental crée par la Conférence de Messine: Rapport de Chefs des Délegation aux Ministres des Affaires Etrangères (Spaak Report), Brussels 1956.
33. Hanns Jürgen Küsters, 'The origins of the EEC Treaty', Serra, *Il rilancio*, pp. 211–38 (219).
34. Milward, *European Rescue*, p. 119.
35. PRO T 234/183 (21 November 1955).

CHAPTER 2   WHAT BUS? THE MESSINA CONFERENCE, 1955

1. PRO CAB 128/29/19th (30 June 1955).
2. PRO CAB 134/1026/33rd (23 August 1955).
3. PRO CAB 134/1029/135 (13 July 1955).
4. PRO CAB 134/1030/201 (24 October 1955).
5. See in particular PRO CAB 134/1044/6 (6 August 1955) and the final report in PRO CAB 134/1030/201 (24 October 1955).
6. PRO CAB 134/1029/135 (13 July 1955).
7. PRO CAB 134/1044/12 (18 August 1955).
8. See in particular PRO CAB 134/1029/135 (13 July 1955).
9. Herbert Schneider, *Großbritanniens Weg nach Europa. Eine Untersuchung über das Verhalten und die Rolle der britischen Handels- und Industrieverbände, Gewerkschaften und Farmerorganisationen zwischen 1955/56 (Spaak-Komitee) und 1961 (EWG-Beitrittsverhandlungen)* (Freiburg: Verlag Rombach, 1968), p. 222.
10. The final MAC report contains an annex with the results of the Industries and Manufactures Department's assessment: PRO CAB 134/1030/201 (24 October 1955).
11. Ibid.
12. PRO CAB 134/1029/136 (14 July 1955).
13. PRO CAB 134/1044/12 (18 August 1955).
14. PRO CAB 134/76/55 (29 June 1955).
15. PRO CAB 134/1030/201 (24 October 1955).
16. PRO CAB 134/1026/35th (2 August 1955).
17. Alec Cairncross, 'The postwar years 1945–1977', in Roderick Floud and Donald MacCloskey (eds), *The Economic History of Britain since 1700. Vol. 2: 1860 to the 1970s* (Cambridge: University Press, 1981), pp. 370–416 (376).
18. PRO CAB 134/1044/12 (18 August 1955).
19. PRO CAB 134/1030/200 (24 October 1955).

20. Anthony Nutting, *Europe Will Not Wait. A Warning and a Way Out* (London: Hollis & Carter, 1960), p. 107.
21. PRO CAB 134/1030/200 (24 October 1955).
22. *Foreign Relations of the United States 1955–1957 (FRUS), Vol. IV: Western European Security and Integration* (Washington, 1986), p. 290.
23. PRO FO 371/116047/204 (2 September 1955).
24. PRO FO 371/116038/1 (14 May 1955).
25. PRO BT 11/5715 (10 November 1955).
26. PRO BT 11/5715 (24 October 1955).
27. PRO CAB 134/889/8th (1 November 1955).
28. PRO CAB 134/1229/11th (11 November 1955).
29. See, for example, Nita Watts to the Economic Adviser, Robert Hall: PRO T 232/433 (14 October 1955).
30. PRO FO 371/116056/369 (December 1955).
31. Anthony Adamthwaite, 'Introduction: The Foreign Office and policy-making', in John W. Young (ed.), *The Foreign Policy of Churchill's Peacetime Administration 1951–1955* (Leicester: University Press, 1988), pp. 1–28 (18).
32. Trend to Clarke: PRO T 234/181 (26 October 1955).
33. PRO FO 371/116039/14 (11 June 1955).
34. PRO CAB 134/889/7th (17 October 1955).
35. PRO CAB 134/889/8th (1 November 1955).
36. PRO T 232/432 (20 September 1955).
37. Harold Macmillan, *Tides of Fortune 1945–1955* (London: Macmillan, 1969), p. 472.
38. See van Loo to Strath: PRO T 232/432 (22 September 1955).
39. PRO FO 371/116048/224 (19 September 1955).
40. HMD (14 December 1955), quoted in Alistair Horne, *Macmillan 1957–1986. Vol. II of the Official Biography* (London: Macmillan, 1989), p. 362.
41. Cf. PRO T 232/431 (29 July 1955).
42. PRO FO 371/116038/1 (14 May 1955).
43. PRO FO 371/116040/52 (29 June 1955).
44. PRO CAB 128/29/19th (30 June 1955).
45. See in connection PRO CAB 134/1026/23rd (28 June 1955), PRO CAB 129/76/55 (29 June 1955), PRO FO 371/116040/61 (1 July 1955).
46. PRO FO 371/116040/39 (22 June 1955); PRO CAB 128/29/19th (30 June 1955).
47. Quoted in Michael Charlton, 'How and why Britain lost the leadership of Europe. "Messina! Messina!" or, the parting of the ways', *Encounter*, Vol. 57, No. 2 (1981), pp. 9–22 (14).
48. See Crookshank to Butler and Macmillan: PRO T 232/432 (21 September 1955) and Macmillan to Butler and Crookshank: PRO T 232/432 (23 September 1955).
49. PRO FO 371/116045/164 (11 August 1955).
50. PRO T 232/431 (29 July 1955), Collier to Nicholls: PRO T 232/431 (10 August).
51. See the remarks by Kirkpatrick and Macmillan on the margins: PRO FO 371/116044/137A (5 August 1955).

52. PRO FO 371/116044/137B (29 August 1955), PRO CAB 134/1026/35th (2 September 1955).

53. Sean Greenwood, *Britain and European Cooperation since 1945* (Oxford: Blackwell, 1992), p. 65.

54. Bretherton to Turnbull: PRO FO 371/116050/281 (10 October 1955).

55. PRO T 234/183 (7 November 1955). The full text of the British statement is contained in PRO FO 371/116055/361 (7 November 1955).

56. PRO CAB 134/1044/8 (9 August 1955).

57. PRO BT 11/5715 (20 September 1955).

58. PRO CAB 129/76/55 Annex B (21 June 1955).

59. PRO CAB 134/1029/146 (30 July 1955).

60. See, for example, PRO T 232/431 (16 June 1955).

61. Cf. PRO FO 371/116045/165 (11 August 1955), PRO FO 371/116046/180 (18 August 1955).

62. PRO CAB 134/1026/26th (11 July 1955).

63. PRO CAB 134/1026/45th (27 October 1955).

64. Quoted in Alistair Horne, *Macmillan 1894–1956. Vol. I of the Official Biography* (London: Macmillan, 1988), p. 363.

65. PRO CAB 134/1226/11th (11 November 1955).

66. Ibid.

67. Dulles to Macmillan: PRO FO 371/116056/380 (12 December 1955).

68. PRO FO 371/116057/390 (31 December 1955).

69. PRO CAB 134/30.I/10th (9 February 1956).

70. Dulles to State Department, quoted in *FRUS*, pp. 367–372.

71. Brentano to Macmillan, quoted in Hanns Jürgen Küsters, *Die Gründung der Europäischen Wirtschaftsgemeinschaft* (Baden-Baden: NOMOS, 1982), p. 211.

72. See Werner Bührer, 'German Industry and European Integration in the 1950s', in Clemens Wurm (ed.), *Western Europe and Germany. The Beginnings of European Integration 1945–1960* (Oxford: Berg, 1995), pp. 87–114.

73. For the Social Democrats see William E. Paterson, *The SPD and European Integration* (Farnborough: Saxon House, 1974).

74. PRO FO 371/121975/3 (23 February 1956).

75. Nutting, p. 89.

76. Coulson to Caccia: PRO FO 371/116038/18 (13 June 1955).

77. PRO CAB 134/1029/199 (24 October 1955).

78. Maudling to Macmillan: PRO FO 371/134498/390 (11 April 1958).

79. Konrad Adenauer, *Erinnerungen. Vol. II: 1955–1959* (Stuttgart: DVA, 1967), pp. 253–5. See also Hans-Peter Schwarz, *Adenauer. Der Staatsmann: 1952–1967* (Stuttgart: DVA, 1991), pp. 288–91.

80. PRO FO 371/116057/384 (15 December 1955).

81. PRO T 234/181 (2 November 1955).

82. See Charlton, 'Messina', p. 20.

83. For Macmillan's role see also Simon Burgess and Geoffrey Edwards, 'The Six plus One: British policy-making and the question of European economic integration, 1955', *International Affairs*, Vol. 64, No. 3 (1988), pp. 393–413 (406).

84. Hoyer Millar to Kirkpatrick: PRO FO 371/116056/369 (2 December 1955).
85. Trend to Clarke: PRO T 234/181 (26 October 1955), PRO CAB 134/1026/45th (27 October 1955).
86. PRO BT 11/5715 (22 October 1955).
87. Trend to Clarke: PRO T 234/181 (26 October 1955).
88. Cf. Bretherton to Thorneycroft: PRO BT 11/5715 (22 October 1955).
89. PRO T 234/183 (19 January 1956).
90. PRO T 234/183 (30 January 1956).
91. See in essence also Anne Deighton, 'Missing the boat. Britain and Europe 1945–1961', *Contemporary Record*, Vol. 3, No. 3 (1990), pp. 15–17. The Brussels talks in 1955 are also interpreted as 'a vital opportunity [that] was missed' in John W. Young, '"The Parting of the Ways"?: Britain, the Messina Conference and the Spaak Committee, June–December 1955', in John W. Young and Michael Dockrill (eds), *British Foreign Policy, 1945–56* (London: Macmillan, 1989), pp. 197–224 (217).
92. HMD (28 February 1956), quoted in Macmillan, *Riding*, p. 56. See also Macmillan to Eden: PRO PREM 11/1337 (3 March 1956).
93. Donald C. Watt, 'Großbritannien und Europa 1951–1959. Die Jahre konservativer Regierung', *Vierteljahreshefte für Zeitgeschichte*, Vol. 28, No. 4 (1980), pp. 389–409 (392/402).
94. Roger Bullen, 'Britain and "Europe" 1950–1957', in Enrico Serra (ed.), *Il rilancio dell'Europa e i trattati di Roma* (Baden-Baden: NOMOS, 1989), pp. 315–38 (334).
95. In a speech at Columbia University on 12 January 1952, quoted in Charlton, 'Messina', p. 16. See also Robert Rhodes James, *Anthony Eden* (London: Weidenfeld & Nicolson, 1986), p. 350.
96. David Sanders, *Losing an Empire, Finding a Role. British Foreign Policy since 1945* (London: Macmillan, 1990), p. 291.
97. William Wallace, *Foreign Policy and the Political Process* (London: Macmillan, 1971), p. 33.
98. Alec Cairncross and Nita Watts, *The Economic Section 1939–1961. A Study in Economic Advising* (London: Routledge, 1989) do not, unfortunately, consider British European policy.
99. See also Bretherton's recollection in Charlton, 'Messina', p. 17.
100. Christopher Coker, 'Dünkirchen und andere britische Mythen', *Europäische Rundschau*, Vol. 19, No. 2 (1991), pp. 107–18 (116).
101. Jeremy Moon, *European Integration in British Politics 1950–1963: A Study of Issue Change* (Aldershot: Gower, 1985), pp. 152–3.
102. Interview with Stephen Blank, quoted in Stephen Blank, *Industry and Government in Britain. The Federation of British Industries in Politics, 1945–65* (Farnborough: Saxon House, 1973), pp. 143.
103. Robert J. Lieber, *British Politics and European Unity. Parties, Elites, and Pressure Groups* (Berkeley: University of California Press, 1970), p. 51.
104. See the letter and statement by the FBI Director General Norman Kipping and the FBI Overseas Director Peter Tennant to Lee: PRO BT 11/5402 (24 February 1956).
105. Cf. *House of Commons Debates*, vol. 554, col. 1209 and vol. 555, col. 1678.

CHAPTER 3   BEST OF ALL WORLDS: THE FREE TRADE AREA PLAN, 1956–7

1. See already Macmillan's and Thorneycroft's initial Cabinet memorandum: PRO CAB 129/82/191 (27 July 1956).
2. PRO T 234/100 (1 February 1956).
3. PRO T 234/183 (6 February 1956).
4. PRO T 234/183 (21 February 1956).
5. PRO T 234/100 (30 January 1956).
6. Lloyd's European policy is only covered briefly in D. R. Thorpe, *Selwyn Lloyd* (London: Cape, 1989), p. 281.
7. PRO FO 371/122024/66 (27 March 1956), PRO CAB 134/1284/64 (18 April 1956).
8. Bretherton to Figgures: PRO T 234/701 (27 January 1956).
9. PRO T 234/101 (29 May 1956).
10. PRO T 234/101 (25 April 1956).
11. Figgures to Clarke: PRO T 234/701 (13 February 1956).
12. See, for example, the protocol of a meeting of the Consultative Committee for Industry: PRO BT 11/5616/48th (29 April 1957).
13. PRO CAB 130/118/GEN 535.
14. Cf. PRO BT 11/5715 (16 May 1956).
15. PRO T 234/183 (21 February 1956).
16. PRO BT 11/5367 (9 November 1955).
17. See in detail Bretherton's early memorandum: PRO BT 11/5367 (26 November 1955).
18. Cf. Clarke's memorandum: PRO T 234/701 (11 February 1956).
19. PRO T 234/100 (13 March 1956).
20. Clarke to Figgures: PRO T 234/701 (13 February 1956).
21. See PRO T 230/395 (November 1955).
22. PRO T 234/100 (13 March 1956).
23. PRO T 234/183 (21 February 1956).
24. See Bretherton's retrospective analysis of the evolution of Plan G within Whitehall: PRO BT 11/5852 (June 1961).
25. Cf. Figgures to Clarke (2 May 1956) and Cohen to Clarke and France (8 May 1956): PRO T 234/101.
26. PRO T 234/101 (31 May 1956).
27. On the origins of Plan G see also Wolfram Kaiser, 'Selbstisolierung in Europa – Die britische Regierung und die Gründung der EWG', in Clemens A. Wurm (ed.), *Wege nach Europa. Wirtschaft und Außenpolitik Großbritanniens im 20. Jahrhundert* (Bochum: Universitätsverlag Dr. N. Brockmeyer, 1992), pp. 125–53 (142–9).
28. PRO BT 11/5715 (10 May 1956).
29. PRO BT 11/5852 (June 1961).
30. PRO BT 11/5715 (22 October 1955).
31. Bretherton to Figgures: PRO T 234/701 (27 January 1956).
32. Meade to Figgures: PRO T 234/701 (24 January 1956).
33. *Manchester Guardian*, 15 February 1956.
34. PRO T 234/701 (15 March 1956).
35. Interview with Cyril Sanders (14 June 1993).

36. Bretherton to Figgures: PRO T 234/701 (27 January 1956).
37. See Bretherton's memorandum for the Clarke Working Group: PRO T 234/101 (4 April 1956).
38. PRO T 234/101 (6 April 1956).
39. PRO CAB 129/82/191 (27 July 1956).
40. PRO CAB 134/1240/87 (20 November 1956).
41. PRO CAB 134/1240/64 (25 October 1956). Cf. Miriam Camps, 'Problems of Freer Trade in Europe', *Political and Economic Planning*, Vol. XXIV, No. 423 (1958), pp. 111–27.
42. PRO CAB 134/1239/13 (16 August 1956).
43. For the evolution of this plan see PRO CAB 129/88/188 (24 August 1957), PRO CAB 128/31.II/62nd (27 August 1957); PRO CAB 129/89/219 (4 October 1957).
44. PRO T 234/101 (31 May 1956).
45. CAB T 234/195 (25 July 1956).
46. See in particular the memorandum by Maudling: PRO CAB 129/93/110 (16 May 1958).
47. De Zulueta to Macmillan: PRO PREM 11/2132 (29 July 1957).
48. See also Thorneycroft's remarks about Plan G in the Economic Policy Committee: PRO CAB 134/1229/15th (1 August 1956).
49. Peter Hennessy, *Whitehall* (London: Secker & Warburg, 1989), p. 162.
50. See Macmillan's press conference about Plan G in October 1956: PRO CAB 134/1240/50 (3 October 1956).
51. Macmillan to Eccles: PRO T 234/196 (12 August 1956).
52. PRO CAB 134/1231/68 (23 August 1956).
53. Cf. PRO BT 11/5716 (25 July 1956).
54. PRO T 234/101 (31 May 1956).
55. ESC Sub-Committee on United Kingdom Initiative in Europe, later renamed ESC Sub-Committee on Closer Economic Association with Europe. See for 1956 PRO CAB 134/1238–40.
56. PRO CAB 129/82/191 (27 July 1956).
57. PRO CAB 129/30.II/65th (14 September 1956), PRO CAB 129/30.II/66th (18 September 1956).
58. PRO CAB 128/30.II/65th (14 September 1956). Interview with Thorneycroft's Principle Private Secretary, Frank Glaves-Smith (19 May 1993).
59. See the meeting of the Economic Policy Committee: PRO CAB 134/1229/16th (5 September 1956).
60. PRO CAB 129/84/256 (6 November 1956).
61. See in particular Butler to Macmillan: PRO PREM 11/2531 (24 August 1957), Home to Macmillan: PRO PREM 11/2531 (25 September 1957).
62. PRO CAB 129/83/207 (7 September 1956).
63. PRO CAB 129/82/172 (9 July 1956), PRO CAB 128/30.II/49th (12 July 1956).
64. Cf. Bretherton's note about the OEEC ministerial meeting: PRO T 234/195 (23 July 1956).
65. PRO CAB 129/83/208 (11 September 1956), PRO CAB 128/30.II/66th (18 September 1956).

66. Cf. Macmillan's report to the Cabinet: PRO CAB 128/30.II/68th (3 October 1956).
67. PRO CAB 134/881/2nd (26 October 1956).
68. PRO BT 11/5402 (13 July 1956).
69. PRO BT 11/5716 (21 September 1956).
70. See the detailed consultations with individual associations of the FBI after the publication of Plan G: PRO BT 258/176, PRO BT 258/229–31 (1956–7), and the demands by the NUM Chairman C. S. Garland in a letter to the new President of the Board of Trade, Eccles: PRO CAB 134/1860/121 (2 April 1957).
71. For the FBI report see PRO CAB 134/1240/74 (31 October 1956).
72. PRO CAB 134/1240/84 (13 November 1956).
73. PRO CAB 134/1240/77 (6 November 1956).
74. Ibid.
75. For the ABCC report see PRO CAB 134/1240/80 (12 November 1956).
76. See also Stephen Blank, *Industry and Government in Britain. The Federation of British Industries in Politics, 1945–65* (Farnborough: Saxon House, 1973), p. 123.
77. See the consultations between Thorneycroft and Hayman, Tennant and Steel of the FBI: PRO BT 11/5716 (21 September 1956).
78. *A Joint Report on the European Free Trade Area* (London: FBI/NUM/ABCC, 1957).
79. Kipping to Lee: PRO BT 11/5402 (24 February 1956).
80. Lee to Kipping: PRO BT 11/5715 (27 February 1956).
81. PRO T 234/720 (17 July 1959, 18 January 1961).
82. For the TUC report see PRO CAB 134/1240/73 (2 November 1956).
83. PRO CAB 134/1857/67 (20 March 1957).
84. See in particular the meeting between Eccles and TUC representatives on 30 March 1957: PRO CAB 134/1860/159. For bilateral consultations between officials and TUC representatives during 1957–8 see PRO T 234/230.
85. For the talks on this matter between the government, the TUC and business associations see PRO BT 241/1115.
86. HMD (5 September 1956), quoted in Harold Macmillan, *Riding the Storm 1956–1959* (London: Macmillan, 1971), p. 82.
87. PRO PREM 11/2679 (29 November 1959).
88. ULB AED (14 September 1956), Avon Papers 20/1/32.
89. PRO CAB 128/30.II/66th (18 September 1956).
90. See also Anthony Seldon, *Churchill's Indian Summer. The Conservative Government, 1951–55* (London: Hodder & Stoughton, 1981), p. 415.
91. Ibid.
92. PRO CAB 129/30.II/65th (14 September 1956).
93. Cf. Peter Clarke, *A Question of Leadership. From Gladstone to Thatcher* (London: Penguin, 1992), p. 223. See also the ironic remarks of Shadow Chancellor Harold Wilson in his memoirs: Harold Wilson, *Memoirs. The Making of a Prime Minister 1916–1964* (London: Weidenfeld & Nicolson, 1986), p. 169.

94. Top Secret and Personal 1957 (18 April 1957), TCL R. A. Butler's Papers G 31.
95. For a critical assessment of Macmillan's internal FTA policy see Richard Lamb, *The Failure of the Eden Government* (London: Sidgwick & Jackson, 1987), p. 97.
96. Thorneycroft to Butler: PRO FO 371/122034/222 (23 August 1956).
97. Beginning with Miriam Camps, *Britain and the European Community 1955–1963* (Oxford: University Press, 1964), p. 509.
98. Cf. Clarke's note: PRO T 234/198 (10 October 1956).

CHAPTER 4   MAKESHIFT SOLUTION: FROM FTA TO EFTA, 1958–9

1. Robert J. Lieber, *British Politics and European Unity. Parties, Elites, and Pressure Groups* (Berkeley: University of California Press, 1970), p. viii.
2. Cf. PRO BT 241/554/12th (12 May 1958).
3. See, for example, PRO BT 241/554/9th (22 January 1958).
4. Butler to Macmillan: PRO PREM 11/2531 (24 August 1957).
5. PRO PREM 11/2827 (6 May 1959).
6. Cf. Stephen Blank, *Industry and Government in Britain. The Federation of British Industries in Politics, 1945–65* (Farnborough: Saxon House, 1973), p. 146.
7. PRO BT 241/554/12th (12 May 1958).
8. Cf. PRO FO 371/134544. See also Derek Urwin, *The Community of Europe. A History of European Integration since 1945*, 2nd edn, (London: Longman, 1995), p. 88 and Miriam Camps, *The European Common Market and Free Trade Area. A Progress Report* (Princeton/NY: Princeton University Press, 1957), p. 22.
9. See the meetings of the CCI: PRO BT 11/5729/55th (27 May 1959), PRO BT 11/5729/56th (29 July 1959) and of the EPB: PRO CAB 134/1813/3rd (1 June 1959).
10. Cf. James Ellison, *Harold Macmillan's Fear of 'Little Europe'. Britain, the Six and the European Free Trade Area*, Discussion Papers on Britain and Europe (Leicester: University of Leicester, 1995), p. 18.
11. For British fears of being sandwiched between West European and Commonwealth economic interests see PRO CAB 134/1835/6th (23 September 1957)
12. Cf. PRO CAB 134/1823/26 (7 May 1960).
13. PRO FO 371/158311/37 (24 February 1961).
14. See in particular the meeting of Commonwealth Economics and Finance Ministers in October 1960: PRO CAB 134/1826/105 (5 October 1960).
15. Reginald Maudling, *Memoirs* (London: Sidgwick & Jackson, 1978), p. 67.
16. Paul-Henri Spaak, *The Continuing Battle: Memoirs of a European, 1936–1966* (London: Weidenfeld & Nicolson, 1971), p. 315.

17. Hans von der Groeben, *Aufbaujahre der Europäischen Gemeinschaft. Das Ringen um den Gemeinsamen Markt und die Politische Union (1958–1966)* (Baden-Baden: NOMOS, 1982), p. 66.
18. Robert Marjolin, *Le Travail d'une Vie. Memoires 1911–1986* (Paris: Laffont, 1986), p. 316.
19. Macmillan to Spaak: PRO FO 371/122035/270 (16 October 1956).
20. Organization for European Economic Cooperation, *Report on the possibility of creating a Free Trade Area in Europe, prepared for the Council of OEEC by a special Working Party* (Paris: OEEC, 1957).
21. *A European Free Trade Area. United Kingdom Memorandum to the OEEC* (London: HMSO, Cmnd. 72, 1957).
22. PRO FO 371/128333/97 (25 January 1957).
23. PRO CAB 129/88/188 (24 August 1957).
24. Cf. PRO CAB 134/1231/75 (3 September 1956).
25. PRO CAB 129/84/256 (6 November 1956).
26. PRO CAB 134/1239/18 (17 August 1956).
27. Cf. Anthony Nutting, *Europe Will Not Wait. A Warning and a Way Out* (London: Hollis & Carter, 1960), p. 91.
28. Serge Bernier, *Relations Politiques Franco-Britanniques (1947–1958)* (Sherbrooke/Quebec: Edition Naaman, 1984), p. 178.
29. PRO FO 371/128339/300 (14 March 1957); PRO FO 371/128351/732 (11 June 1957); PRO FO 371/128354/801 (30 July 1957).
30. PRO FO 371/128365/1086 (21 October 1957).
31. BBC interview with Con O'Neill, quoted in Michael Charlton, 'How (and why) Britain lost the leadership of Europe (II). A last step sideways', *Encounter*, Vol. 57, No. 3 (1981), pp. 22–33 (26).
32. Konrad Adenauer, *Erinnerungen. Band III: 1959–1963* (Stuttgart: DVA, 1968), p. 160.
33. PRO FO 371/128343/495 (3 May 1957).
34. See, for example, the bilateral negotiations between the British and a German delegation under the State-Secretary in the Economics Ministry, Professor Müller-Armack: PRO CAB 134/1866/81+85 (17–18 April 1958).
35. Diplomatically expressed in a roundabout way in Charles de Gaulle, *Mémoires d'espoir. Le renouveau 1958–1962* (Paris: Plon, 1970), p. 190; Konrad Adenauer, *Erinnerungen. Band II: 1955–1959* (Stuttgart: DVA, 1967), p. 433. See also Hans-Peter Schwarz, *Adenauer. Der Staatsmann: 1952–1967* (Stuttgart: DVA, 1991), p. 466 and Daniel Koerfer, *Kampf ums Kanzleramt. Erhard und Adenauer* (Stuttgart: DVA, 1987), p. 206.
36. PRO CAB 129/84/6 (5 January 1957).
37. PRO CAB 128/30.II/3rd (8 January 1957).
38. On the question of a possible WEU nuclear force see also Gustav Schmidt, '"Tying" (West) Germany into the West – But to what? NATO? WEU? The European Community?', in Clemens Wurm (ed.), *Western Europe and Germany. The Beginnings of European Integration 1945–1960* (Oxford: Berg, 1995), pp. 137–74 (156–8).
39. On Macmillan's policy towards the United States after Suez see also Alistair Horne, 'The Macmillan years and afterwards', in W. M. Roger Louis and Hedley Bull (eds), *The 'Special Relationship'. Anglo-American*

Relations since 1945 (Oxford: Clarendon Press, 1986), pp. 87–102 and Christopher John Bartlett, '*The Special Relationship*'. *A Political History of Anglo-American Relations since 1945* (London: Longman, 1992), p. 88.

40. See also Ellison, p. 13.
41. Horne, *Macmillan II*, p. 21.
42. PRO CAB 129/96/27 (20 February 1959).
43. Eccles to Macmillan: PRO PREM 11/2531 (14 July 1958).
44. See already de Zulueta to Macmillan: PRO PREM 11/2532 (3 December 1958).
45. PRO CAB 130/123/GEN 580/4th (5 March 1959).
46. HMD (7 July 1959), quoted in Harold Macmillan, *Pointing the Way 1959–1961* (London: Macmillan, 1972), p. 54.
47. PRO CAB 128/33/30th (7 May 1959).
48. Cf. PRO CAB 130/123/GEN 580/4th (5 March 1959), PRO CAB 128/33/30th (7 May 1959).
49. Donald Maclean, *British Foreign Policy since Suez 1956–1968* (London: Hodder & Stoughton, 1970), p. 19.
50. For the internal acceleration debate within the EEC see in greater detail Camps, *Britain and the European Community*.
51. Of all solutions, the Luns Plan, therefore, was least unattractive for the British. Cf. PRO BT 11/5562 (8 January 1960).
52. PRO CAB 134/1825/61 (12 July 1960).
53. PRO CAB 134/1826/114 (10–12 October 1960).
54. PRO CAB 134/1829/25 (23 February 1961).
55. PRO CAB 134/1240/11 (14 August 1956).
56. Cf., for example, PRO FO 371/128346/567 (10 May 1957).
57. Maudling to Macmillan: PRO PREM 11/2678 (27 November 1959).
58. PRO PREM 11/3002 (19 October 1958).
59. PRO FO 371/150279/278 (11 May 1960).

CHAPTER 5   DUAL APPEASEMENT: TOWARDS THE EEC APPLICATION, 1960–1

1. PRO CAB 129/99/188 (14 December 1959).
2. B. W. E. Alford, *British Economic Performance 1945–1975* (London: Macmillan, 1988), p. 15.
3. Donald Maclean, *British Foreign Policy since Suez 1956–1968* (London: Hodder & Stoughton, 1970), p. 81.
4. Herbert Schneider, *Großbritanniens Weg nach Europa. Eine Untersuchung über das Verhalten und die Rolle der britischen Handels- und Industrieverbände, Gewerkschaften und Farmerorganisationen zwischen 1955/56 (Spaak-Komitee) und 1961 (EWG-Beitrittsverhandlungen)* (Freiburg: Verlag Rombach, 1968), p. 245.
5. *House of Commons Debates*, vol. 645, col. 1653, 3 August 1961.
6. Cf. Alec Cairncross, *The British Economy, since 1945* (Oxford: Blackwell, 1992), p. 142.

7. Interview with the Deputy Under-Secretary of State, Roderick Barclay (28 April 1993).
8. See PRO FO 371/150279/278 (11 May 1960).
9. See also John Turner, *Macmillan* (London: Longman, 1994), p. 217.
10. PRO CAB 134/1819/27 (27 May 1960).
11. PRO CAB 129/102.I/107 (6 July 1960).
12. The influence of Lee and of the Treasury on the reorientation of British policy towards the EEC is, however, exaggerated and domestic pressures outside Whitehall are ignored in Anne Deighton, 'La Grande-Bretagne et la Communauté Économique Européenne (1958–1963)', *Histoire économie et société*, Vol. 13, No. 1 (1994), pp. 113–30.
13. Alec Cairncross, 'The postwar years, 1945–1977', in Roderick Floud and Donald McCloskey (eds), *The Economic History of Britain since 1700. Vol. 2: 1860 to the 1970s* (Cambridge: University Press, 1981), p. 376.
14. Sidney Pollard, *The Wasting of the British Economy. British Economic Policy 1945 to the Present* (London: Croom Helm, 1982), p. 47.
15. PRO CAB 134/1819/27 (27 May 1960).
16. Explicitly in PRO CAB 134/1821/3rd (9 May 1961).
17. See also Michael Pinto-Duschinsky, 'From Macmillan to Home, 1959–1964', in Peter Hennessy and Anthony Seldon (eds), *Ruling Performance. British Governments from Attlee to Thatcher* (Oxford: Blackwell, 1987), pp. 150–85 (151).
18. *House of Commons Debates*, vol. 640, col. 1387, 17 May 1961.
19. PRO CAB 134/1819/27 (27 May 1960). See also PRO CAB 129/102.I/107 (6 July 1960), particularly question 10.
20. PRO CAB 134/1819/27 (27 May 1960).
21. Ibid.
22. PRO CAB 134/1819/7th (16 May 1960).
23. See in particular PRO FO 371/150362/12 (29 June 1960).
24. PRO CAB 134/1819/8th (27 May 1960).
25. PRO CAB 129/102.I/107 (6 July 1960), question 22.
26. Olivier Wormser, Head of Economic Affairs in the French Foreign Ministry and leader of the French delegation in the bilateral talks with Britain at the official level in the first half of 1961.
27. PRO PREM 11/3325 (29 December 1960 – 3 January 1961). On the growing importance of foreign policy considerations see also Joseph Frankel, *British Foreign Policy 1945–1973* (Oxford: University Press, 1975), p. 241.
28. See for example Stephen George, *Britain and European Integration since 1945* (Oxford: Blackwell, 1991), pp. 33/62.
29. See also Macmillan's 'Grand Design': PRO PREM 11/3325 (29 December 1960 – 3 January 1961).
30. See the answers of the Economic Steering (Europe) Committee to Macmillan's questions about British European policy: PRO CAB 129/102.I/107 (6 July 1960), questions 3 and 4.
31. PRO PREM 11/2985 (Autumn 1959).
32. Cf. *House of Commons Debates*, vol. 645, col. 1481, 2 August 1961.

33. For the problem of the domestic presentation of the EEC application see in particular PRO CAB 134/1821/4th (17 May 1961).

34. The Macmillan government's increasing preoccupation with Britain's status rather than its actual influence in international relations and the reasons for this change are discussed in Wolfram Kaiser, '"Das Gesicht wahren": Die Konservativen und die Rolle Großbritanniens in der Welt, 1945–1964', in Hans-Heinrich Jansen and Ursula Lehmkuhl (eds), *Grossbritannien, das Empire und die Welt: Britische Außenpolitik zwischen 'Größe' und 'Selbstbehauptung', 1850–1990* (Bochum: Universitätsverlag Dr. N. Brockmeyer, 1995), pp. 245–61.

35. PRO PREM 11/3325 (29 December 1960 – 3 January 1961).

36. For Churchill's summit diplomacy see in greater detail Klaus Larres, *Politik der Illusionen. Churchill, Eisenhower und die deutsche Frage 1945–1955* (Göttingen/Zurich: Vandenhoeck & Ruprecht, 1995).

37. See also Donald C. Watt, *Succeeding John Bull: America in Britain's Place 1900–1975. A Study of the Anglo-American Relationship and World Politics in the Context of British and American Foreign Policy-Making in the Twentieth Century* (Cambridge: University Press, 1984), pp. 115–6.

38. Konrad Adenauer, *Erinnerungen. Vol. II: 1955–1959* (Stuttgart: DVA, 1967), pp. 468–71; Dwight D. Eisenhower, *The White House Years. Waging Peace 1956–1961* (London: Heinemann, 1965), pp. 402/407. On the importance of domestic electoral considerations for Macmillan's foreign policy see in general Christopher John Bartlett, *British Foreign Policy in the Twentieth Century* (London: Macmillan, 1989), p. 106.

39. See also Peter Hennessy, *Cabinet* (Oxford: Blackwell, 1986), p. 60.

40. Interview with de Zulueta in Michael Charlton, *The Price of Victory* (London: BBC, 1983), p. 237.

41. PRO CAB 129/102.I/107 (6 July 1960); PRO CAB 128/34/41st (13 July 1960).

42. PRO PREM 11/2679 (29 November 1959).

43. On decolonization see John Darwin, *Britain and Decolonisation: The Retreat from Empire in the Post-War World* (London: Macmillan, 1988).

44. At the time of Macmillan's questionnaire the Commonwealth Relations Office was naturally still more attached to the idea that the Commonwealth was the essential pillar of Britain's world power status. See, for example, PRO CAB 129/102.I/107 (6 July 1960), question 18 and annex E. Under the influence of the new, pro-European Commonwealth Secretary Duncan Sandys, the CRO subsequently modified its policy in view of the crisis over South African membership and merely insisted that essential Commonwealth interests should be safeguarded in any future negotiations with the EEC.

45. PRO PREM 11/2986 (5 January 1960); Lloyd to Macmillan: ibid. (1 February 1960).

46. PRO PREM 11/2879 (8–9 December 1959).

47. PRO PREM 11/2985 (Autumn 1959).

48. Cf. William Wallace, *The Foreign Policy Process in Britain* (London: Royal Institute of International Affairs, 1975), p. 78.

49. PRO CAB 129/102.I/107 (6 July 1960).
50. Jackling to Home: PRO FO 371/150364/56 (28 August 1960).
51. De Zulueta wrote to Macmillan: 'Its conclusions are broadly ones that you had already reached.' De Zulueta to Macmillan: PRO PREM 11/2985 (Autumn 1959).
52. PRO PREM 11/2679 (29 November 1959).
53. HMD (9 July 1960), quoted in Alistair Horne, *Macmillan 1957–1986. Vol. II of the Official Biography* (London: Macmillan, 1989), p. 256.
54. CAC Duncan Edwin Duncan-Sandys' Papers 9/3/22 (29 January 1952).
55. For an introduction to Anglo-American nuclear cooperation see Margaret Gowing, 'Nuclear Weapons and the "Special Relationship"', in W. M. Roger Louis and Hedley Bull (eds), *The 'Special Relationship'. Anglo-American Relations since 1945* (Oxford: University Press, 1986), pp. 117–128; for British nuclear policy see Lawrence Freedman, *Britain and Nuclear Weapons* (London: Macmillan, 1990).
56. David Dimbleby and David Reynolds, *An Ocean Apart. The Relationship between Britain and America in the Twentieth Century* (London: BBC, 1988), p. 225.
57. Michael Dockrill, *British Defence since 1945* (Oxford: Blackwell, 1988), pp. 72–4; Freedman, pp. 8–10.
58. Cf. Arthur M. Schlesinger, *A Thousand Days. John F. Kennedy in the White House* (London: André Deutsch, 1965), p. 734.
59. See ibid., p. 724; George Ball, *The Past Has Another Pattern. Memoirs* (New York/London: Norton, 1982), p. 261.
60. Schlesinger, p. 723.
61. HMD (1 December 1960).
62. See also Gustav Schmidt, 'Die politischen und die sicherheitspolitischen Dimensionen der britischen Europapolitik 1955/56–1963/64', in Gustav Schmidt (ed.), *Grossbritannien und Europa – Grossbritannien in Europa* (Bochum: Universitätsverlag Dr. N. Brockmeyer, 1989), pp. 169–252 (179).
63. See in particular PRO CAB 128/35.I/24th (26 April 1961).
64. PRO CAB 134/1821/4th (17 May 1961).
65. See also Robert Holland, *The Pursuit of Greatness. Britain and the World Role, 1900–1970* (London: Fontana, 1991), pp. 359–60.
66. PRO PREM 11/3311 (6 April 1961).
67. The transatlantic character of the first British EEC application is stressed in Wolfram Kaiser, 'To join, or not to join: the "Appeasement" policy of Britain's first EEC application', in Brian Brivati and Harriet Jones (eds), *From Reconstruction to Integration. Britain and Europe since 1945* (Leicester: University Press, 1993), pp. 144–56.
68. PRO FO 371/158162/45 (30 March 1961).
69. PRO CAB 134/1854/4th (25 April 1961).
70. PRO FO 371/158162/45 (30 March 1961).
71. Ibid.
72. PRO FO 371/158161/34 (16 March 1961).
73. See, for example, *Daily Telegraph*, 29 April 1961.

74. For example, when talking to Heath in May 1961: PRO FO 371/158163/79 (18 May 1961).
75. On the European policy of the Kennedy government see Pascaline Winand, *Eisenhower, Kennedy, and the United States of Europe* (New York: St. Martin's Press, 1993), especially Chapter Six.
76. In a BBC interview, quoted in Charlton, *The Price*, p. 304.
77. PRO CAB 128/34/41st (13 July 1960).
78. In essence, this is still argued in Deighton, *Missing*, p. 17 as well as in Bernard Porter, *Britain, Europe and the World 1850–1986: Delusions of Grandeur*, 2nd edn, (London: Allen & Unwin, 1987), p. 124. In contrast, the degree of continuity in official thinking on British foreign policy goals during 1944–60 is emphasized in John W. Young, 'British Officials and European Integration, 1944–60', in Anne Deighton (ed.), *Building Postwar Europe. National Decision-Makers and European Institutions, 1948–63* (London: Macmillan, 1995), pp. 87–106.
79. David Sanders, *Losing an Empire, Finding a Role. British Foreign Policy since 1945* (London: Macmillan, 1990), pp. 136/156.
80. PRO PREM 11/3132 (21 December 1959).
81. For the balance between political and economic motives see also the BBC interview with Heath, quoted in Charlton, *The Price*, p. 234.
82. Cf. PRO CAB 128/34/41st (13 July 1960).
83. *House of Commons Debates*, vol. 627, col. 1099, 25 July 1960.
84. Cf. Miriam Camps, *Britain and the European Community, 1955–1963* (Oxford: University Press, 1964), p. 289.
85. *Neue Züricher Zeitung*, 4 June 1960.
86. Heath to Macmillan: PRO FO 371/158264/12 (7 February 1961).
87. PRO CAB 134/1821/2nd (14 March 1961).
88. The detailed study 'The Implications of Signing the Treaty of Rome' is summarized in PRO CAB 134/1821/4 (26 April 1961).
89. Kilmuir to Heath: PRO FO 371/150369/133 (14 December 1960).
90. PRO CAB 134/1821/6 (26 April 1961). See PRO CAB 129/102.I/107 (6 July 1960), questions 19–21 and Annex F.
91. Ibid.
92. For the political significance of the Commonwealth and British agriculture see also Macmillan's remarks in the ministerial committee: PRO CAB 134/1821/3rd (9 May 1961).
93. The consequences of British EEC entry for the Commonwealth are discussed in detail in PRO CAB 134/1821/18 (12 June 1961); see also PRO CAB 134/1821/17 (Spring 1961).
94. On the especially precarious position of New Zealand see the 1960 Lee Committee report in PRO CAB 129/102.I/107 (6 July 1960), in particular Annex C.
95. PRO CAB 134/1821/18 (12 June 1961).
96. The political consequences of British EEC entry for the Commonwealth are discussed in greater detail in PRO CAB 134/1821/4 (26 April 1961).
97. The reports of ministers on their talks with Commonwealth governments were discussed by ministers in mid-July 1961: PRO CAB 134/1821/5th (19 July 1961).

98. But see the differentiated analysis in PRO CAB 129/102.I/107 (6 July 1960), questions 13–15.

99. See for greater detail the study 'The Common Market and United Kingdom Food and Agriculture': PRO CAB 134/1821/13–14 (12 May 1961) and Soames' earlier statement in the Cabinet: PRO CAB 128/35.I/24th (26 April 1961). For the policy-making process within the Ministry of Agriculture, Fisheries and Food see in particular PRO MAF 255/961 (15 May 1961) and PRO MAF 255/961 (5 June 1961).

100. Cf. PRO CAB 134/1821/13–14 (12 May 1961) and the discussion in the ministerial committee: PRO CAB 134/1821/4th (17 May 1961). Particularly revealing is the discussion between Heath and Soames on 25 January 1961, which was recorded by the Deputy Secretary in the Ministry of Agriculture, Eric Roll: PRO MAF 155/430 (6 February). See also the BBC interviews with Soames and Roll, quoted in Charlton, *The Price*, pp. 242/252.

101. Soames to Butler: TCL R.A. Butler's Papers F 123 (31 July 1961).

102. PRO CAB 129/102.I/107 (6 July 1960), question 15.

103. Cf. Eric Roll, *Crowded Hours* (London: Faber, 1985), p. 102.

104. PRO CAB 134/1821/13 (12 May 1961).

105. Winnifrith to Soames: PRO MAF 255/430 (7 September 1960).

106. See already PRO MAF 255/430 (29 June 1960).

107. See in particular Butler to Macmillan: TCL R.A. Butler's Papers F 123 (25 July 1961) as well as the BBC interview with Butler, quoted in Charlton, *The Price*, p. 245. See also Roll, p. 107.

108. PRO CAB 128/35.I/22nd (18 April 1961) and PRO CAB 128/35.I/24th (26 April 1961).

109. *Daily Telegraph*, 29 April 1961. See also Butler to Macmillan: PRO PREM 11/3554 (29 April 1961).

110. PRO CAB 134/1821/21 (18 June 1961). See also the BBC interview with Soames, quoted in Charlton, *The Price*, p. 255.

111. PRO CAB 128/35.II/42nd (21 July 1961).

112. HMD (21 August 1962).

113. *House of Commons Debates*, vol. 645, col. 1481, 2–3 August 1961. Macmillan had already announced his government's intention to apply for full membership on 31 July 1961. Cf. *House of Commons Debates*, vol. 645, col. 928 (31 July 1961).

114. Jeremy Moon, *European Integration in British Politics 1950–1963: A Study of Issue Change* (Aldershot: Gower, 1985), p. 155.

115. For the different motivations see in particular the meetings of the Conservative Parliamentary Foreign Affairs Committee: BLO CPA CRD 2/34/2–4, especially those on 25 May 1960, 22 June 1960 and 22 March 1961.

116. Cf. Nigel Ashford, *The Conservative Party and European Integration 1945–1975* (University of Warwick: PhD thesis, 1983), pp. 102–4.

117. Conservative Central Office to Heath: PRO FO 371/158267/70 and 80 (Spring 1961).

118. Ronald Butt, 'The Common Market and Conservative Party politics, 1961–2', *Government and Opposition*, Vol. 2, No. 3 (1967), pp. 372–86 (383). For internal opposition to EEC entry see also David Dutton,

'Anticipating Maastricht: The Conservative Party and Britain's first application to join the European Community', *Contemporary Record*, Vol. 7, No. 3 (1993), pp. 522–40.

119. Examples are collected in Ashford, p. 150.
120. HMD (5 August 1961), quoted in Harold Macmillan, *At the End of the Day 1961–1963* (London: Macmillan, 1973), p. 26.
121. For the meetings of the Agricultural Policy Committee see BLO CPA CRD 2/11/12.
122. Hurd to Butler: BLO CPA CRD 2/11/12 (21 July 1961).
123. See also the meetings of the Parliamentary Agricultural Committee: BLO CPA CRD 1/11/9, particularly those on 5 July 1960, 16 May 1961 and 31 July 1961.
124. BLO CPA CCO 500/31/2.
125. Barclay to Heath: PRO FO 371/158277/225 (18 July 1961). See also PRO FO 371/158270/131 (24 May 1961).
126. For the question of a party political advantage see, for example, the interview with the Colonial Secretary (1959–61) and Leader of the House of Commons (1961–3), Ian Macleod, quoted in Ashford, p. 139; see also the discussion in the Parliamentary Foreign Affairs Committee: BLO CPA CRD 2/34/4 (22 March 1961).
127. On Labour and European integration see Michael Newman, *Socialism and European Unity. The Dilemma of the Left in Britain and France* (London: Junction Books, 1983).
128. PRO FO 371/158269/102 (1 May 1961).
129. Cf. Clemens A. Wurm, 'Sozialisten und europäische Integration: Die britische Labour Party 1945–1984', *Geschichte in Wissenschaft und Unterricht*, Vol. 38, No. 5 (1987), pp. 280–95 (284).
130. *House of Commons Debates*, vol. 645, col. 1590, 2 August 1961.
131. See also Robert J. Lieber, *British Politics and European Unity. Parties, Elites, and Pressure Groups* (Berkeley: University of California Press, 1970), p. 167.
132. Cf. Newman, p. 163.
133. *House of Commons Debates*, vol. 645, col. 1494, 2 August 1961.
134. Quoted in David Butler and Anthony King, *The British General Election of 1964* (London: Macmillan, 1965), p. 79.
135. Roy Jenkins, *A Life at the Centre* (London: Pan/Macmillan, 1991), p. 324.
136. Moon, p. 205.
137. Cf. Gabriel A. Almond and Sidney Verba, *The Civic Culture. Political Attitudes and Democracy in Five Nations* (Princeton/NY: University Press, 1963), p. 315.
138. Cf. in particular Heath to Macmillan: PRO FO 371/158264/12 (7 February 1961).
139. Macmillan to Lloyd: PRO PREM 11/2679 (22 October 1959).
140. Macmillan to Lloyd and Heathcoat-Amory: PRO PREM 11/2315 (24 June 1958). See also PRO PREM 11/3133 (4 April 1960).
141. Macmillan to Lloyd: PRO PREM 11/2678 (22 October 1959).
142. PRO PREM 11/2328 (8 October 1958). For the evolution of British policy towards the Federal Republic see also Wolfram Kaiser: 'Wie

nach Austerlitz? London–Bonn–Paris und die britische EWG-Politik bis 1961', *Integration*, Vol. 16, No. 1 (1993), pp. 19–32 (26–7).

143. Macmillan to Adenauer: PRO PREM 11/2706 (25 October 1958).
144. PRO PREM 11/2993 (3 August 1960).
145. Macmillan to Lloyd: PRO FO 371/134545/3 (15 October 1958).
146. PRO PREM 11/3334 (16 September 1960).
147. Ibid.
148. ULB Avon Papers 23/3/18 (1 May 1968).
149. Adenauer to Heuss (20 April 1960), quoted in Daniel Koerfer, *Kampf ums Kanzleramt. Erhard und Adenauer* (Stuttgart: DVA, 1987), p. 399.
150. PRO PREM 11/2993 (10 August 1960).
151. On Anglo-German relations see also Sabine Huth, 'Anglo-German relations 1958–59: The postwar turning point?', *Diplomacy and Statecraft*, Vol. 6, No. 3 (1995), pp. 787–808.
152. PRO PREM 11/2676 (12–13 March 1959).
153. Cf. Dockrill, p. 65.
154. See in detail Wolfram Kaiser, 'Money, money, money. The economics and politics of the stationing costs, 1955–1965', in Gustav Schmidt (ed.), *Zwischen Bündnissicherung und privilegierter Partnerschaft: Die deutsch-britischen Beziehungen und die Vereinigten Staaten von Amerika, 1955–1963* (Bochum: Universitätsverlag Dr. N. Brockmeyer, 1995), pp. 1–31.
155. HMD (23 February 1961), quoted in Harold Macmillan, *Pointing the Way 1959–61* (London: Macmillan, 1972), p. 327.
156. HMD (28 May 1959), quoted in Macmillan, *Pointing*, p. 64.
157. Steel to Macmillan: PRO PREM 11/2706 (27 June 1959).
158. Macmillan to Lloyd: PRO PREM 11/2679 (22 October 1959).
159. See for example Philip G. Cerny, *The Politics of Grandeur. Ideological Aspects of de Gaulle's Foreign Policy* (Cambridge: University Press, 1980).
160. Wilfried Loth, 'De Gaulle und Europa. Eine Revision', *Historische Zeitschrift*, Vol. 253, No. 3 (1991), pp. 629–60.
161. Macmillan to Lloyd: PRO PREM 11/2679 (22 October 1959).
162. Lloyd to Macmillan: PRO PREM 11/2998 (15 February 1960).
163. Macmillan to Eisenhower: PRO PREM 11/2998 (17 February 1960).
164. Amery to Lennox-Boyd and Macmillan: PREM 11/2696 (December 1958).
165. PRO PREM 11/2679 (29 November 1959).
166. For French nuclear policy see Jean Lacouture, *De Gaulle. The Ruler 1945–1970* (London: Harvill, 1991), pp. 413–33.
167. PRO PREM 11/2998 (12–13 March 1960).
168. Dixon to Foreign Office: PRO PREM 11/3322 (21 January 1961). The former French Foreign Minister Couve de Murville has since hinted in his memoirs that these talks had been intended as a platform for a possible Anglo-French nuclear programme. See Maurice Couve de Murville, *Une Politique Étrangère 1958–1969* (Paris: Plon, 1971), p. 397.
169. Cf. Macmillan to de Zulueta: PRO PREM 11/3131 (22 August 1960); PRO PREM 11/3322 (27–9 January 1961); de Zulueta to Macmillan: PRO PREM 11/3553 (4 February 1961).
170. PRO PREM 11/3325 (29 December 1960 – 3 January 1961).

171. HMD (29 January 1961), quoted in Macmillan, *Pointing*, p. 327.
172. The link between the European and defence issues is examined in detail in Wolfram Kaiser, 'The Bomb and Europe. Britain, France, and the EEC entry negotiations, 1961–63', *Journal of European Integration History*, Vol. 1, No. 1 (1995), pp. 65–85. See also Simona Toschi, 'Washington–London–Paris. An untenable Triangle (1960–1963)', *Journal of European Integration History*, Vol. 1, No. 2 (1995), pp. 81–109.
173. PRO PREM 11/3554 (6 April 1961).
174. Ibid.
175. Caccia to Hoyer Millar and Macmillan: PRO PREM 11/3326 (30 January 1961).
176. Kennedy to Macmillan: PRO PREM 11/3319 (8 May 1961).
177. Caccia to Macmillan: PRO PREM 11/3319 (5 May 1961).
178. Caccia to Macmillan: PRO PREM 11/3319 (12 May 1961).
179. Macmillan to Kennedy. PRO PREM 11/3311 (15 May 1961).
180. Kennedy to Macmillan: PRO PREM 11/3311 (22 May 1961).
181. JFKL Orals, Bundy, quoted in Horne, *Macmillan II*, p. 439.
182. De Zulueta to Macmillan: PRO PREM 11/3709 (24 June 1962).
183. On the 'culture of dependency' in Anglo-American relations after Suez see also Kenneth O. Morgan, *The People's Peace. British History 1945–1990* (Oxford: University Press, 1992), p. 168.
184. Thorneycroft to Macmillan: PRO FO 371/163516/24 (24 October 1962).
185. PRO FO 371/163516/23 (17 October 1962).
186. See Macmillan's meeting with Kennedy: PRO PREM 11/3783 (28 April 1962).
187. Ormsby-Gore to Macmillan: PRO PREM 11/3712 (17 May 1962).
188. Ormsby-Gore to Foreign Office: PRO PREM 11/3712 (11 September 1962).
189. PRO PREM 11/3712 (12 September 1962).
190. Thorneycroft to Macmillan: PRO FO 371/163516/24 (24 October 1962).
191. De Zulueta to Macmillan: PRO PREM 11/3712 (18 October 1962).
192. See in particular de Zulueta to Caccia: PRO PREM 11/3255 (29 April 1961). ·
193. Kennedy to Macmillan: PRO PREM 11/3319 (8 May 1961).
194. See in particular Shuckburgh to Macmillan: PREM 11/3325 (26 December 1960).
195. De Zulueta to Macmillan: PRO PREM 11/3325 (17 January 1961).
196. Macmillan to Caccia: PRO PREM 11/3319 (9 May 1961).
197. HMD (15 June 1961), quoted in Macmillan, *Pointing*, p. 374. See also HMD (22 July 1961), quoted in Macmillan, *At the End of the Day*, p. 17.
198. PRO PREM 11/3557 (18 June 1961).
199. PRO CAB 128/35.I/24th (26 April 1961).
200. PRO CAB 129/102.I/107 (6 July 1960).
201. PRO CAB 128/35.I/30th (6 July 1961).
202. HMD (11 June 1961).
203. Dixon to Heath: PRO PREM 11/3557 (14 July 1961).
204. PRO PREM 11/3559 (25 July 1961).

205. Cf. Richard Lamb, *The Macmillan Years. The Emerging Truth* (London: John Murray, 1995), pp. 150–1.
206. HMD (29 November 1961), quoted in Macmillan, *Pointing*, p. 428.
207. HMD (11 June 1961).
208. *House of Commons Debates*, vol. 645, cols. 935 and 938, 31 July 1961.
209. Wallace, *The Foreign Policy Process*, p. 100.
210. Ibid.
211. For the development of press opinion see Moon, p. 198.
212. See also Wallace, *The Foreign Policy Process*, p. 81.
213. PRO FO 371/158269/108 (4 May 1961).
214. Interview with Edward Heath (1 April 1993).
215. Robinson to Heath: PRO FO 371/158274/186 (28 June 1961).
216. Cf. Kipping to Heath: PRO FO 371/158277/222 (13 July 1961); Federation of British Industries, *British Industry and Europe* (London: FBI, 1961).
217. Cf. PRO FO 371/158277/222 (13 July 1961), in particular the hand-written remarks on the margins by Robinson (25 July 1961) and Barclay (27 July 1961).
218. Ashford, p. 186.
219. PRO MAF 255/430 (30 June 1960).
220. PRO MAF 255/961/42th (15 May 1961).
221. Hutchinson to Home: PRO FO 371/158274/189 (28 June 1961).
222. Cf. also Brown to Barclay: PRO FO 371/158278/236 (21 July 1961).
223. PRO CAB 134/1815/6th (4 July 1960).
224. Cf. Lieber, p. 106.
225. Cf. HMD (26–7 April 1961).

CHAPTER 6   FAILURE, YET SUCCESS: THE EEC ENTRY NEGOTIATIONS, 1961–3

1. On the role of the Commission during the negotiations see Piers Ludlow, *Influence and vulnerability: the role of the EEC Commission in the enlargement negotiations*, European University Institute DOC 23 (1994).
2. PRO FO 371/158162/52 (14 April 1961).
3. Krag to Home: PRO FO 371/158188/70 (14 April 1961).
4. PRO PREM 11/3555 (26 May 1961).
5. Ibid.
6. Cf. PRO FO 371/158188/61 (29 March 1961).
7. See Dermot Keogh, *Ireland and Europe 1919–1989: A Diplomatic and Political History* (Cork: University Press, 1990), pp. 232–3.
8. *Irish Independent*, 26 January 1962.
9. PRO FO 371/164771/4 (4 February 1962). See also the meeting between Macmillan and Lemass: PRO PREM 11/4320 (19 March 1963).
10. Caccia (Washington) to Foreign Office: PRO PREM 11/3554 (3 May 1961).
11. Kennedy to Macmillan: PRO PREM 11/3555 (22 May 1961).

12. On the negotiations over agriculture see in greater detail Piers Ludlow, 'A Problem of Trust: British agriculture and the Brussels negotiations', unpublished paper presented to the Cambridge University Centre for International Studies/European University Institute conference, 28 June 1993.
13. Cf. the interview with Hallstein in *The Observer*, 4 March 1963.
14. PRO CAB 134/1821/3rd (9 May 1961).
15. PRO FO 371/158316/125 (21 May 1961); PRO PREM 11/3556 (12 June 1961).
16. Macmillan to Menzies and Holyoake: PRO FO 371/158163/61 (15 April 1961).
17. PRO CAB 134/1821/5th (19 July 1961).
18. PRO CAB 128/35.II/42nd (21 July 1961).
19. See the statements by the Canadian representatives at the meeting of Commonwealth economic and finance ministers in October 1960: PRO CAB 134/1826/105 (5 October 1960); see also PRO CAB 134/1821/5th (9 July 1961).
20. Menzies to Macmillan: PRO PREM 11/3556 (30 May 1961).
21. Cf. PRO CAB 129/106/111 (21 July 1961).
22. PRO FO 371/158312/47 (10 May 1961).
23. Holyoake to Macmillan: PRO FO 371/158312/44 (27 April 1961); PRO PREM 11/3557 (22 June 1961).
24. PRO CAB 129/106/111 (21 July 1961).
25. PRO CAB 129/106/104 (18 July 1961).
26. PRO CAB 129/105/96 (11 July 1961).
27. PRO CAB 129/106/103 (18 July 1961).
28. PRO CAB 129/106/108 (19 July 1961).
29. See, for example, the report by Sandys: PRO CAB 129/106/111 (21 July 1961); PRO FO 371/158312/43 (21 April 1961).
30. PRO FO 371/158313/65 (2 June 1961).
31. Quoted in Dennis Austin, 'Regional associations and the Commonwealth', in W. B. Hamilton et al. (eds), *A Decade of the Commonwealth 1955–1964* (Durham, NC: Duke University Press, 1966), pp. 325–48 (325).
32. Cf. Ludlow, 'A Problem of Trust'.
33. Too much is made of the negative effect of the initial maximalist British demands over agriculture on the negotiations in Anne Deighton and Piers Ludlow, '"A conditional application": British management of the first attempt to seek membership of the EEC, 1961–3', in Anne Deighton (ed.), *Building Postwar Europe. National Decision-Makers and European Institutions, 1948–63* (London: Macmillan, 1995), pp. 107–26.
34. See the remarks by Roger Lavelle, Special Assistant to Edward Heath during the negotiations, at the conference 'The Brussels Breakdown: Europe divided or saved?' at Cambridge in June 1993.
35. See Wilfried Loth, 'De Gaulle und Europa. Eine Revision', *Historische Zeitschrift*, Vol. 253, No. 3 (1991), pp. 629–60. The importance of the nuclear issue for de Gaulle is also stressed in Françoise de Serre, 'De Gaulle et la Candidature Britannique aux Communautés

Européennes', *Histoire économie et société*, Vol. 13, No. 1 (1994), pp. 132–42.

36. PRO PREM 11/3792 (19 April 1962).
37. PRO PREM 11/3775 (9 May 1962).
38. PRO PREM 11/3712 (3 June 1962).
39. PRO PREM 11/3712 (4 July 1962).
40. In a conversation with Walter Lippman. Cf. UK Washington Embassy to Lee: PRO PREM 11/3775 (15 March 1962).
41. PRO CAB 129/84/6 (5 January 1957).
42. See also Alistair Horne, *Macmillan 1957–1986. Vol. II of the Official Biography* (London: Macmillan, 1989), p. 439.
43. Watkinson to Macmillan: PRO PREM 11/3712 (12 April 1962). See also Macmillan's remarks to de Courcel: PRO PREM 11/3775 (9 May 1962).
44. PRO PREM 11/3775 (3 June 1962).
45. Jean Lacouture, *De Gaulle. The Ruler 1945–1970* (London: Harvill, 1991), p. 336.
46. De Zulueta to Macmillan: PRO PREM 11/3557 (18 June 1961).
47. PRO PREM 11/3783 (28 April 1962).
48. Ibid.
49. PRO PREM 11/3790 (14 July 1962).
50. Dixon to Home and Macmillan: PRO PREM 11/3775 (22 May 1962); Dixon to Foreign Office: PRO FO 371/164839/142 (1 October 1962).
51. Dixon to Home and Macmillan: PRO PREM 11/3775 (22 May 1962). See also Roll to Lee: PRO PREM 11/3775 (10 May 1962).
52. See in connection Dixon to Foreign Office: PRO PREM 11/3775 (23 May 1962); Home to Macmillan: PRO PREM 11/3712 (13 July 1962); de Zulueta to Macmillan: PRO PREM 11/3712 (6 September 1962); de Zulueta to Macmillan: PRO PREM 11/3712 (7 December 1962).
53. de Zulueta to Macmillan: PRO PREM 11/3712 (7 December 1962). See the attached report on 'Considerations affecting possible Anglo-French nuclear collaboration in the military field'.
54. Quoted in Lacouture, p. 358.
55. PRO PREM 11/3338 (16 November 1961).
56. PRO FO 371/164832/2 (12 December 1961).
57. PRO PREM 11/3775 (2–3 June 1962).
58. Ibid.
59. HMD (29 November 1961), quoted in Harold Macmillan, *Pointing the Way 1959–1961* (London: Macmillan, 1972), p. 428.
60. PRO PREM 11/3775 (19 May 1962).
61. Charles de Gaulle, *Mémoires d'espoir. Le renouveau 1958–1962* (Paris: Plon, 1970), p. 182.
62. Maurice Couve de Murville, *Une Politique Étrangère 1958–1969* (Paris: Plon, 1971), pp. 100–1.
63. PRO PREM 11/3783 (28 April 1962).
64. PRO PREM 11/3775 (2–3 June 1962).
65. Ibid.

66. Lacouture, p. 345.
67. Dixon to Home and Macmillan: PRO PREM 11/3775 (22 May 1962).
68. HMD (28 January 1963), quoted in Horne, *Macmillan II*, p. 427.
69. See also Christopher Hill, 'Public opinion and British Foreign Policy since 1945: Research in Progress?', *Millennium. Journal of International Studies*, Vol. 10, No. 1 (1981), pp. 53–62 (57).
70. See, for example, Hallstein's speech to the European Parliament on 5 February 1963, in *Débats de l'Assemblée Parlementaire Européenne 1962–3*, Vol. 2, pp. 25–32.
71. HMD (4 February 1963).
72. *Svenska Dagbladet*, 5 March 1963, quoted in Cartledge (Stockholm) to Foreign Office: PRO FO 371/172022/17 (12 March 1963).
73. Baker (EFTA Geneva) to Foreign Office: PRO FO 371/171328/40 (15 March 1963).
74. Heath (Lisbon) to Foreign Office: PRO FO 371/171330/79 (11 May 1963).

CHAPTER 7   EPILOGUE: BRITAIN AND EUROPEAN INTEGRATION, 1963–96

1. For example, in Simon Bulmer, 'Britain and European integration: of sovereignty, slow adaptation, and semi-detachment', in Stephen George (ed.), *Britain and the European Community. The Politics of Semi-Detachment* (Oxford: Clarendon Press, 1992), pp. 1–29 (8–10).
2. See Nigel Ashford, 'The political parties', in Stephen George (ed.), *Britain and the European Community. The Politics of Semi-Detachment* (Oxford: Clarendon Press, 1992), pp. 119–48 (139–40).
3. According to the pioneering, if controversial, comparative study of the political cultures of five industrialized nations by Gabriel A. Almond and Sidney Verba, *The Civic Culture. Political Attitudes and Democracy in Five Nations* (Princeton, NJ: University Press, 1963), p. 315. Here, Britain still appears as a model democracy with an adequate mix of 'subject' and 'participant' roles. For a more critical appreciation see Dennis Kavanagh, 'Political culture in Britain: the decline of the civic culture', in Gabriel A. Almond and Sidney Verba (eds), *The Civic Culture Revisited* (London: Sage, 1989), pp. 124–76.
4. Jim Bulpitt, 'Conservative leaders and the "Euro-ratchet": five doses of scepticism', *Political Quarterly*, Vol. 63, No. 3 (1992), pp. 258–75 (265).
5. William E. Paterson, 'Britain and the European Union revisited: some unanswered questions', *Scottish Affair*, Vol. 9 (1994), pp. 1–12 (6).
6. *House of Commons Debates*, vol. 627, col. 1111, 25 July 1960.
7. See the fascinating discussion between George Bush, Mikhail Gorbachev, François Mitterrand and Thatcher about their policies towards German unification in 1989–90, published in *Die Zeit*, 8 March 1996 – originally published in the *Los Angeles Times*.

8. On Edward Heath's European policy see also Christopher Lord, *British Entry to the European Community under the Heath Government of 1970–4* (Aldershot: Dartmouth, 1993) and John Campbell, *Edward Heath* (London: Pimlico, 1994), Part Four, Chapters 17 and 20.

9. Willy Brandt, *People in Politics, 1960–75* (London: Collins, 1978), p. 161.

10. Richard Crossman, *Diaries of a Cabinet Minister* (London: Methuen, 1979), pp. 159–61.

11. Tony Benn, *Office Without Power* (London: Hutchinson, 1988), p. 194. For a scathing but nonetheless differentiated analysis of the assumption of a natural British leadership role see Christopher Coker, *Who Only England Know. The Conservatives and Foreign Policy* (London: Alliance Publishers, 1990).

12. *House of Commons Debates*, vol. 643, col. 546, 28 June 1961.

13. Christopher Lord, 'Sovereign or confused? The "great debate" about British entry to the European Community 20 years on', *Journal of Common Market Studies*, Vol. 30, No. 4 (1992), pp. 419–36 (420–1).

14. Ibid., p. 421.

15. National Union of Conservative and Unionist Associations, 81st Annual Conference, Llandudno (10–13 October 1962), p. 53.

16. For overviews of the Labour Party and European integration see William E. Paterson et al., *The European Policies of Labour and Conservative Party in Great Britain* (Sankt Augustin: Interne Studien Nr. 109 der Konrad-Adenauer-Stiftung, 1995), pp. 9–60 and Andrew Geddes, 'Labour and the European Community 1973–93: Pro-Europeanism, "Europeanisation" and their implications', *Contemporary Record*, Vol. 8, No. 2 (1994), pp. 370–80.

17. PRO PREM 11/3132 (March 1960).

18. Cf. Hugo Young, *One of Us. A Biography of Margaret Thatcher* (London: Macmillan, 1989), p. 184.

19. PRO T 234/100 (1 February 1956); Harold Macmillan, *Riding the Storm 1956–1959* (London: Macmillan, 1971), p. 74.

20. Margaret Thatcher, *The Downing Street Years* (London: HarperCollins, 1993), pp. 790–6.

21. See, for example, Thatcher's Bruges speech: Margaret Thatcher, *Britain and Europe* (London: Conservative Political Centre, 1989).

22. PRO PREM 11/2679 (29 November 1959).

23. Cf. *The Times*, 20 October 1995, 13 January 1996.

24. Thatcher, *Downing Street Years*, p. 81.

25. 'Tories line up to play anti-European card', *The Guardian*, 11 October 1995.

26. Cf. T. F. Lindsay and Michael Harrington, *The Conservative Party 1918–1979* (London: Macmillan, 1979), p. 13.

27. For an analysis of the views on Europe in the Conservative parliamentary party see John Garry, 'The British Conservative Party: divisions over European policy', *West European Politics*, Vol. 18, No. 4 (1995), pp. 170–89 and David Baker et al., 'Backbench Conservative attitudes to Europe', *The Political Quarterly*, Vol. 66, No. 2 (1995), pp. 221–33.

28. See also Andrew Scott, John Peterson and David Millar, 'Subsidiarity: A "Europe of the Regions" v. the British constitution?' *Journal of Common Market Studies*, Vol. 32, No. 1 (1994), pp. 47–67.
29. This possibility is discussed in comparative historical perspective in David Baker et al., '1846...1906...1996? Conservative splits and European integration', *Political Quarterly*, Vol. 64, No. 4 (1993), pp. 420–34.

Bibliography

UNPUBLISHED SOURCES

Public Record Office, Kew, Surrey (PRO)

Prime Minister's Office (PREM)
PREM 11 (Prime Minister's Files)
1337, 1365, 1366, 1829A, 1830A, 1831A, 1838, 1841, 1844, 1853, 2132, 2133, 2136, 2315, 2326, 2328, 2336, 2341, 2343, 2345, 2531, 2532, 2676, 2678, 2679, 2695, 2696, 2699, 2701, 2705–7, 2714, 2826–8, 2870, 2978, 2985, 2986, 2993, 2994, 2998, 3002, 3024, 3025, 3131–3, 3136, 3255, 3311, 3318, 3319, 3321, 3322, 3325, 3326, 3328, 3334, 3338, 3345, 3553–61, 3709, 3712, 3772–3, 3775–8, 3780, 3782–3, 3790–2, 3800, 4052, 4055, 4224, 4320

Cabinet (CAB)
CAB 128 (Cabinet Meetings)
29–37
CAB 129 (Cabinet Memoranda)
75–112
CAB 130 (Ad-hoc Committees)
120 GEN 549, 123–4 GEN 580, 132–6 GEN 613, 154–7 GEN 670–1, 168 GEN 699, 173 GEN 717
CAB 134 (Cabinet Committees)
889, 1026–30, 1044, 1226–30, 1236–7, 1238–41, 1282–6, 1520–44, 1546–7, 1674–92, 1767–9, 1811–17, 1818–30, 1835–40, 1852–4, 1884–5, 2201–5, 2392–3

Foreign Office (FO)
FO 371 (Mutual Aid Department/European Economic Organizations)
116038–57, 121972, 121975, 122022–43, 122044–6, 128331–74, 134486–520, 134544, 134545, 142425, 142561–9, 142588–600, 142609–15, 142616–19, 142628, 142629, 150166–70, 150172–80, 150217–24, 150263–99, 150306–32, 150360–9, 158160–9, 158170–84, 158185–212, 158213–6, 158238–43, 158264–309, 158312–6, 158357–63, 163515–16, 164698–727, 164735–43, 164771, 164832–41, 171328–30, 172022

Treasury (T)
T 230 (Economic Advisory Section)
335–6, 394–401

T 231 (Exchange Control Division)
793–801
T 232 (European Economic Co-Operation Committee)
430–3
T 234 (Home and Overseas Planning Staff Division)
67, 100–4, 181–7, 195–205, 207–21, 230, 235, 357–62, 367, 369, 373–9, 715, 717–21
T 236 (Overseas Finance Division)
4080–1, 4369–70, 4760–6, 4865–8, 6018–38, 6317–23, 6530–47, 6550–4

Board of Trade (BT)
BT 11 (Commercial Relations and Exports Department)
5367, 5402, 5484–7, 5514, 5516, 5519, 5520, 5530, 5538–9, 5544, 5545, 5552–9, 5562–8, 5570–2, 5580, 5591–3, 5596, 5597, 5602, 5612, 5616, 5622, 5624, 5648–50, 5693, 5708–10, 5714–17, 5729, 5734, 5735, 5783–7, 5800–4, 5813, 5820, 5852, 5891
BT 205 (Tariff Division)
261–5, 306–8
BT 213 (Commodity and General Division)
70, 95
BT 241 (Commercial Relations and Exports Division)
554, 555, 1115
BT 258 (Industries and Manufactures Department)
28, 176, 229–31

Ministry of Agriculture, Fisheries and Food (MAF)
MAF 247 (External Relations Division)
21, 22, 32, 36
MAF 255 (Minister's Papers)
430, 431, 442, 961

Bodleian Library, Oxford (BLO)

Conservative Party Archives (CPA)
CCO 3 (Organization Department/Outside Organizations)
5/115, 6/149, 6/150
CCO 4 (Special Subjects)
7/428, 8/94, 9/152
CCO 500 (Director of Organization's Office)
31/1–4
CRD 2 (Conservative Research Department)
8/4, 9/41, 11/8, 11/9, 11/12, 34/2–4, 34/7, 34/8
Paul Gore-Booth Papers
Harry Crookshank Papers
Anthony Rumbold Papers

University Library, Birmingham (ULB)

Avon Papers
13/3/51, 13/3/52, 20/1/1–32, 20/2/5, 20/20/1–149, 20/21/1–237,
20/29/2–3, 20/49/1–17, 20/50/88–104, 23/3/1–18

Trinity College Library, Cambridge (TCL)

R. A. Butler's Papers
F 1–130, G 1–46, H 1–118

Churchill Archives Centre, Cambridge (CAC)

Duncan Edwin Duncan-Sandys Papers
6/30, 6/33, 6/37, 9, 15/4, 15/5
David Maxwell Fyfe Papers

INTERVIEWS

Barclay, Roderick (28 April 1993)
France, Arnold (4 May 1993)
Glaves-Smith, Frank W. (19 May 1993)
Heath, Edward (1 April 1993)
Sanders, Cyril W. (14 June 1993)

PUBLISHED SOURCES AND MEMOIRS

Acheson, Dean, *Present at the Creation. My Years in the State Department* (New York: Norton, 1969).

Adenauer, Konrad, *Erinnerungen. Vol. II: 1955–1959* (Stuttgart: DVA, 1967).

Adenauer, Konrad, *Erinnerungen. Vol. III: 1959–1963* (Stuttgart: DVA, 1968).

A European Free Trade Area. United Kingdom Memorandum to the OEEC (London: HMSO, Cmnd. 72, 1957).

Ball, George W., *The Past Has Another Pattern. Memoirs* (New York/London: Norton, 1982).

Barclay, Roderick, *Ernest Bevin and the Foreign Office 1932–1969* (London: Latimer, 1975).

Benn, Tony, *Office Without Power* (London: Hutchinson, 1988).

Brandt, Willy, *People in Politics, 1960–75* (London: Collins, 1978).

Butler, Richard Austen, *The Art of the Possible. The Memoirs of Lord Butler* (London: Hamilton, 1971).

Comité Intergouvernemental crée par la Conférence de Messine, Rapport des Chefs de Délegation aux Ministres des Affaires Etrangères (Spaak Report), Brussels 1956.

Crossman, Richard, *Diaries of a Cabinet Minister* (London: Methuen, 1979).
Douglas-Home, Alec, *The Way the Wind Blows. An Autobiography* (London: Collins, 1976).
Eden, Anthony, *Full Circle. The Memoirs of Anthony Eden* (London: Cassell, 1960).
Eisenhower, Dwight D., *The White House Years. Waging Peace 1956–1961* (London: Heinemann, 1966).
Evans, Harold, *Downing Street Diary. The Macmillan Years 1957–1963* (London: Hodder & Stoughton, 1981).
Federation of British Industries, *British Industry and Europe*, London 1961.
Federation of British Industries/NUM/ABCC, *A Joint Report on the European Free Trade Area*, London 1957.
Foreign Relations of the United States (FRUS), 1955–1957, Vol. IV: Western European Security and Integration, Washington 1986.
Gaulle, Charles de, *Mémoires d'espoir. Le renouveau 1958–1962* (Paris: Plon, 1970).
House of Commons Debates, 1945–63.
James, Robert Rhodes (ed.), *Churchill Speaks. Winston S. Churchill in Peace and War. Collected Speeches 1897–1963* (Leicester: Winward, 1981).
Jebb, Herbert Gladwyn, *The Memoirs of Lord Gladwyn* (London: Weidenfeld & Nicolson, 1972).
Jenkins, Roy, *A Life at the Centre* (London: Pan/Macmillan, 1992).
Kirkpatrick, Ivone, *The Inner Circle. Memoirs of Ivone Kirkpatrick* (London: Macmillan, 1959).
Lloyd, Selwyn, *Suez 1956. A Personal Account* (London: Cape, 1978).
Macmillan, Harold, *Tides of Fortune 1945–1955* (London: Macmillan, 1969).
Macmillan, Harold, *Riding the Storm 1956–1959* (London: Macmillan, 1971).
Macmillan, Harold, *Pointing the Way 1959–1961* (London: Macmillan, 1972).
Macmillan, Harold, *At the End of the Day 1961–1963* (London: Macmillan, 1973).
Marjolin, Robert, *Le Travail d'une Vie. Mémoires 1911–1986* (Paris: Laffont, 1986).
Maudling, Reginald, *Memoirs* (London: Sidgwick & Jackson, 1978).
Maxwell-Fyfe, David, *Political Adventure. The Memoirs of the Earl of Kilmuir* (London: Wiedenfeld & Nicolson, 1964).
Monnet, Jean, *Memoirs* (London: Collins, 1978).
Murville, Maurice Couve de, *Une Politique Étrangère 1958–1969* (Paris: Plon, 1971).
Organization for European Economic Cooperation, *Report on the possibility of creating a Free Trade Area in Europe*, prepared for the Council of OEEC by a special Working Party, Paris 1957.
Roll, Eric, *Crowded Hours* (London: Faber, 1985).
Schuman, Robert, *Pour l'Europe* (Paris: Genève, 1963).
Shuckburgh, Evelyn, *Descent to Suez. Diaries 1951–56* (London: Weidenfeld & Nicolson, 1986).
Spaak, Paul-Henri, *The Continuing Battle: Memoirs of a European, 1936–1966* (London: Weidenfeld & Nicolson, 1971).
Thatcher, Margaret, *Britain and Europe* (London: Conservative Political Centre, 1989).

Thatcher, Margaret, *The Downing Street Years* (London: HarperCollins, 1993).

Wilson, Harold, *Memoirs, The Making of a Prime Minister 1916–64* (London: Weidenfeld & Nicolson, 1986).

Wolff, Michael (ed.), *The Collected Essays of Sir Winston Churchill, Vol. II* (London: Buckram, 1976).

BOOKS AND ARTICLES

Adamthwaite, Anthony, 'Introduction: The Foreign Office and policy-making', in Young, *The Foreign Policy*, pp. 1–28.

Alford, B. W. E., *British Economic Performance 1945–1975* (London: Macmillan, 1988).

Allen, David, 'Britain and Western Europe', in Smith et al., *British Foreign Policy*, pp. 168–92.

Almond, Gabriel A. and Sidney Verba, *The Civic Culture. Political Attitudes and Democracy in Five Nations* (Princeton, NJ: University Press, 1963).

Almond, Gabriel A. and Sidney Verba (eds), *The Civic Culture Revisited* (London: Sage, 1989).

Archer, Clive, *Organizing Western Europe* (London: Edward Arnold, 1990).

Ashford, Nigel, 'The political parties', in George, *Britain and the European Community*, pp. 119–48.

Ashford, Nigel, *The Conservative Party and European Integration 1945–1975* (University of Warwick: PhD, 1983).

Aster, Sidney, *Anthony Eden* (London: Weidenfeld & Nicolson, 1976).

Austin, Dennis, 'Regional associations and the Commonwealth', in Hamilton, *A Decade*, pp. 325–48.

Baker, David et al., '1846...1906...1996? Conservative splits and European integration', *Political Quarterly*, Vol. 64, No. 4 (1993), pp. 420–34.

Baker, David et al., 'The parliamentary siege of Maastricht 1993: Conservative divisions and British ratification', *Parliamentary Affairs*, Vol. 47, No. 1 (1994), pp. 37–60.

Baker, David et al., 'Backbench Conservative attitudes to Europe', *Political Quarterly*, Vol. 66, No. 2 (1995), pp. 221–33.

Barker, Elisabeth, *Britain in a Divided Europe 1945–1970* (London: Weidenfeld & Nicolson, 1971).

Barnes, John, 'From Eden to Macmillan, 1955–1959', in Hennessy & Seldon, *Ruling Performance*, pp. 98–149.

Bartlett, Christopher John, *A History of Postwar Britain 1945–1974* (London: Longman, 1977).

Bartlett, Christopher John, *British Foreign Policy in the Twentieth Century* (London: Macmillan, 1989).

Bartlett, Christopher John, *'The Special Relationship'. A Political History of Anglo-American Relations since 1945* (London: Longman, 1992).

Baylis, John, *Anglo-American Defence Relations 1939–1984. The Special Relationship*, 2nd edn (London: Macmillan, 1984).

Beloff, Max, *New Dimensions in Foreign Policy. A Study in British Administrative Experience 1947–59* (London: Allen & Unwin, 1961).

Beloff, Nora, *The General Says No. Britain's Exclusion from Europe* (London: Penguin, 1963).

Benoit, Emile, *Europe at the Sixes and Sevens. The Common Market, the Free Trade Association and the United States* (New York: Columbia University Press, 1961).

Bernier, Serge, *Relations Politiques Franco-Britanniques (1947–1958)* (Sherbrooke/Quebec: Edition Naaman, 1984).

Blank, Stephen, *Industry and Government in Britain. The Federation of British Industries in Politics, 1945–65*, (Farnborough: Saxon House, 1973).

Bogdanor, Vernon and Robert Skidelsky (eds), *The Age of Affluence 1951–1964* (London: Macmillan, 1970).

Boyle, Peter, 'The "Special Relationship" with Washington', in Young, *The Foreign Policy*, pp. 29–54.

Brenke, Gabriele, 'Europakonzeptionen im Widerstreit. Die Freihandelszonen-Verhandlungen 1956–1958', *Vierteljahrshefte für Zeitgeschichte*, Vol. 42, No. 4 (1994), pp. 595–633.

Brittan, Samuel, *The Treasury under the Tories, 1951–1964* (Harmondsworth: Penguin, 1964).

Brivati, Brian and Harriet Jones (eds), *From Reconstruction to Integration: Britain and Europe since 1945* (Leicester: University Press, 1993).

Bührer, Werner, 'German industry and European integration in the 1950s', in Wurm, *Western Europe*, pp. 87–114.

Bullen, Roger, 'Britain and "Europe" 1950–1957', in Serra, *Il rilancio*, pp. 315–38.

Bulmer, Simon, 'Britain and European integration: of sovereignty, slow adaptation, and semi-detachment', in George, *Britain and the European Community*, pp. 1–29.

Bulpitt, Jim, 'Conservative leaders and the "Euro-ratchet": five doses of scepticism', *Political Quarterly*, Vol. 63, No. 3 (1992), pp. 258–75.

Burgess, Simon and Geoffrey Edwards, 'The Six plus One: British policy-making and the question of European economic integration, 1955', *International Affairs*, Vol. 64, No. 3 (1988), pp. 393–413.

Butler, David and Anthony King, *The British General Election of 1964* (London: Macmillan, 1965).

Butler, Lawrence J., 'Winds of change: Britain, Europe and the Commonwealth, 1959–61', in Brivati and Jones, *From Reconstruction*, pp. 157–65.

Butt, Ronald, 'The Common Market and Conservative Party politics, 1961–2', *Government and Opposition*, Vol. 2, No. 3 (1967), pp. 372–86.

Cairncross, Alec, 'The postwar years 1945–1977', in Floud and McCloskey, *The Economic History*, pp. 370–416.

Cairncross, Alec, *The British Economy since 1945* (Oxford: Blackwell, 1992).

Cairncross, Alec and Nita Watts, *The Economic Section 1939–1961. A Study in Economic Advising* (London: Routledge, 1989).

Campbell, John, *Edward Heath* (London: Pimlico, 1994).

Camps, Miriam, *The European Common Market and Free Trade Area. A Progress Report* (Princeton University: Centre of International Studies, 1957).

Camps, Miriam, *Problems of Freer Trade in Europe, Political and Economic Planning*, Vol. XXIV, No. 423 (1958), pp. 111–27.

Camps, Miriam, *Britain and the European Community 1955–1963* (Oxford: University Press, 1964).

Carlton, David, *Anthony Eden. A Biography* (London: Allen Lane, 1981).

Cerny, Philip G., *The Politics of Grandeur. Ideological Aspects of de Gaulle's Foreign Policy* (Cambridge: University Press, 1980).

Charlton, Michael: 'How and why Britain lost the leadership of Europe. "Messina! Messina!" or, the parting of the ways', *Encounter*, Vol. 57, No. 2 (1981), pp. 9–22.

Charlton, Michael, 'How (and why) Britain lost the leadership of Europe (II). A last step sideways', *Encounter*, Vol. 57, No. 3 (1981), pp. 22–33.

Charlton, Michael, *The Price of Victory* (London: BBC, 1983).

Childs, David, *Britain since 1945: A Political History*, 2nd edn (London: Methuen, 1986).

Clark, Ian, *Nuclear Diplomacy and the Special Relationship. Britain's Deterrent and America, 1957–1962* (Oxford: Clarendon Press, 1994).

Clarke, Peter, *A Question of Leadership. From Gladstone to Thatcher* (London: Penguin, 1992).

Coker, Christopher, *Who Only England Know. The Conservatives and Foreign Policy* (London: Alliance Publishers, 1990).

Coker, Christopher, 'Dünkirchen und andere britische Mythen', *Europäische Rundschau*, Vol. 19, No. 2 (1991), pp. 107–18.

Cosgrave, Patrick, *R. A. Butler. An English Life* (London: Quartet Books, 1981).

Crafts, N. F. R. und N. W. C. Woodward (eds), *The British Economy since 1945* (Oxford: Clarendon Press, 1991).

Darwin, John, *Britain and Decolonisation. The Retreat from Empire in the Post-War World* (London: Macmillan, 1988).

Deighton, Anne, 'Missing the boat. Britain and Europe 1945–1961', *Contemporary Record*, Vol. 3, No. 3 (1990), pp. 15–17.

Deighton, Anne, 'La Grande-Bretagne et la Communauté Économique Européenne (1958–1963)', *Histoire économie et société*, Vol. 13, No. 1 (1994), pp. 113–30.

Deighton, Anne (ed.), *Building Postwar Europe. National Decision-Makers and European Institutions, 1948–1963* (London: Macmillan, 1995).

Deighton, Anne and Piers Ludlow, '"A conditional application": British management of the first attempt to seek membership of the EEC, 1961–3', in Deighton, *Building*, pp. 107–26.

Dell, Edmund, *The Schuman Plan and the British Abdication of Leadership in Europe* (Oxford: University Press, 1995).

Dimbleby, David and David Reynolds, *An Ocean Apart. The Relationship between Britain and America in the Twentieth Century* (London: BBC, 1988).

Dixon, Piers, *Double Diploma. The Life of Sir Pierson Dixon. Don and Diplomat* (London: Hutchinson, 1968).

Dockrill, Michael, *British Defence since 1945* (Oxford: Blackwell, 1988).

Dockrill, Saki, *Britain's Policy for West German Rearmament 1950–1955* (Cambridge: University Press, 1991).

Dumoulin, Michel, 'Les travaux du Comité Spaak (juillet 1955 – avril 1956)', in Serra, *Il rilancio*, pp. 195–210.

Ellison, James, *Harold Macmillan's Fear of 'Little Europe'. Britain, the Six and the European Free Trade Area,* Discussion Papers on Britain and Europe (Leicester: University of Leicester, 1995).

Fisher, Nigel, *Harold Macmillan* (London: Weidenfeld & Nicolson, 1982).

Floud, Roderick and Donald McCloskey (eds), *The Economic History of Britain since 1700. Vol. 2: 1860 to the 1970s* (Cambridge: University Press, 1981).

Frankel, Joseph, *British Foreign Policy 1945–1973* (Oxford: University Press, 1975).

Freedman, Lawrence, *Britain and Nuclear Weapons* (London: Macmillan, 1980).

Garry, John, 'The British Conservative Party: divisions over European policy', *West European Politics,* Vol. 18, No. 4 (1995), pp. 170–89.

Geddes, Andrew, 'Labour and the European Community 1973–93: Pro-Europeanism, "Europeanisation" and their implications', *Contemporary Record,* Vol. 8, No. 2 (1994), pp. 370–80.

George, Stephen, *An Awkward Partner. Britain and the European Community* (Oxford: Clarendon Press, 1990).

George, Stephen, *Britain and European Integration since 1945* (Oxford: Blackwell, 1991).

George, Stephen (ed.), *Britain and the European Community. The Politics of Semi-Detachment* (Oxford: Clarendon Press, 1992).

Gillingham, John, *Coal, Steel and the Rebirth of Europe, 1945–1955. The Germans and French from Ruhr Conflict to Economic Community* (Cambridge: University Press, 1991).

Gowing, Margaret, 'Nuclear weapons and the "Special Relationship"', in Louis and Bull, *The 'Special Relationship',* pp. 117–28.

Grayling, Christopher and Christopher Langdon, *Just Another Star? Anglo-American Relations since 1945* (London: Harrap, 1988).

Greenwood, Sean, *Britain and European Cooperation since 1945* (Oxford: Blackwell, 1992).

Groeben, Hans von der, *Aufbaujahre der Europäischen Gemeinschaft. Das Ringen um den Gemeinsamen Markt und die Politische Union (1958–1966)* (Baden-Baden: NOMOS, 1982).

Hamilton, W. B. et al. (eds), *A Decade of the Commonwealth 1955–1964* (Durham, NC: Duke University Press, 1966).

Hennessy, Peter, *Cabinet* (Oxford: Blackwell, 1986).

Hennessy, Peter, *Whitehall* (London: Secker & Warburg, 1989).

Hennessy, Peter and Anthony Seldon (eds), *Ruling Performance. British Governments from Attlee to Thatcher* (Oxford: Blackwell, 1987).

Hill, Christopher, 'Public opinion and British Foreign Policy since 1945: research in progress?', *Millennium. Journal of International Studies,* Vol. 10, No. 1 (1981), pp. 53–62.

Hogan, Michael J., *The Marshall Plan: America, Britain, and the Reconstruction of Western Europe, 1947–1952* (Cambridge: University Press, 1987).

Holland, Robert, *The Pursuit of Greatness. Britain and the World Role, 1900–1970* (London: Fontana, 1991).

Horne, Alistair: 'The Macmillan years and afterwards', in Louis and Bull, *The 'Special Relationship',* pp. 87–102.

Horne, Alistair, *Macmillan 1894–1956. Vol. I of the Official Biography* (London: Macmillan, 1988).

Horne, Alistair, *Macmillan 1957–1986. Vol. II of the Official Biography* (London: Macmillan, 1989).

James, Robert Rhodes, *Anthony Eden* (London: Weidenfeld & Nicolson, 1986).

Jansen, Jürgen, *Britische Konservative und Europa. Debattenaussagen im Unterhaus zur westeuropäischen Integration 1945–1972* (Baden-Baden: NOMOS, 1978).

Jebb, Herbert Gladwyn, *The European Idea* (London: Weidenfeld & Nicolson, 1966).

Kaiser, Wolfram, 'To join, or not to join: the 'Appeasement' policy of Britain's first EEC application', in Brivati and Jones, *From Reconstruction*, pp. 144–56.

Kaiser, Wolfram, 'Money, Money, Money: the Economics and Politics of the Stationing Costs, 1955–1965', in Schmidt, *Bündnissicherung*, pp. 1–31.

Kaiser, Wolfram, 'Selbstisolierung in Europa. Die britische Regierung und die Gründung der EWG', in Wurm, *Wege nach Europa*, pp. 125–53.

Kaiser, Wolfram, 'Wie nach Austerlitz? London–Bonn–Paris und die britische EWG-Politik bis 1961', *Integration*, Vol. 16, No. 1 (1993), pp. 19–32.

Kaiser, Wolfram, 'Using Europe and Abusing the Europeans: The Conservatives and the European Community 1957–1994', *Contemporary Record*, Vol. 8, No. 2 (1994), pp. 381–99.

Kaiser, Wolfram, 'The Bomb and Europe. Britain, France, and the EEC Entry Negotiations, 1961–63', *Journal of European Integration History*, Vol. 1, No. 1 (1995), pp. 65–85.

Kaiser, Wolfram, '"Das Gesicht wahren": Die Konservative Partei und die Rolle Großbritanniens in der Welt, 1945–1964', in Ursula Lehmkuhl and Hans-Heinrich Jansen (eds), *Großbritannien, das Empire und die Welt: Britische Außenpolitik zwischen 'Größe' und 'Selbstbehauptung', 1850–1990* (Bochum: Universitätsverlag Dr. N. Brockmeyer, 1995), pp. 245–61.

Kavanagh, Dennis, 'Political culture in Britain: the decline of the civic culture', in Almond and Verba, *The Civic Culture Revisited*, pp. 124–76.

Kent, John, *British Imperial Strategy and the Origins of the Cold War* (Leicester: University Press, 1994).

Keogh, Dermot, *Ireland and Europe 1919–1989: A Diplomatic and Political History* (Cork: University Press, 1990).

Koerfer, Daniel, *Kampf ums Kanzleramt. Erhard und Adenauer* (Stuttgart: DVA, 1987).

Küsters, Hanns Jürgen, 'The origins of the EEC Treaty', in Serra, *Il rilancio*, pp. 211–38.

Küsters, Hanns Jürgen, *Die Gründung der Europäischen Wirtschaftsgemeinschaft* (Baden-Baden: NOMOS, 1982).

Lacouture, Jean, *De Gaulle. The Ruler 1945–1970* (London: Harvill, 1991).

Lamb, Richard, *The Failure of the Eden Government* (London: Sidgwick & Jackson, 1987).

Lamb, Richard, *The Macmillan Years 1957–1963. The Emerging Truth* (London: John Murray, 1995).

Larres, Klaus, *Politik der Illusionen. Churchill, Eisenhower und die deutsche Frage 1945–1955* (Göttingen: Vandenhoeck & Ruprecht, 1995).

La Serre, Françoise de, 'De Gaulle et la Candidature britannique aux Communautés Européennes', *Histoire économie et société*, Vol. 13, No. 1 (1994), pp. 131–42.

Lee, Sabine, 'Anglo-German relations 1958–59: the postwar turning point?', *Diplomacy and Statecraft*, Vol. 6, No. 3 (1995), pp. 787–808.

Lieber, Robert J., *British Politics and European Unity. Parties, Elites, and Pressure Groups* (Berkeley: University of California Press, 1970).

Lindsay, T. F. and Michael Harrington, *The Conservative Party 1918–1979* (London: Macmillan, 1979).

Lord, Christopher, 'Sovereign or confused? The "Great Debate" about British entry to the European Community 20 years on', *Journal of Common Market Studies*, Vol. 30, No. 4 (1992), pp. 419–36.

Lord, Christopher, *British Entry to the European Community under the Heath Government of 1970–74* (Aldershot: Dartmouth, 1993).

Loth, Wilfried, *The Division of the World, 1941–1955* (London: Routledge, 1988).

Loth, Wilfried, *Der Weg nach Europa. Geschichte der europäischen Integration 1939–1957* (Göttingen: Vandenhoeck & Ruprecht, 1990).

Loth, Wilfried, 'De Gaulle und Europa. Eine Revision', *Historische Zeitschrift*, Vol. 253, No. 3 (1991), pp. 629–60.

Louis, W. M. Roger und Hedley Bull (eds), *The 'Special Relationship'. Anglo-American Relations since 1945* (Oxford: Clarendon Press, 1986).

Ludlow, Piers, 'A Problem of Trust: British agriculture and the Brussels negotiations', unpublished paper presented to the Cambridge University Centre for International Studies/European University Institute Conference, Cambridge, 28 June 1993.

Ludlow, Piers, *Influence and Vulnerability: The Role of the EEC Commission in the Enlargement Negotiations* (Florence: European University Institute Doc. 23, 1994).

MacDermott, Geoffrey, *The Eden Legacy and the Decline of British Diplomacy* (London: Frewin, 1969).

Maclean, Donald, *British Foreign Policy since Suez 1956–1968* (London: Hodder & Stoughton, 1970).

Manderson-Jones, R. B., *The Special Relationship. Anglo-American Relations and Western European Unity, 1947–56* (London: Weidenfeld & Nicolson, 1972).

Medlicott, William N., *Contemporary England 1914–1964* (London: Longman, 1967).

Medlicott, William N., *British Foreign Policy since Versailles 1919–1963* (London: Methuen, 1968).

Middlemas, Keith, *Power, Competition and the State. Vol. 1: Britain in Search of Balance 1940–61* (London: Macmillan, 1986).

Milward, Alan S., *The Reconstruction of Western Europe 1945–51* (London: Methuen, 1984).

Milward, Alan S., *The European Rescue of the Nation-State* (London: Alan Steele, 1992).

Milward, Alan S., *The Frontier of National Sovereignty. History and Theory, 1945–1992* (London: Routledge, 1993).

Moon, Jeremy, *European Integration in British Politics 1950–1963: A Study of Issue Change* (Aldershot: Gower, 1985).

Morgan, Kenneth O., 'The Second World War and British culture', in Brivati and Jones, *From Reconstruction*, pp. 33–46.

Morgan, Kenneth O., *The People's Peace. British History 1945–1990* (Oxford: University Press, 1992).

Newman, Michael, *Socialism and European Unity. The Dilemma of the Left in Britain and France* (London: Junction Books, 1983).

Northedge, F. S., *Descent From Power. British Foreign Policy 1945–1973* (London: Allen & Unwin, 1974).

Nutting, Anthony, *Europe Will Not Wait. A Warning and a Way Out* (London: Hollis & Carter, 1960).

Ovendale, Ritchie (ed.), *The Foreign Policy of the British Labour Governments, 1945–1951* (Leicester: University Press, 1984).

Ovendale, Ritchie, *The English-Speaking Alliance: Great Britain, the US, the Dominions and the Cold War* (London: Allen & Unwin, 1985).

Paterson, William E., *The SPD and European Integration* (Farnborough: Saxon House, 1974).

Paterson, William E., 'Britain and the European Union revisited: some unanswered questions', *Scottish Affairs*, Vol. 9 (1994), pp. 1–12.

Paterson, William et al., *The European Policies of Labour and Conservative Party in Great Britain* (Sankt Augustin: Interne Studien Nr. 109 der Konrad-Adenauer-Stiftung, 1995), pp. 9–60.

Pelling, Henry, *Britain and the Marshall Plan* (London: Macmillan, 1988).

Pinto-Duschinsky, Michael, 'From Macmillan to Home, 1959–1964', in Hennessy and Seldon, *Ruling Performance*, pp. 150–85.

Poidevin, Raymond (ed.), *Histoire des Débuts de la Construction Européenne (mars 1948–mai 1950)* (Baden-Baden: NOMOS, 1984).

Pollard, Sidney, *European Economic Integration 1815–1970* (London: Thames & Hudson, 1974).

Pollard, Sidney, *The Wasting of the British Economy. British Economic Policy 1945 to the Present* (London: Croom Helm, 1982).

Pollard, Sidney, *The Development of the British Economy, 1914–1990*, 4th edn (London: Edward Arnold, 1992).

Porter, Bernard, *Britain, Europe and the World 1850–1986: Delusions of Grandeur*, 2nd edn (London: Allen & Unwin, 1987).

Ramsden, John, 'From Churchill to Heath', in Richard Austen Butler (ed.), *The Conservatives. A History from Their Origins to 1965* (London: Allen & Unwin, 1977), pp. 405–78.

Ramsden, John, *The Making of Conservative Party Policy. The Conservative Research Department since 1929* (London: Longman, 1980).

Reynolds, David, 'A "special relationship"? America, Britain and the international order since the Second World War', *International Affairs*, Vol. 62, No. 1 (1985/86), pp. 1–20.

Sampson, Anthony, *Macmillan. A Study in Ambiguity* (London: Penguin, 1967).

Sanders, David, *Losing an Empire, Finding a Role. British Foreign Policy since 1945* (London: Macmillan, 1990).

Schlesinger, Arthur M., *A Thousand Days. John F. Kennedy in the White House* (London: André Deutsch, 1965).

Schmidt, Gustav, 'Die politischen und sicherheitspolitischen Dimensionen der britischen Europapolitik 1955/56–1963/64', in Schmidt, *Grossbritannien*, pp. 169–252.

Schmidt, Gustav, '"Tying" (West) Germany into the West – But to what? NATO? WEU? The European Community?', in Wurm, *Western Europe*, pp. 137–74.

Schmidt, Gustav (ed.), *Grossbritannien und Europa – Grossbritannien in Europa. Sicherheitsbelange und Wirtschaftsfragen in der britischen Europapolitik nach dem Zweiten Weltkrieg* (Bochum: Universitätsverlag Dr. N. Brockmeyer, 1989).

Schmidt, Gustav (ed.), *Zwischen Bündnissicherung und privilegierter Partnerschaft: Die deutsch-britischen Beziehungen und die Vereinigten Staaten von Amerika, 1955–1963* (Bochum: Universitätsverlag Dr. N. Brockmeyer, 1995).

Schneider, Herbert, *Großbritanniens Weg nach Europa. Eine Untersuchung über das Verhalten und die Rolle der britischen Handels- und Industrieverbände, Gewerkschaften und Farmerorganisationen zwischen 1955/56 (Spaak-Komitee) und 1961 (EWG-Beitrittsverhandlungen)* (Freiburg: Verlag Rombach, 1968).

Schwabe, Klaus (ed.), *Die Anfänge des Schuman-Plans, 1950–51* (Baden-Baden: NOMOS, 1986).

Scott, Andrew, John Peterson and David Millar, 'Subsidiarity: a "Europe of the Regions" v. the British constitution?', *Journal of Common Market Studies*, Vol. 32, No. 1 (1994), pp. 47–67.

Seldon, Anthony, *Churchill's Indian Summer. The Conservative Government, 1951–1955* (London: Hodder & Stoughton, 1981).

Serra, Enrico (ed.), *Il rilancio dell'Europa e i trattati di Roma* (Baden-Baden: NOMOS, 1989).

Sked, Alan and Chris Cook, *Post-War Britain: A Political History*, 4th edn (London: Penguin, 1993).

Smith, Michael, Steve Smith and Brian White (eds), *British Foreign Policy* (London: Unwin Hyman, 1988).

Spierenburg, Dirk and Raymond Poidevin, *The History of the High Authority of the European Coal and Steel Community. Supranationality in Operation* (London: Weidenfeld & Nicolson, 1994).

Steininger, Rolf, '1961, "Europe at Sixes and Sevens". Die EFTA und Großbritanniens Entscheidung für die EWG', *Vierteljahrschrift für Sozial- und Wirtschaftsgeschichte*, Vol. 80, No. 1 (1993), pp. 4–29.

Stephenson, Jill, 'Britain and Europe in the later twentieth century: identity, sovereignty, peculiarity', in Mary Fulbrook (ed.), *National Histories and European History* (London: University Press, 1993), pp. 230–54.

Stevenson, John, *Third Party Politics since 1945. Liberals, Alliance and Liberal Democrats* (Oxford: Blackwell, 1993).

Thorpe, D. R., *Selwyn Lloyd* (London: Cape, 1989).

Toschi, Simona, 'Washington–London–Paris. An untenable triangle (1960–1963)', *Journal of European Integration History*, Vol. 1, No. 2 (1995), pp. 81–109.

Turner, John, *Macmillan* (London: Longman, 1994).

Urwin, Derek W., *The Community of Europe. A History of European Integration since 1945*, 2nd edn (London: Longman, 1995).

Vital, David, *The Making of British Foreign Policy* (London: Allen & Unwin, 1968).

Wallace, William, *Foreign Policy and the Political Process* (London: Macmillan, 1971).

Wallace, William, *The Foreign Policy Process in Britain* (London: Royal Institute of International Affairs, 1975).

Warner, Geoffrey, 'The Labour Governments and the unity of Western Europe, 1945–51', in Ovendale, *The Foreign Policy*, pp. 61–82.

Watt, Donald C., 'Großbritannien und Europa 1951–1959. Die Jahre konservativer Regierung', *Vierteljahrshefte für Zeitgeschichte*, Vol. 28, No. 4 (1980), pp. 389–409.

Watt, Donald C., *Succeeding John Bull, America in Britain's Place 1900–1975. A study of the Anglo-American Relationship and World Politics in the Context of British and American Foreign Policy-Making in the Twentieth Century* (Cambridge: University Press, 1984).

Weilemann, Peter, *Die Anfänge der Europäischen Atomgemeinschaft. Zur Gründungsgeschichte von Euratom 1955–1957* (Baden-Baden: NOMOS, 1983).

Winand, Pascaline, *Eisenhower, Kennedy, and the United States of Europe* (New York: St. Martin's Press, 1993).

Wurm, Clemens A., 'Großbritannien, Westeuropa und die Anfänge der europäischen Integration 1945–1951: ein Überblick', in Schmidt, *Großbritannien*, pp. 57–88.

Wurm, Clemens A., 'Two paths to Europe: Great Britain and France from a comparative perspective', in Wurm, *Western Europe*, pp. 175–200.

Wurm, Clemens A., 'Sozialisten und europäische Integration: Die britische Labour Party 1945–1984, *Geschichte in Wissenschaft und Unterricht*, Vol. 38, No. 5 (1987), pp. 280–95.

Wurm, Clemens A. (ed.), *Wege nach Europa. Wirtschaft und Außenpolitik Großbritanniens im 20. Jahrhundert* (Bochum: Universitätsverlag Dr. N. Brockmeyer, 1992).

Wurm, Clemens A. (ed.), *Western Europe and Germany. The Beginnings of European Integration 1945–1960* (Oxford: Berg, 1995).

Young, Hugo, *One of Us. A Biography of Margaret Thatcher* (London: Macmillan, 1989).

Young, John W., 'British officials and European integration, 1944–60', in Deighton, *Building*, pp. 87–106.

Young, John W., 'German rearmament and the European Defence Community', in Young, *The Foreign Policy*, pp. 81–107.

Young, John W., 'The Schuman Plan and British association', in Young, *The Foreign Policy*, pp. 109–34.

Young, John W., '"The parting of the ways"?: Britain, the Messina Conference and the Spaak Committee, June–December 1955', in Young and Dockrill, *British Foreign Policy*, pp. 197–224.

Young, John W., *Britain, France and the Unity of Europe 1945–1951* (Leicester: University Press, 1984).

Young, John W., 'Churchill's 'No' to Europe: the 'rejection' of European union by Churchill's post-war government, 1951–52', *Historical Journal*, Vol. 28, No. 4 (1985), pp. 923–37.

Young, John W. (ed.), *The Foreign Policy of Churchill's Peacetime Administration 1951–1955* (Leicester: University Press, 1988).

Young, John W., *Britain and European Unity, 1945–1992* (London: Macmillan, 1993).

Young, John W. and Michael Dockrill (eds), *British Foreign Policy 1945–56* (London: Macmillan, 1989).

Index

268